Get the eBook FREE!

(PDF, ePub, Kindle, and liveBook all included)

We believe that once you buy a book from us, you should be able to read it in any format we have available. To get electronic versions of this book at no additional cost to you, purchase and then register this book at the Manning website.

Go to https://www.manning.com/freebook and follow the instructions to complete your pBook registration.

That's it!
Thanks from Manning!

Go in Practice

Go in Practice

MATT BUTCHER
MATT FARINA

MANNING
SHELTER ISLAND

For online information and ordering of this and other Manning books, please visit
www.manning.com. The publisher offers discounts on this book when ordered in quantity.
For more information, please contact

Special Sales Department
Manning Publications Co.
20 Baldwin Road
PO Box 761
Shelter Island, NY 11964
Email: orders@manning.com

Manning Publications Co.
20 Baldwin Road
PO Box 761
Shelter Island, NY 11964

Development editor: Susanna Kline
Technical development editors: Ivan Kirkpatrick, Kim Shrier,
Glenn Burnside, Alain Couniot
Review editor: Aleksandar Dragosavljevic
Project editor: Karen Gulliver
Copy editor: Sharon Wilkey
Proofreader: Melody Dolab
Technical Proofreader: James Frasché
Typesetter: Dottie Marsico
Cover designer: Marija Tudor

ISBN 9781633430075
Printed in the United States of America

brief contents

v

contents

foreword

When I heard that Matt Farina and Matt Butcher were starting a new book on Go, I was excited. Both have been key contributors in the Go ecosystem for years, and have extensive work experience and backgrounds that flavor the prose in this book with the spice of past learnings. The book is intended as a spiritual successor to *Go in Action,* taking you beyond the basics that we introduced there and into more practical learning.

The book is broken into four easily digestible parts, each with a different focus. Part 1 is a refresher on key Go concepts. If you're in a hurry and comfortable with your Go skills, you can safely skip this section, but I discourage that. In reviewing the final manuscript, I found nuggets of such value that I think everyone would benefit from these chapters.

Part 2 dives into the mechanics of managing a Go application in the real world. The chapter on errors is one of the best treatises on Go errors I've ever read, and the chapter on debugging and testing provides useful information on that crucial middle step of application development that takes your application from proof of concept to reliable production system.

In part 3, you'll learn about ways to create user interfaces for your application. The chapter on templates is an excellent guide to what many find to be a complicated part of Go's ecosystem. You'll see practical ways to reuse your templates and make your web interfaces more *dry.* The examples alone are worth the price of the book, as it's difficult to find examples of template usage that can be easily mapped to a real-world application. Later, you'll see how to create and consume a standards-compliant REST API and learn the tricks to properly versioning that API.

The final section of the book moves into the interoperability layer that's required in nearly every application today. You'll dive deep into cloud infrastructure and see where Go fits in the cloud-computing model. You'll finish with great coverage of microservices and service-to-service communication patterns.

Whether you're just coming to Go or you've been writing Go applications for years, this book has vital knowledge that will help you take your application development to the next level. The authors do a great job of presenting complex information with a unified voice and in a manner that's easy to digest. I'm excited for the publication of this book and the value that it brings to the Go community. I hope that you'll enjoy reading it as much as I have.

—BRIAN KETELSEN
CO-AUTHOR OF *GO IN ACTION*
CO-FOUNDER OF GOPHER ACADEMY

preface

When we first started using Go, we saw a language with a lot of potential. We wanted to build applications with it. But it was a new language, and many companies are wary of introducing a new programming language.

This is especially true in the enterprise, where Go has the potential to have a huge impact. New languages are challenged to be trusted, accepted, and adopted. There are hundreds of thousands of developers in businesses where leaders need to be swayed to try a new language and developers need to learn it well enough to build applications and see a benefit.

Open source projects, conferences, training, and books all help to make a programming language more palatable. We wanted to write a book that teaches Go in order to help the Go community, help those trying to learn Go or to convince their organizations' leadership, and help us in the companies that we work for and with.

When we first started the book, it was targeted squarely at cloud development with Go. Go is a language built for the cloud, and we've spent years working in cloud computing. Once we started working with Manning Publications, we saw an opportunity to expand beyond the cloud, into more useful and helpful patterns. And so the book shifted from being cloud-focused to pattern-focused. Yet it still retains its cloud roots.

Go in Practice is our attempt to help developers move from being familiar with the language to being productive with it. To help the community of developers grow, while helping organizations write better software.

acknowledgments

We've spent about two years writing this book, but none of the effort would have been possible without the commitment of our families. They've supported us through the early mornings, late nights, and weekends when we were focused on writing. They were there as we were fixated on solving problems, even when we weren't sitting down to write.

Good code is never created in a vacuum. We're also grateful to the women and men of the Go community who have so generously given their time to create a great language, great libraries, and a thriving ecosystem. It has been exciting to be a part of such a diverse, burgeoning community of developers. In particular, Rob Pike, Brian Ketelsen, and Dave Cheney all reached out to us early in our Go learning process. They're admirable ambassadors of the language. Special thanks to Brian for contributing the foreword to the book and for endorsing our work.

We appreciate the many individuals who gave time and effort to the creation of this book. It has been an arduous process, and thanks to many careful readers, including our MEAP readers, we found and corrected numerous mistakes.

We'd like to thank everyone at Manning, especially our development editor, Susanna Kline; our technical development editors, Ivan Kirkpatrick, Kim Shrier, Glenn Burnside, and Alain Couniot; and our technical proofreader, James Frasché; as well as everyone who worked on our book behind the scenes. Thanks also to the many reviewers who took the time to read our manuscript at various stages of its development and who provided invaluable feedback: Anthony Cramp, Austin Riendeau, Brandon Titus, Doug Sparling, Ferdinando Santacroce, Gary A. Stafford, Jim Amrhein, Kevin Martin, Nathan Davies, Quintin Smith, Sam Zaydel, and Wes Shaddix.

Finally, we owe a debt of gratitude to the Glide community, which has grown with us as we worked to build a top-tier package manager for Go. Thank you for your support.

Matt Butcher

I began writing this book at Revolv, continued when Google/Nest acquired us, and finished at Deis. Thanks to all three for supporting the writing of this book. Thanks to Brian Hardock, Cristian Cavalli, Lann Martin, and Chris Ching, all of whom served as early sounding boards. Matt Boersma provided helpful feedback for several chapters. Kent Rancourt and Aaron Schlesinger each inspired particular code examples in this book. Matt Fisher, Sivaram Mothiki, Keerthan Mala, Helgi Þorbjörnsson (yes, Helgi, I copied and pasted that), Gabe Monroy, Chris Armstrong, Sam Boyer, Jeff Bleiel, Joshua Anderson, Rimas Mocevicius, Jack Francis, and Josh Lane all (wittingly or unwittingly) influenced specific portions of this book. The impact of Michelle Noorali and Adam Reese cannot be understated; I've learned a lot watching a couple of Ruby developers master Go. And thanks to Angie, Annabelle, Claire, and Katherine for their unflagging support and understanding.

Matt Farina

I would like to thank Kristin, my beautiful and amazing wife, along with our wonderful daughters, Isabella and Aubrey, for their love and support.

I wrote this book while working at Hewlett Packard Enterprise, formerly Hewlett-Packard. Working at HPE has taught me invaluable lessons while providing me with the opportunity to work alongside and learn from those far wiser than myself. Specifically, I need to thank Rajeev Pandey, Brian Aker, Steve McLellan, Erin Handgen, Eric Gustafson, Mike Hagedorn, Susan Balle, David Graves, and many others. They have affected the way I write and operate applications, and that has shown up in these chapters in subtle ways.

There have been many others who influenced portions of this book, sometimes without realizing it. Thanks to Tim Pletcher, Jason Buberel, Sam Boyer, Larry Garfield, and all those I may have forgotten who had a positive influence.

Finally, I want to thank Matt Butcher. I never imagined authoring books until you suckered me into it. Thanks!

about this book

Go in Practice is a book about practical development using the Go programming language. Developers already familiar with the basics of Go will find patterns and techniques for creating Go applications. Chapters are organized around central themes (for example, chapter 10, "Communicating between cloud services"), but then explore a variety of techniques related to that theme.

How the book is organized

The 11 chapters are divided into four parts.

Part 1, "Background and fundamentals," provides a foundation for building applications. Chapter 1 provides the background of Go for those not already familiar with it or those with a passing understanding who would like to learn more. Building console applications and servers is the topic of chapter 2, and concurrency in Go is the topic of chapter 3.

Part 2, "Well-rounded applications," contains chapters 4 and 5. These chapters cover errors, panics, debugging, and testing. The goal of this section is to build applications you trust that handle problems well.

Part 3, "An interface for your applications," contains three chapters with topics ranging from generating HTML and to serving assets to providing and working with APIs. Many Go applications provide web applications and REST APIs for interaction. These chapters cover patterns to aid in their construction.

Part 4, "Taking your applications to the cloud," contains the remaining chapters, which focus on cloud computing and generating code. Go is a language built with cloud needs in mind. This section showcases patterns that enable working with those services and operating applications, sometimes as microservices, in them. It also covers generating code and metaprogramming.

There are 70 techniques explored in the book, each with its own Problem, Solution, and Discussion sections.

Code conventions and downloads

All source code in the book is presented in a `mono-spaced typeface like this`, which sets it off from the surrounding text. In many listings, the code is annotated to point out key concepts, and numbered bullets are sometimes used in the text to provide additional information about the code.

Source code for the examples in the book is available for download from the publisher's website at www.manning.com/books/go-in-practice and from GitHub at github.com/Masterminds/go-in-practice.

Author Online Forum

The purchase of *Go in Practice* includes free access to a private web forum run by Manning Publications, where you can make comments about the book, ask technical questions, and receive help from the authors and from other users. To access the forum and subscribe to it, point your web browser to www.manning.com/books/go-in-practice. This page provides information on how to get on the forum after you're registered, what kind of help is available, and the rules of conduct on the forum.

Manning's commitment to our readers is to provide a venue where a meaningful dialogue between individual readers and between readers and the authors can take place. It's not a commitment to any specific amount of participation on the part of the authors, whose contribution to the forum remains voluntary (and unpaid). We suggest you try asking the authors some challenging questions lest their interest stray!

The Author Online forum and the archives of previous discussions will be accessible from the publisher's website as long as the book is in print.

about the authors

 MATT BUTCHER is an architect at Deis, where contributing to open source projects is his day job. He has written several books and dozens of articles. Matt holds a PhD in philosophy and teaches in the Computer Science department at Loyola University Chicago. Matt is passionate about building strong teams and developing elegant solutions to complex problems.

 MATT FARINA is a Principal Engineer in the Advanced Technology Group at Hewlett Packard Enterprise. He is an author, speaker, and regular contributor to open source software who has been developing software for over a quarter century. He likes to solve problems for regular people by creating solutions using both the latest technology and the mundane that can be easily overlooked.

about the cover illustration

The figure on the cover of *Go in Practice* is captioned "Habit of the Wife of a Russian Peasant in 1768." The illustration is taken from Thomas Jefferys' *A Collection of the Dresses of Different Nations, Ancient and Modern*, published in London between 1757 and 1772. The title page states that these are hand-colored copperplate engravings, heightened with gum arabic.

Thomas Jefferys (1719–1771) was called "Geographer to King George III." An English cartographer, he was the leading map supplier of his day. He engraved and printed maps for government and other official bodies and produced a wide range of commercial maps and atlases, especially of North America. His work as a map maker sparked an interest in local dress customs of the lands he surveyed and mapped, and these are brilliantly displayed in his four-volume collection.

Fascination with faraway lands and travel for pleasure were relatively new phenomena in the late 18th century, and collections such as this one were popular, introducing the tourist as well as the armchair traveler to the inhabitants of other countries. The diversity of the drawings in Jefferys' volumes speaks vividly of the uniqueness and individuality of the world's nations some 200 years ago. Dress codes have changed since then, and the diversity by region and country, so rich at the time, has faded away. It's now often hard to tell the inhabitant of one continent from another. Perhaps, trying to view it optimistically, we've traded a cultural and visual diversity for a more varied personal life, or a more varied and interesting intellectual and technical life.

At a time when it's hard to tell one computer book from another, Manning celebrates the inventiveness and initiative of the computer business with book covers based on the rich diversity of regional life of two centuries ago, brought back to life by Jefferys' pictures.

Part 1

Background and fundamentals

This opening part of the book provides some background about Go and a foundation for building applications. Chapter 1 starts with an overview of Go for those not already familiar with it.

Chapters 2 and 3 move into base components for an application. Chapter 2 provides the foundation for building an application, including working with console applications and servers, and handling configuration. Chapter 3 focuses on using goroutines. Goroutines are one of the more powerful and useful elements in Go. They're regularly used in Go applications, and you'll see them through the rest of this book.

Getting into Go

1

The way we build and run software is changing. Innovation has swept in, disrupting long-standing assumptions about the computing environments that software runs in. To fully take advantage of these innovations, you need languages and tools that support them at their core.

When most mainstream programming languages and supporting toolchains were developed, they were designed for single-core processing. That's what we had. Now desktop computers, servers, and even our phones have processors with multiple cores. Running software with operations taking place concurrently can happen anywhere.

Toolchains around building applications have changed. Increased functionality and complexity in software requires environments that can build and execute the code rapidly and efficiently. Testing larger and more complicated codebases needs to happen quickly so it doesn't become a development blocker. Many applications are developed using libraries. Libraries and their versions are managed differently, thanks to solutions to disk-space problems that hampered this in the past.

The way infrastructure and software are delivered has changed. Using colocated servers, managing your own hardware, or getting simple virtual private servers used to be the norm. Standing up a service at scale often meant you needed an investment in running your own hardware, including load balancers, servers, and storage. Getting everything ordered, assembled, and connected to the world would take weeks or months. Now it's available in a matter of seconds or minutes via the cloud.

This chapter introduces the Go programming language for those not already familiar with it. In this chapter, you'll learn about the language, the toolchain that accompanies it, where Go fits into the landscape of languages, and how to install Go and get it running.

1.1 *What is Go?*

Go, sometimes referred to as *golang* to make it easier to find on the web, is a statically typed and compiled open source programming language initially developed by Google. Robert Griesemer, Rob Pike, and Ken Thompson were attempting to create a language for modern systems programming that solved real-world problems they encountered while building large systems at scale.

Instead of attempting to attain theoretical pureness, these designers engineered Go around real-world practical situations. It's inspired by a host of languages that came before it, including C, Pascal, Smalltalk, Newsqueak, C#, JavaScript, Python, Java, and many others.

Go isn't the typical statically typed and compiled language. The static typing has features that make it feel dynamic, and the compiled binaries have a runtime that includes garbage collection. The design of the language took into account the types of projects that Google would need to use it for: large codebases operating at scale and being developed by large developer teams.

At its core, Go is a programming language defined by a specification that can be implemented by any compiler. The default implementation is shipped via the go tool. But Go is more than a programming language. As figure 1.1 illustrates, layers are built on top of the language.

Developing applications requires more than a programming language—for example, testing, documentation, and formatting. Each of these areas needs tools to support it. The go tool that's used to compile applications also provides functionality to support these elements. It's a toolchain for application development. One of the most notable aspects of the toolchain is package management. Out of the box, the programming language Go and the go toolchain provide for packages. A built-in package system, along with a common toolchain for the essential elements of development, has enabled an ecosystem to form around the programming language.

One of the defining characteristics of Go is its simplicity. When Griesemer, Pike, and Thompson were originally designing the language, a feature didn't go in until all three

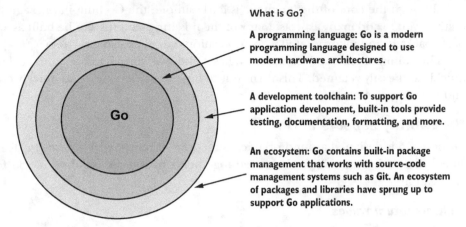

What is Go?

A programming language: Go is a modern programming language designed to use modern hardware architectures.

A development toolchain: To support Go application development, built-in tools provide testing, documentation, formatting, and more.

An ecosystem: Go contains built-in package management that works with source-code management systems such as Git. An ecosystem of packages and libraries have sprung up to support Go applications.

Figure 1.1   The layers of Go

agreed that it should be a feature of the language. This style of decision-making, along with their years of experience, led to a simple but powerful language. It's simple enough to keep in your head yet powerful enough to write a wide variety of software.

An example of this philosophy can be seen in the variable syntax:

```
var i int = 2
```

Here a variable is created as an integer and set to a value of 2. Because an initial value is given, you can shorten the syntax as follows:

```
var i = 2
```

When an initial value is provided, the compiler is smart enough to figure out the type. In this case, the compiler sees the value of 2 and knows the type is an integer.

Go doesn't stop there. Do we need the `var` keyword? Go provides something called *short variable declarations*:

```
i := 2
```

This is a concise equivalent to the first variable statement. It's less than half the length of the first example, easy to read, and happens because the compiler figures out the missing parts.

Simplicity means Go doesn't have all the features of every other programming language. For example, Go has neither a ternary operator (usually `? :`) nor type generics. Lacking some features present in other modern languages has opened Go to occasional criticism, but this shouldn't deter you from using Go. With software, there's often more than one way to solve a programming problem. Although Go may lack a feature that another language contains, Go provides ways to solve the same problems in a well-thought-out manner.

Although the core of the language is fairly simple, the Go built-in package system enables you to add many aspects. Many of the missing elements can be built as a third-party package and incorporated into applications via the package system.

The minimal size and complexity has benefits. The language can be learned quickly and easily retained. This turns out to be quite a benefit when quickly crafting and iterating over a codebase.

1.2   Noteworthy aspects of Go

Because Go is designed around practical situations, it has several noteworthy features. These useful characteristics, when used together, provide the building blocks for Go applications.

1.2.1   Multiple return values

One of the first things you'll learn in Go is that functions and methods can return multiple values. Most programming languages support returning a single value from a function. When you need to return multiple values, they're shoehorned into a tuple, hash, or other type, and that value is returned. Go is one of the few languages natively supporting multiple return values. This feature is regularly used, and something you'll see in virtually every part of Go and the libraries and applications written in it. For example, consider the following function that returns two string names.

Listing 1.1   Multiple returns: `returns.go`

```go
package main

import (
    "fmt"
)

func Names() (string, string) {        ← ❶ Two strings defined for return
    return "Foo", "Bar"                ← ❷ Two strings are returned.
}

func main() {
    n1, n2 := Names()                  ❸ Variables get two values
    fmt.Println(n1, n2)                   and print them.

    n3, _ := Names()                   ← ❹ Gets first return value and skips second
    fmt.Println(n3)
}
```

TIP   Imported packages used in this chapter, such as `fmt`, `bufio`, `net`, and others, are part of the standard library. More details, including their APIs and how they work, can be found at https://golang.org/pkg.

In this example, each `return` is defined in the function definition after the arguments ❶. In this case, there are two string values. When `return` is called, it returns two strings ❷ to match the definition. When the `Names` function is called, you need to have a variable for each `return` to capture the value ❸. But if you want to ignore one of the returned values, use _ instead of a variable name ❹. (Don't worry too much about the details of this example. You'll come back to these concepts, libraries, and tools in the coming chapters.)

Building on the idea of multiple returned values, you can name them and work with these names the same way you do variables. To illustrate, let's rework the previous example to use named return values in the next listing.

Listing 1.2   Named return values: `returns2.go`

```
package main
import (
    "fmt"
)
func Names() (first string, second string) {  ◁─────  ❶ Returned values have names.
    first = "Foo"
    second = "Bar"                                     ❷ Values assigned to named
    return                                               return variables
}                                            ◁─────── 
func main() {                                   ❸ return is called with no values.
    n1, n2 := Names()           ◁──── ❹ Variables are filled with values.
    fmt.Println(n1, n2)
}
```

As the Names function executes, the named return variables ❶ are available to have values assigned to them ❷. When return is called ❸ with no values, the current values for the return names are returned. For code calling the function, getting the response ❹ and using it works the same as without using names.

1.2.2   *A modern standard library*

Modern applications have common themes, such as being networked and dealing with encryption. Instead of burdening you, the developer, with the task of hunting for commonly needed libraries, the Go standard library provides useful modern functionality out of the box. Let's take a look at a few elements in the standard library so you can get an idea of what's included.

> **NOTE** The entire standard library is documented, with examples, at http://golang.org/pkg/.

NETWORKING AND HTTP

Building applications in a networked world means applications need to work as both a client that can connect to other networked devices, and as a server that other applications can connect to (see listing 1.3). The Go standard library makes this easy, whether you're working with HTTP or dealing directly with Transmission Control Protocol (TCP), User Datagram Protocol (UDP), or other common setups.

Listing 1.3   Read TCP status: `read_status.go`

```
package main

import (
    "bufio"
    "fmt"
    "net"
)

func main() {
    conn, _ := net.Dial("tcp", "golang.org:80")      ❶ Connects over TCP
    fmt.Fprintf(conn, "GET / HTTP/1.0\r\n\r\n")       ❷ Sends string over
    status, _ :=                                         the connection
        ➥bufio.NewReader(conn).ReadString('\n')
    fmt.Println(status)                               ❸ Prints the first response line
}
```

Connecting directly to a port is part of the `net` package, in which Go provides a common setup for different types of connections. The `Dial` function ❶ connects using the type and endpoint specified. In this case, it makes a TCP connection to golang.org on port 80. Over the connection, a `GET` request is sent ❷, and the first line of the response is printed ❸.

The ability to listen on a port is similarly easy to work with. Instead of calling out to an endpoint by using `Dial`, the `Listen` function in the `net` package enables an application to listen on a port and act on incoming connections.

HTTP, Representational State Transfer (REST), and web servers are incredibly common. To handle this common case, Go has the `http` package for providing both a client and a server (see the following listing). The client is simple enough to use that it meets the needs of the common everyday cases and extensible enough to use for the complex cases.

Listing 1.4   HTTP `GET`: `http_get.go`

```
package main

import (
    "fmt"
    "io/ioutil"
    "net/http"
)

func main() {
    resp, _ :=                                        Makes an HTTP GET request
        ➥http.Get("http://example.com/")
    body, _ :=                              Prints the body as a string
        ➥ioutil.ReadAll(resp.Body)                   Reads the body from the response
    fmt.Println(string(body))
    resp.Body.Close()                                Closes the connection
}
```

This example shows how to print the body of a simple HTTP GET request. The HTTP client can go far beyond this to deal with proxies, perform TLS handling, set headers, handle cookies, create client objects, and even swap out the transport layer altogether.

Creating an HTTP server with Go is a common task. What Go provides in the standard library is powerful enough to operate at scale, easy to get started with, and flexible enough to handle complex applications. Chapter 3 is dedicated to getting up and running with an HTTP server.

HTML

If you're working with web servers, you're likely going to work with HTML as well. The `html` and `html/template` packages provide a great start to generating web pages. Whereas the `html` package deals with escaping and unescaping HTML, the `html/template` package deals with creating reusable HTML templates. The security model for handling the data is documented, and helper functions exist for working with HTML, JavaScript, and more. The template system is extensible, making it an ideal base for more-complicated functionality, while providing a good set of functionality for anyone to get started.

CRYPTOGRAPHY

Cryptography has become a common component of an application, whether you're dealing with hashes or encrypting sensitive information. Go provides the common functionality including MD5, multiple versions of Secure Hash Algorithm (SHA), Transport Layer Security (TLS), Data Encryption Standard (DES), Triple Data Encryption Algorithm (TDEA), Advanced Encryption Standard (AES, formerly known as Rijndael), Keyed-Hash Message Authentication Code (HMAC), and many others. Additionally, a cryptographically secure random number generator is provided.

DATA ENCODING

When you share data between systems, an immediate concern is encoding. Did the data come in with base64 encoding? Does JavaScript Object Notation (JSON) or Extensible Markup Language (XML) data need to be turned into a local object? These are common situations, especially in our modern networked world.

Go was designed with encoding in mind. Internally, Go is entirely handled as UTF-8. This should be no surprise, as the creators of UTF-8 also created Go. But not everything passed around between systems is in UTF-8, and you have to deal with data formats that add meaning to the text. To handle the transitions and manipulations, Go has packages and interfaces. The packages provide features such as the ability to turn a JSON string into instantiated objects, and the interfaces provide a way to switch between encodings or add new ways to work with encodings via external packages.

1.2.3 Concurrency with goroutines and channels

Computer processors with multiple processing cores have become commonplace. They're in devices from servers to cell phones. Yet most programming languages were designed for processors with a single core, because that's what existed at the time.

Some programming languages even have a runtime with a global thread lock hampering the ability to easily run routines in parallel. Go was designed with parallel and concurrent processing in mind.

Go has a feature called a *goroutine,* a function that can be run concurrently to the main program or other goroutines. Sometimes dubbed *lightweight threads,* goroutines are managed by the Go runtime, where they're mapped and moved to the appropriate operating system thread and garbage-collected when no longer needed. When multiple processor cores are available, the goroutines can be run in parallel because various threads are running on different processing cores. But from the developer's point of view, creating a goroutine is as easy as writing a function. Figure 1.2 illustrates how goroutines work.

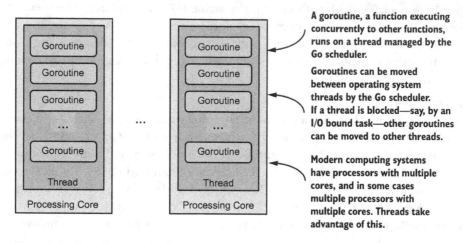

Figure 1.2   Goroutines running in threads distributed on the available processing cores

To further illustrate how this works, let's look at a goroutine that counts from 0 to 4 while the main program prints `Hello World` concurrently, as shown in the following listing.

Listing 1.5   Concurrent output

```
0
1
Hello World
2
3
4
```

This printed output is a mix of two functions printing concurrently. The code to make this happen is similar to normal procedural programming, but with a small twist, as shown next.

Listing 1.6   Printing concurrently

```
package main

import (
     "fmt"
     "time"
)

func count() {
     for i := 0; i < 5; i++ {
          fmt.Println(i)
          time.Sleep(time.Millisecond * 1)
     }
}

func main() {
     go count()
     time.Sleep(time.Millisecond * 2)
     fmt.Println("Hello World")
     time.Sleep(time.Millisecond * 5)
}
```

❶ **Function to execute as goroutine**

❷ **Starts goroutine**

The count function ❶ is a normal function that counts from 0 to 4. To run count in parallel rather than in order, you use the go keyword ❷. This causes main to continue executing immediately. Both count and main execute concurrently.

Channels provide a way for two goroutines to communicate with each other. By default, they block execution, allowing goroutines to synchronize. Figure 1.3 shows a simple example.

Step I: A goroutine has an instance of a type.

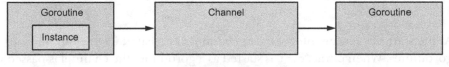

Step 2: The goroutine passes the instance into a channel.

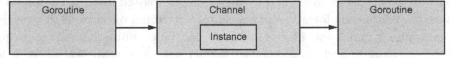

Step 3: The channel passes the instance into another goroutine.

Figure 1.3   Passing variables between goroutines via a channel

In this example, a variable is passed from one goroutine to another through a channel. This operation works even when goroutines are running in parallel on different processor cores. Although this example shows one-directional information passing, channels can be one-directional or bidirectional.

The following listing is an example of taking advantage of a channel.

Listing 1.7   Using channels: `channel.go`

```go
package main

import (
    "fmt"
    "time"
)

func printCount(c chan int) {              ◄──❶ An int type channel passed in
    num := 0
    for num >= 0 {
        num = <-c                          ◄──❷ Waits for value to come in
        fmt.Print(num, " ")
    }
}

func main() {
    c := make(chan int)                    ◄──❸ A channel is created.
    a := []int{8, 6, 7, 5, 3, 0, 9, -1}

    go printCount(c)                       ◄──❹ Starts the goroutine

    for _, v := range a {                  ❺ Passes ints into channel
        c <- v
    }
    time.Sleep(time.Millisecond * 1)       ◄──❻ main pauses before ending.
    fmt.Println("End of main")
}
```

At the start of `main`, an integer-typed channel `c` is created ❸ to communicate between goroutines. When `printCount` is started as a goroutine, the channel is passed in ❹. As an argument to `printCount`, the channel needs to be identified as an integer channel ❶. In the `for` loop inside `printCount`, `num` waits for channel `c` to send in integers ❷. Back in `main`, a list of integers is iterated over and passed into the channel `c` one at a time ❺. When each integer is passed into the channel on `main` ❺, it's received into `num` within `printCount` ❷. `printCount` continues until the `for` loop goes into another iteration and comes to the channel statement again ❷, where it waits for another value to come in on the channel. After `main` is done iterating over the integers, it continues on. When `main` is finished executing, the entire program is done, so you pause for a second ❻ before exiting so `printCount` can complete before `main` is done. Running this code produces the following listing.

Listing 1.8   Channel output

```
8 6 7 5 3 0 9 -1 End of main
```

Using channels and goroutines together provides functionality similar to lightweight threads or internal micro-services that communicate over a type-defined API. These can be chained or pieced together by using various techniques.

You'll return to goroutines and channels, two of Go's most powerful concepts, several times in this book. You'll see how they're used to write servers, handle message passing, and delay the execution of tasks. You'll also examine design patterns for working with goroutines and channels.

1.2.4 Go the toolchain—more than a language

Developing modern scalable and maintainable applications requires many elements. Compiling isn't the only common step. From the beginning, Go had this in mind. Go is more than a language and compiler. The go executable is a toolchain enabling lightweight package management, testing, documentation generation, and more, in addition to being able to compile a Go codebase into an executable. To illustrate, let's look at a few of the components in the toolchain.

PACKAGE MANAGEMENT

Many modern programming languages have package managers, but how many have package management built right in? Go does, and this proves to be useful for two important reasons. The obvious reason is programmer productivity. The second reason is faster compile time. Package handling was designed with a compiler in mind. It's one of the reasons the compiler is so fast.

The easiest way to ease into packages is to look at the standard library (see the following listing), which is built on the package system.

Listing 1.9 Single package import

```
package main

import "fmt"                            ◁──────  The fmt package is imported.

func main() {
    fmt.Println("Hello World!")         ◁──────  A function from fmt is used.
}
```

Packages are imported by their name. In this case, fmt is the format package. Everything in the package that can be referenced is available with the package name as the prefix. Here you have fmt.Println:

```
import (
    "fmt"
    "net/http"
)
```

Package imports can be grouped together and should be in alphabetical order. In this case, the net/http package is referenced with the http. prefix.

The import system works with packages from outside the Go standard library, and those packages are referenced just like any other package:

```
import (
    "golang.org/x/net/html"              ⟵——— External package referenced by URL
    "fmt"
    "net/http"
)
```

Package names are unique strings and can be anything. Here they're URLs to external packages. This enables Go to know this unique resource and to go out and get it for you:

```
$ go get ./...
```

The go get command can accept a path, such as golang.org/x/net/html, to get an individual package or ./... can be used, which will walk through the codebase and get any referenced external packages. Here Go looks at the import statement, sees an external reference, gets the package, and makes it available in the current workspace.

Go can talk to version-control systems to get the packages. It can speak to Git, Mercurial, SVN, and Bazaar when you have them installed in your local environment. In this case, Go retrieves the codebase from Git and checks out the latest commit from the default branch.

This package system isn't designed to be everything anyone would ever want in a package system. It provides the basics that can be used directly or as a basis for a more fully featured system.

TESTING

Testing is a common element of software development—some would say it's essential. Go provides a system for testing that includes a package in the standard library, a command-line runner, code-coverage reporting, and race-condition detection.

Creating and executing tests is fairly straightforward, as shown in the next listing.

Listing 1.10   Hello World: hello.go

```
package main

import "fmt"

func getName() string {
    return "World!"
}

func main() {
    name := getName()
    fmt.Println("Hello ", name)
}
```

Starting with a variant form of a Hello World application, you have a function, get-Name, that can be tested. Go's naming convention for test files is that they end in _test.go. This suffix tells Go that this is a file to be run when tests execute, and excluded when the application is built, as shown in the next listing.

Listing 1.11   Hello World test: `hello_test.go`

```
package main

import "testing"

func TestName(t *testing.T) {
    name := getName()

    if name != "World!" {
        t.Error("Respone from getName is unexpected value")
    }
}
```

❶ Functions starting with Test are run.

❷ Report error if test fails

When `go test` is run, it executes the function that begins with Test ❶. In this case, `TestName` is executed, and a struct `t` is passed in to help with testing. It contains useful functionality such as reporting an error. For more details, see the full `testing` package. If the name isn't correct, the test reports an error ❷.

The output of `go test` shows the packages tested and how they fared, as shown in the following listing. To test the current package and the ones nested in subdirectories, `go test ./...` can be used.

Listing 1.12   Running `go test`

```
$ go test
PASS
ok    go-in-practice/chapter1/hello      0.012s
```

If `getName` had returned something different from `World!`, you'd see something different. In the next example, the test system reports the location where the test error occurs, indicating the failed test, the file the test is in, and the line where the error happens. In this case, `getName` has been altered to return something different from `World!`.

Listing 1.13   Running `go test` **failure**

```
$ go test
--- FAIL: TestName (0.00 seconds)
      hello_test.go:9: Response from getName is unexpected value
FAIL
exit status 1
FAIL    go-in-practice/chapter1/hello             0.010s
```

Go provides the basic tooling and processes needed to get up and running quickly with tests. Go itself uses these tools. For those who want something more opinionated, such as behavior-driven development or something found in a framework from another language, external packages can be used that build atop the built-in functionality. Tests in Go have the full power of the language available, which includes packages.

CODE COVERAGE

In addition to executing tests, the test system can generate code-coverage reports and provide a view of the coverage down to the statement level, as shown in listing 1.14.

> **NOTE**   As of Go 1.5, the coverage commands are part of the core Go toolchain. Prior to 1.5, cover had been an add-on tool.

To see the code coverage from the tests, run the following command:

```
$ go test -cover
```

Adding the -cover flag to the go test command causes it to report code coverage alongside the other details about the tests.

Listing 1.14   Testing with code coverage

```
$ go test -cover
PASS
Coverage: 33.3% of statements
ok    go-in-practice/chapter1/hello          0.011s
```

Code coverage doesn't stop there. Coverage can be exported into files that other tools can use. Those reports can be displayed using built-in tools. Figure 1.4 shows a report displayed in a web browser that indicates which statements were executed in the tests.

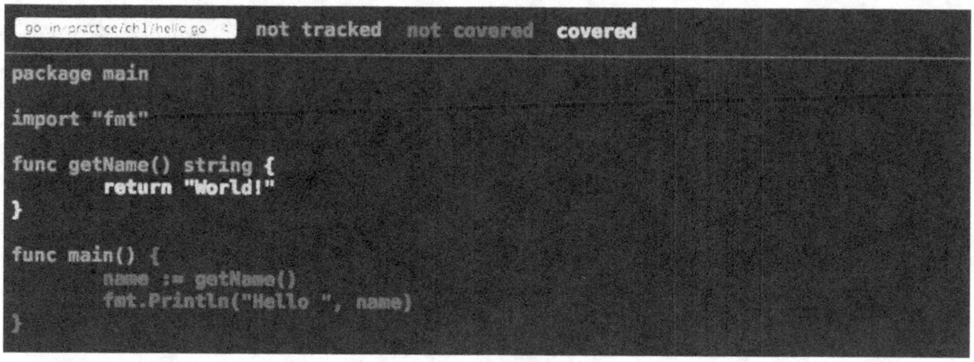

Figure 1.4   Code coverage displayed in a web browser

Quite often test coverage reports provide details down to the line level. Multiple statements can be on the same line. A simple example can be seen in if and else statements. Go will display which statements were executed and which don't have coverage in the tests.

> **TIP**   More information about the cover tool can be found on the Go blog at http://blog.golang.org/cover.

Testing is an important feature in Go and one we spend some time on in chapter 4.

FORMATTING

Should block indentations use tabs or spaces? Formatting and style questions are regularly discussed and debated when it comes to coding conventions. How much time would we save if these discussions didn't need to happen? With Go, you don't need to spend time debating formatting or other idioms.

Effective Go, available at http://golang.org/doc/effective_go.html, is a guide to writing idiomatic Go. It describes styles and conventions used throughout the Go community. Using these conventions makes it easier to read and interact with Go programs.

Go has a built-in tool for reformatting code to meet many of the style guidelines. Running the `go fmt` command from the root of a package causes Go to go through each of the `.go` files in a package and rewrite them into the canonical style. The `go fmt` command can have a path to a package or `./...` (iterate over all subdirectories) appended to it.

Numerous editors have commands, either built in or through add-on packages, to handle formatting for you. These include Vim, Sublime Text, Eclipse, and many others. For example, the Sublime Text package GoSublime updates the formatting of a file when it's saved.

1.3 Go in the vast language landscape

GitHub, the popular code-hosting service, holds projects in hundreds of languages. The TIOBE index, a listing of the most popular programming languages, indicates that those popular languages are capturing a diminishing percent of the market. More languages have traction. With so many languages available, it's useful to know where Go fits in.

Go was designed to be a systems language. What we call *cloud computing* is often considered a form of systems programming. Go was designed with systems programming use cases in mind, which is where it excels.

Being a systems language narrows its focus. For example, although Go is useful in situations where C or C++ has been used, it's not a good language for embedded systems. Go has a runtime and a garbage-collection system that don't run well on embedded systems with limited resources.

Comparing Go to other popular programming languages can provide insight into where it sits relative to those languages. Although we believe Go is great for some applications, this isn't a debate about which programming languages to use. Choosing the right languages needs to take into account more than the characteristics of those languages.

1.3.1 C and Go

Go initially came to life as an alternative to C for developing applications. Because the original inspiration came out of developing in C (and C is one of the most popular languages, if not the most popular), it's helpful to show the similarities and differences in these languages.

Both Go and C compile into machine code for a target operating system and architecture. Both share many style similarities, but Go goes well beyond what C does.

Go provides a runtime that includes features such as managing threads and garbage collection. When writing Go applications, you give up control over thread management and work around interruptions for garbage collection as you would with other garbage-collected languages. In C, you manage threads and memory yourself. Any threads and the corresponding work on them are handled by the application. Memory is intentionally managed without a garbage collector.

C and its object-oriented derivatives such as C++ enable a wide variety of applications to be written. High-performance embedded systems,

> **C + Go = cgo**
>
> Go provides support for binding C libraries to Go programs. Go provides a library of C compatibility tools. This library eases the transition between, for example, C-style strings and Go strings. Furthermore, the Go tools can build mixed C and Go programs. Go also has support for Simplified Wrapper and Interface Generator (SWIG) wrappers. You can get a feel for the features by running `go help c` and `go doc cgo` to read a brief overview.

large-scale cloud applications, and complicated desktop applications can all be written in C. Go is useful as a systems and cloud-platform language. Go applications have a sweet spot that provides real productivity.

The Go runtime and toolchain provide a lot out of the box. This functionality enables Go applications to be written fairly quickly and with less tedious work than a comparable C counterpart. For example, a Go application taking advantage of all four cores in a server can use goroutines. The C version would need to start threads and manage the work moved between them in addition to the application code.

Compiling C applications can take time. This is especially true when working with outside dependencies and the need to compile them. Speed when compiling applications in Go was a design goal, and Go applications compile faster than their C counterparts. When applications scale in size to the point that compiling can take minutes or hours, saving time while compiling can make a real difference in the productivity of your development. Compiling Go applications is fast enough that many applications and their dependent packages can compile in seconds or less.

1.3.2   *Java and Go*

Java, which is consistently one of the most popular programming languages on the planet, is used for a wide variety of projects, ranging from server applications to mobile and Android applications to cross-platform desktop applications. Go was originally designed as a systems language. Although its use has expanded into areas such as web and mobile development, Go still isn't a language that you can use to easily write a desktop application. It excels the most when used as originally intended.

Given that Java is so popular and can be used for a wider variety of applications, why would anyone want to use Go? Although the basic syntax is similar, Java and Go are quite different. Go compiles to a single binary for an operating system. This binary contains the Go runtime, all the imported packages, and the entire application—everything needed to run the program. Java takes a different approach. With Java, you have a runtime installed on the operating system. Java applications are packaged into a file that can be run on any system with the runtime. The applications need to be executed in a compatible runtime version.

These differing approaches, depicted in figure 1.5, have practical applications. Deploying a Go application to a server entails deploying the one file. Deploying a Java application requires installing and maintaining Java on the system along with deploying the application.

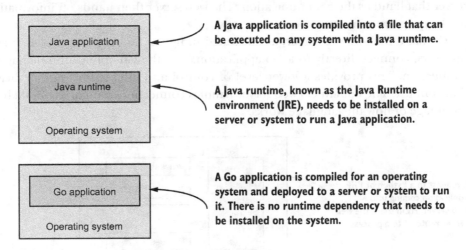

Figure 1.5   Java and Go running in an operating system

Another key difference between Java and Go has to do with how applications are executed. Go programs are compiled into a system binary and executed by the operating system. Java applications are executed in a virtual machine (VM) typically containing a just-in-time (JIT) compiler. A JIT can look at how the code is executing in context and optimize it accordingly.

This raises an important question: is code running a VM with a JIT faster than a compiled binary? The answer isn't straightforward because it depends on the JIT, the code being executed, and more. In tests comparing similar functionality side by side, no clear-cut winner emerges.

1.3.3   Python, PHP, and Go

Python and PHP are two of the most popular dynamic languages in the world. Python has become one of the most popular languages taught and used in universities. It can be used for a wide variety of purposes, from building cloud applications to websites to command-line utilities. PHP is the most popular programming language used to build websites with a focus on the web. Although these two languages have many differences, they have a few similarities that highlight some of the ways Go works.

Python and PHP are dynamically typed languages, whereas Go is a statically typed language with dynamic-like features. Dynamic languages check type at runtime and even perform what appear to be type conversions on the fly. Statically typed languages do type checking based on static code analysis. Go has the ability to do some type switching. Under some circumstances, variables of one type can be turned into variables of a different type. This may seem unorthodox for a statically typed language, but it's useful.

When Python and PHP are used to build a website or application, they typically sit behind a web server such as Nginx or Apache. A web browser connects to the web server that handles the communication. The web server then hands off information to the language runtime and program.

Go has a built-in web server, as illustrated in figure 1.6. Applications, such as web browsers, connect directly to a Go application, and the Go application manages the connection. This provides a lower level of control and interaction with applications that connect. The built-in Go web server handles connections concurrently, taking full advantage of how the language works.

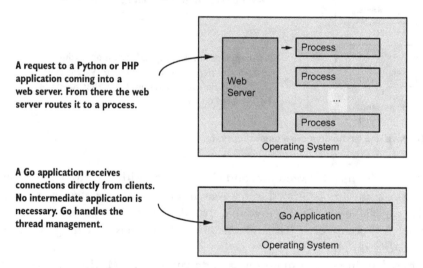

Figure 1.6   Python, PHP, and Go paths of a client request

One of the reasons it's useful to put Python and PHP behind a web server has to do with threads and concurrent connections. Python has a global interpreter lock that allows only one thread to execute at a time. PHP applications tend to run from start to end in a process. To enable multiple connections to an application concurrently, a web server can sit in front of the application and handle running the concurrent connections in separate processes.

The built-in Go web server takes advantage of goroutines to run connections concurrently. The Go runtime manages the goroutines across application threads. You'll see this in more detail in chapter 3. Whereas Python and PHP end up with separate processes for the different connections, Go shares an environment, allowing you to share resources where it makes sense.

Under the hood in the primary implementation, Python and PHP are built in C. Built-in objects, methods, and functions, whose implementation is in C, execute more quickly than application objects, methods, and functions. The code written for an application takes a different path that includes an intermediate format that's interpreted. One of the performance tips for both Python and PHP is to take performance-critical code and rewrite it in C.

Go applications compile into a binary. Software in the standard library and application code are both compiled into machine code. There's no distinction.

1.3.4 JavaScript, Node.js, and Go

JavaScript came into being in just over 10 days. It went on to be one of the most popular languages in the world, as it was baked into all the major web browsers. More recently, JavaScript has been used on servers, in desktop applications, and in other areas. This was driven by the Node.js platform.

Go and JavaScript, primarily through Node.js, can fill a similar space but do so in different ways. Exploring how they fill the space differently helps to highlight where Go fits in the space.

JavaScript has a single-threaded model. Although asynchronous I/O may use separate threads, the main program executes in a single thread. When code in the main thread takes a significant amount of time, it blocks other code from executing. Go uses a multithreaded model in which the runtime manages goroutines running concurrently on the different threads. The Go model, with multiple threads running across multiple cores, can take advantage of more of the available hardware than the single thread used in JavaScript.

Node.js uses the V8 engine created by Google and used in Google Chrome. The V8 engine contains a virtual machine with a JIT compiler. This is conceptually similar to Java. The virtual machine and JIT can lead to some performance improvements. As V8 watches a long-running program execute, it can improve performance over time. For example, it can look at the execution of a loop and see ways to improve the performance beyond the direct machine code because it knows the context. V8 also knows a variable type even though JavaScript is dynamically typed. The longer a program runs, the more V8 can learn and improve the performance.

On the other hand, Go programs are compiled machine code and execute at statically typed machine-code speeds. No JIT is looking to improve runtime execution. As in C, there's no practical need for a JIT.

PACKAGE HANDLING

The Node.js ecosystem has a community and tooling surrounding the handling and distribution of packages. These can range from libraries to command-line utilities to full applications. The package manager npm is often bundled with installation of Node.js. A central repository of information about packages is available at www.npmjs.org. When a package is fetched, metadata about the package is received from the central repository, and the package is downloaded from its source location.

As we touched on earlier, Go has a package-handling system. Unlike Node.js, which has metadata and content in a central repository, Go has no central repository, and packages are fetched from their source location.

1.4 Getting up and running in Go

You have a few options for getting into Go, depending on your level of commitment.

The easiest way to get started with Go is through a tour at http://tour.golang.org, which walks you through using some of its main features. What separates the Go tour from typical tutorials is in how the examples work. You can execute the examples right in your browser. If you want to change them and execute your changes, you can do that as well.

If you want to try executing simple Go applications, you can do that through the Go Playground at https://play.golang.org. The Go Playground is what enables the tour examples to be executable. Here you can test code and share a link to it. The examples in this book that represent a program can be executed in the Playground.

1.4.1 Installing Go

Installing Go is a fairly straightforward process. Everything you need to know about getting and installing Go is documented at http://golang.org/doc/install. This includes the operating systems supported, the hardware architectures that can be targeted for these systems, and more.

For Microsoft Windows and Mac OS X, installers take care of the installation. It's as easy as installing any other program. Users of Homebrew on OS X can install Go by using the command `brew install go`.

Installing Go on Linux includes a wider variety of options. You can install go using built-in package managers, such as `apt-get` and `yum`. The version available is usually an older version, and newer versions are faster or contain new features. Through the Go install instructions, you can download the most recent version of Go, put it on your system, and add the Go executables to your path. On versions of Linux that support the Debian package system, such as Ubuntu, you can use the `godeb` tool to install the latest version of Go. The author of `godeb` explains the process at http://blog.labix .org/2013/06/15/in-flight-deb-packages-of-go.

1.4.2 Working with Git, Mercurial, and version control

To work with packages and external imports stored in version-control systems, Go expects these systems to be installed on the local system. Go doesn't reimplement any software configuration management (SCM) tools; rather, it knows about them and takes advantage of them when installed.

Two of the dominant version-control systems used by Go developers for packages are Git and Mercurial (`hg`). Git is widely popular and is used by numerous Google developers and by the packages they release to GitHub. You'll need to have Git installed, but Go doesn't require a specific version. Any recent version should do.

1.4.3   Exploring the workspace

The go toolchain expects Go code to be in a workspace. A *workspace* is a directory hierarchy with the src, pkg, and bin directories, as shown in the following listing.

```
Listing 1.15    Workspace layout
```

```
$GOPATH/                        ◀──❶ The base directory, or $GOPATH
      ┌──▸  src/
      │        github.com/
      │              Masterminds/
      │                    cookoo/
      │                    glide/
      │    bin/                  ◀────── Compiled programs
      │        glide
      │    pkg/                  ◀────── Compiled libraries
      │        darwin_amd64/
      github.com/
                    Masterminds/
                          cookoo.a
```

The source code to external dependencies

The one environment variable that you need to set is $GOPATH ❶. This points go to the base directory for the workspace. Source code, including both the code you're working on and any dependent code, goes in the src directory. Although you'll do some management of this directory, the Go tools will help manage external source code repositories. The other two directories are almost always managed by the Go tools themselves. When you run go install on a project, executables (like the one in listing 1.15) will be compiled and written to bin. In this example, the Glide project compiles into an executable named *glide*. The Cookoo project, though, doesn't have a standalone executable. It provides only libraries that other Go programs can use. Running go install on it will create an archive file suffixed with .a, and that's stored in the pkg directory.

1.4.4   Working with environment variables

GOPATH is one environment variable that the go executable expects to exist. GOPATH tells Go where your workspace is to import packages, install binaries, and store intermediate archives. The following example creates a workspace in a directory named *go* on a UNIX-like system:

```
$ mkdir $HOME/go
$ export GOPATH=$HOME/go
```

Inside GOPATH, the go program will create a bin directory where executables are installed. For convenience, it's useful to add this directory to your path. For example, on UNIX-like systems:

```
$ export PATH=$PATH:$GOPATH/bin
```

If you'd like to install binaries to an alternative location, the GOBIN environment variable can be set to that path. This is an optional environment variable.

1.5 *Hello, Go*

In an obvious twist on the standard Hello World program, the next listing shows a simple application that prints Hello, my name is Inigo Montoya through a web server.

Listing 1.16 Hello World web server: inigo.go

```
package main                              ──❶ The main package is used for applications.

import (
    "fmt"
    "net/http"                                      ❷ Import
)                                                      needed
                                                       packages.

func hello(res http.ResponseWriter, req *http.Request) {      Handler for
    fmt.Fprint(res, "Hello, my name is Inigo Montoya")        an HTTP
}                                                             request

func main() {
    http.HandleFunc("/", hello)                             ❸ Main
    http.ListenAndServe("localhost:4000", nil)                application
}                                                             execution
```

This simple application has three parts. It opens with a package declaration ❶. Where libraries are declared with a short name describing what they do—for example, net or crypto—applications have the package main. To write strings and operate as a web server, the fmt and http packages are imported ❷. Importing these packages makes them available in the code and in the compiled application.

The application execution begins with the main function ❸ that has no arguments or returned values. Following the first line of main, the http.HandleFunc function is called, telling the web server to execute the function hello when the path / is matched. The hello function follows an interface for handlers. It receives an object for the HTTP request and response. This is followed by a call to http.ListenAndServe, telling the web server to start up and listen on port 4000 of the domain localhost.

You can execute this application in two ways. In the next listing you use go run, which compiles the application into a temp directory and executes it.

Listing 1.17 Running inigo.go

```
$ go run inigo.go
```

The temporary file is cleaned up when the application is done running. This is useful in development of new versions of applications that are regularly tested.

After the application has started, you can open a web browser and visit http://localhost:4000 to view the response, as shown in figure 1.7.

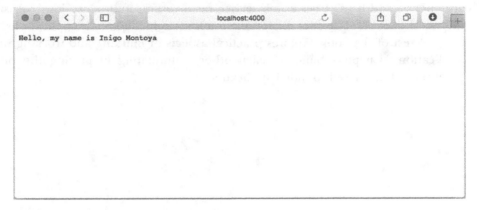

Figure 1.7 **"Hello, my name is Inigo Montoya" viewed in web browser**

Alternately, an application can be built and run as in the following listing.

Listing 1.18 Building `inigo.go`

```
$ go build inigo.go
$ ./inigo
```

Here the first step is to build the application. Using `go build` without filenames will build the current directory. Using a filename, or set of filenames, only builds the selection. From there, the built application needs to be executed.

1.6 Summary

Go is a language designed for modern hardware and application development. It takes advantage of recent advances in technology while providing a toolchain so that Go development just works. In this chapter, you took a peek at what makes Go a powerful language worth using to develop applications, and learned the following:

- The Go philosophy of simplicity plus extensibility that created a useful language and enables an ecosystem to surround it
- Features of Go that take advantage of modern hardware, such as goroutines that enable concurrent execution
- The toolchain accompanying the Go language, including testing, package management, formatting, and documentation
- How Go compares to languages such as C, Java, JavaScript, Python, PHP, and others, as well as when to use it and when to use something else
- How to install and get up and running in Go

Chapter 2 starts with the foundation necessary to build applications from console utilities through web services. How should you handle applications that have commands, arguments, and flags? Does a web service need to gracefully shut down? Answering questions like these provides the foundation for production-ready applications.

The rest of the book explores practical aspects of building and working with Go applications. Chapters build on each other, culminating in putting the practices together to build a well-rounded application.

A solid foundation

This chapter covers

- Working with command-line flags, options, and arguments
- Passing configuration into an application
- Starting and gracefully stopping a web server
- Path routing for web and API servers

The foundation an application is built upon can be as important as any feature. Handling the way an application shuts down so you don't lose data or create a bad user experience is an example of a step you take when building a strong foundation.

This chapter covers four foundational areas. You'll start with console applications, also known as *CLI applications*. You'll learn about handling command-line options, sometimes called *flags* or *getopts*, in a way that's consistent with modern applications on Linux and other POSIX systems. As part of this, you'll explore a setup that enables you to focus on application code rather than structure while developing console applications.

You'll follow that up by looking at several ways to pass configuration into an application. This includes various popular file and content formats used to store configuration.

From there, you'll move onto servers and practical measures for starting and stopping them. This may seem fairly straightforward, but addressing certain situations early (for example, stopping a server before data has finished being saved) can cut down on future problems.

The chapter ends with path-matching techniques for servers. URL path matching is common for websites and servers providing a Representational State Transfer (REST) API. You'll learn how and when to implement a few of the common methods for path matching.

By the end of this chapter, you'll know the best practices for building command-line clients and web servers that can serve as a foundation for building robust applications in Go.

2.1 Working with CLI applications, the Go way

Whether you're using a console application (such as the source-control management system Git or an application such as the MySQL database or the Apache web server), command-line arguments and flags are part of the application user interface. The Go standard library has built-in functionality for working with these, but it comes with a twist.

> ### Windowed applications
> Designed as a systems language, Go doesn't provide native support for building windowed applications like the ones you find in Microsoft Windows or Mac OS X. The Go community has dabbled in windowed development, but no clear direction has presented itself.

2.1.1 Command-line flags

The argument and flag handling in the Go standard library is based on Plan 9, which has a different style from the systems based on GNU/Linux and Berkeley Software Distribution (BSD), such as Mac OS X and FreeBSD, that are in wide use today. For example, on Linux and BSD systems, you can use the command ls -la to list all files in a directory. The -la part of the command contains two flags, or options. The l flag tells ls to use the long form listing, and the a flag causes the list to include hidden files. The Go flag system won't let you combine multiple flags, and instead sees this as one flag named la.

GNU-style commands (such as Linux's ls) support long options (for example, --color) that require two dashes in order to tell the program that the string color isn't five options, but one.

A debate has arisen over whether the Go (or Plan 9) system offers any real advantages over the style that dominates GNU, Linux, and BSD. Honestly, it boils down to a matter of preference. GNU-style double-dashes feel clunky and error-prone to some.

Plan 9

Developed at Bell Labs as a successor to UNIX, Plan 9 is an open source operating system primarily developed between the 1980s and 2002. Ken Thompson and Rob Pike, two of the creators of Go, were initial members of the team leading the development of Plan 9. Their influence over both projects has led to similarities.

But Go's single-dash long options eliminate the ability (as you just saw) of grouping single-character options into one.

This built-in flag system doesn't differentiate between short and long flags. A flag can be short or long, and each flag needs to be separated from the others. For example, if you run `go help build`, you'll see flags such as -v, -race, -x, and -work. For the same option, you'll see a single flag rather than a long or short name to use.

To illustrate the default flag behavior, the following listing shows a simple console application using the `flag` package.

Listing 2.1   Hello World CLI using `flag` package

```
$ flag_cli
Hello World!
$ flag_cli -s -name Buttercup
Hola Buttercup!
$ flag_cli --spanish -name Buttercup
Hola Buttercup!
```

Each flag is separate from the rest and begins with either a - or --, as they're interchangeable. A method is available for defining a flag with either a short or long name, but as you can see in the next listing, it's an implicit method.

Listing 2.2   Source of Hello World using `flag` package: `flag_cli.go`

```
package main

import (
    "flag"              ← Imports the standard flag package
    "fmt"
)

var name = flag.String("name", "World", "A name to say hello to.")   ← ❶ Creates a new variable from a flag

var spanish bool        ← ❷ New variable to store flag value

func init() {
    flag.BoolVar(&spanish, "spanish", false, "Use Spanish language.")
    flag.BoolVar(&spanish, "s", false, "Use Spanish language.")   ┐
}                                                                  ┘ Sets variable to the flag value ❸

func main() {
    flag.Parse()        ← ❹ Parses the flags, placing values in variables
```

```
        if spanish == true {
                fmt.Printf("Hola %s!\n", *name)
        } else {
                fmt.Printf("Hello %s!\n", *name)
        }
}
```

◄── **Accesses name**
 ❺ **as a pointer**

Here you can see two ways to define a flag. In the first, a variable can be created from a flag. In this example, it's done using flag.String() ❶. flag.String takes a flag name, default value, and description as arguments. The value of name is an address containing the value of the flag. To access this value, you'll need to access name as a pointer ❺.

The second method for handling a flag is the one that implicitly lets you have a long and short flag. Start by creating a normal variable ❷ of the same type as the flag. This will be used to store the value of a flag. Then use one of the flag functions that places the value of a flag into an existing variable ❸. In this case, flag.BoolVar is used twice, once for the long name and once for the short name.

TIP Flag functions exist for each variable type. To learn about each of them, see the flag package (http://golang.org/pkg/flag).

Finally, for the flag values to be in the variables, flag.Parse() needs to be run ❹.

TIP Command-line arguments aren't registered with the flag package but are available via the Args or Arg function from the flag package.

The flag package doesn't create help text for you but does help with the flags. This package has two handy functions you can use. The PrintDefaults function generates help text for flags. For example, the line of help text for the preceding name option ❶ reads as follows:

```
-name string
    A name to say hello to. (default "World")
```

This is a nicety in Go that makes it easier to keep your user informed about how your program works.

Flags also have a VisitAll function that accepts a callback function as an argument. This iterates over each of the flags executing the callback function on it and allows you to write your own help text for them. For example, the following listing would instead display -name: A name to say hello to. (Default: 'World').

Listing 2.3   Custom flag help text

```
flag.VisitAll(func(flag *flag.Flag) {
    format := "\t-%s: %s (Default: '%s')\n"
    fmt.Printf(format, flag.Name, flag.Usage, flag.DefValue)
})
```

TECHNIQUE 1   GNU/UNIX-style command-line arguments

Although the built-in `flag` package is useful and provides the basics, it doesn't provide flags in the manner most of us have come to expect. The difference in user interaction between the style used in Plan 9 and the style in Linux- and BSD-based systems is enough to cause users to stop and think. This is often due to problems they'll encounter when trying to mix short flags, such as those used when executing a command like `ls -la`.

PROBLEM

Those of us who write for non-Windows systems will likely be working with a UNIX variant, and our users will expect UNIX-style flag processing. How do you write Go command-line tools that meet users' expectations? Ideally, you want to do this without writing one-off specialized flag processing.

SOLUTION

This common problem has been solved in a couple of ways. Some applications, such as Docker, the software container management system, have a subpackage containing code to handle Linux-style flags. In some cases, these are forks of the Go `flag` package, in which the extra needs are added in. But maintaining per-project implementations of argument parsing results is an awful lot of duplicated effort to repeatedly solve the same generic problem.

The better approach is to use an existing library. You can import several standalone packages into your own application. Many are based on the `flag` package provided by the standard library and have compatible or similar interfaces. Importing one of these packages and using it is faster than altering the `flag` package and maintaining the difference.

DISCUSSION

In the following examples, you'll see two packages with slightly different approaches. The first attempts to keep API compatibility with the Go `flag` package, whereas the second breaks from it.

GNUFLAG

Similar to the `flag` package, the `launchpad.net/gnuflag` package brings GNU-style (Linux) flags to Go. Don't let the name fool you. The license isn't the GPL license, typical of GNU-based programs and libraries, but rather a BSD-style license in line with the Go license.

Several forms of flags are supported when using `gnuflag`, including these:

- `-f` for a single-letter or short flag
- `-fg` for a group of single-letter flags
- `--flag` for a multiletter or long flag name
- `--flag x` for a long flag with a value passed in as `x`
- `-f x` or `-fx` for a short flag with a passed-in value

The gnuflag package has almost the exact same API as the flag package, with one notable difference. The Parse function has an additional argument. Otherwise, it's a drop-in replacement. The flag package will parse flags between the command name and the first nonflag argument. For example, in listing 2.4, the -s and -n flags are defined, and -n takes a value. When flag parses foo, it has reached a nonflag argument and stops parsing. That means -bar won't be parsed to see if it's a flag. The gnuflag package has an option to continue parsing that would allow it to find flags positioned where -bar is.

> **Listing 2.4   `flag` package flag parsing**

```
$ flag_based_cli -s -n Buttercup foo -bar
```

To switch from the flag package to the gnuflag package, you need to change only two things in an application. First, instead of importing the flag package, import launchpad.net/gnuflag. Then, add an additional first argument to the Parse function of either true or false. A value of true looks for flags anywhere in the command, and false behaves like the flag package. That's it.

> **NOTE** lanuchpad.net uses the Bazaar version-control system. You need to have this installed in order for Go to fetch the package. More details are available at http://bazaar.canonical.com/.

GO-FLAGS

Some community flag packages break from the conventions used in the flag package within the standard library. One such package is github.com/jessevdk/go-flags. It provides Linux- and BSD-style flags, providing even more features than those in gnuflag, but uses an entirely different API and style. Features include the following:

- Short flags, such as -f, and groups of short flags, such as -fg.
- Multiple-letter or long flags, such as --flag.
- Supporting option groups.
- Generating well-formed help documentation.
- Passing values for flags in multiple formats such as -p/usr/local, -p /usr /local, and -p=/usr/local.
- The same option can, optionally, appear more than once and be stored multiple times on a slice.

To illustrate using this flag package, the following listing shows our Spanish-capable Hello World console application rewritten using go-flags.

> **Listing 2.5   Using `go-flags`**

```
package main

import (
    "fmt"
```

```
        flags "github.com/jessevdk/go-flags"
)

var opts struct {
    Name    string `short:"n" long:"name" default:"World"
 description:"A name to say hello to."`
            Spanish bool   `short:"s" long:"spanish"
 description:"Use Spanish Language"`
}

func main() {
    flags.Parse(&opts)

    if opts.Spanish == true {
        fmt.Printf("Hola %s!\n", opts.Name)
    } else {
        fmt.Printf("Hello %s!\n", opts.Name)
    }
}
```

Imports go-flags aliased to the name flags

❶ Struct containing the defined flags

❷ Parses the flag values into the struct

❸ Properties on opts used with flag values

The first big difference you'll notice from previous techniques is how flags are defined. In this instance, they're defined as properties on a struct ❶. The property names provide access to the values in your application. Information about a flag, such as short name, long name, default value, and description, are gathered using reflection to parse the space-separated key-value pairs following a property on a struct. This key-value-pair parsing capability is provided by the `reflect` package in the standard library. For example, opts.Name is mapped to a flag that has a short name -n, a long name --name, a default value of World, and a description used for help text.

For the values to be available on the opts struct, the Parse function needs to be called with the opts struct passed in ❷. After that, the properties on the struct can be called normally with flag values or their defaults available ❸.

2.1.2 Command-line frameworks

Processing flags certainly isn't the only important part of building a command-line application. Although Go developers learn as a matter of course how to begin with a main function and write a basic program, we often find ourselves writing the same set of features for each new command-line program we write. Fortunately, tools can provide a better entry point for creating command-line programs, and you'll look at one of those in this section.

TECHNIQUE 2   **Avoiding CLI boilerplate code**

You know the drill: You need a quick command-line tool for doing some light processing. You start from scratch and build that same old, bare-minimum boilerplate code. And it works. Unfortunately, it works well enough that you soon find yourself writing a more advanced version. This one has new options. But to add these new features, you refactor the boilerplate code into something just flexible enough to get the new job done. And the cycle repeats.

PROBLEM

Repeatedly, we find ourselves writing the same kinds of command-line programs. At first, we think of them as disposable, but some of the tools we write end up growing far beyond our initial expectations. Why keep writing the same boilerplate, only to be faced later with refactoring the top level of the program? Are there tools that can provide a simple and repeatable pattern for rapidly building CLI programs?

SOLUTION

If you want something more opinionated and full of features for building a console application, frameworks are available to handle command routing, help text, subcommands, and shell autocompletion, in addition to flags. A popular framework used to build console-based applications is `cli` (https://github.com/urfave/cli). This framework has been used by projects such as the open source platform-as-a-service (PaaS) project Cloud Foundry, the container management system Docker, and the continuous integration and deployment system Drone.

DISCUSSION

Combining routing, flag and option parsing, and help documentation into a setup that's self-documenting, `cli.go` is one of the easiest ways to get started building a console application that works the way you'd expect it to.

A SIMPLE CONSOLE APPLICATION

Before looking at a console application with multiple commands, it's useful to look at a console application that executes a single action. You'll use this foundation in an expansion to multiple commands and subcommands. Figure 2.1 shows the structure that a single-action application can use from the command line.

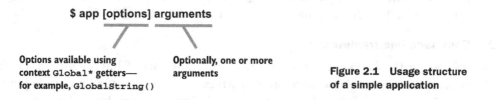

Figure 2.1   Usage structure of a simple application

The following listing is a simple console application that displays `Hello World!` or says hello to a name you choose.

Listing 2.6   Hello World CLI: `hello_cli.go`

```
$ hello_cli
Hello World!
$ hello_cli --name Inigo
Hello Inigo!
$ hello_cli -n Inigo
Hello Inigo!
$ hello_cli -help
NAME:
   hello_cli - Print hello world
```

```
USAGE:
   hello_cli [global options] command [command options] [arguments...]
VERSION:
   0.0.0
COMMANDS:
   help, h   Shows a list of commands or help for one command
GLOBAL OPTIONS:
   --name, -n 'World'      Who to say hello to.
   --help, -h             show help
   --version, -v          print the version
```

Using cli.go, the application-specific code needed to generate this application is only 26 lines long and can be seen in the following listing. The rest of the work and user interface is handled by cli.go.

Listing 2.7   Hello World CLI: hello_cli.go

```go
package main

import (
    "fmt"
    "os"

    "gopkg.in/urfave/cli.v1"        ◁── Includes the
)                                         cli.go package

func main() {
    app := cli.NewApp()                            ❶ Creates a new
    app.Name = "hello_cli"                             application
    app.Usage = "Print hello world"
    app.Flags = []cli.Flag{                        ❷ Sets up a
        cli.StringFlag{                                global flag
            Name:  "name, n",
            Value: "World",
            Usage: "Who to say hello to.",
        },
    }
    app.Action = func(c *cli.Context) error {      ❸ Defines the action
        name := c.GlobalString("name")                 to run
        fmt.Printf("Hello %s!\n", name)
        return nil
    }

    app.Run(os.Args)        ◁──❹ Runs the application
}
```

After cli.go is imported, a new application is created using cli.NewApp. The returned variable is the basis for the application. Setting the Name and Usage properties is useful for documentation ❶.

> **TIP**   If the Name property is left unset, cli.go will attempt to determine the name by using the name of the application. If an application may be renamed, it's useful to use the default behavior.

The Flags property is a slice of `cli.Flag` containing the global flags ❷. Each flag has a long name, short name, or both. Some flags, such as a `cli.StringFlag`, have a `Value` property for the default value. `cli.BoolFlag` is an example of a flag without a default value. Its presence sets the value to `true`, and its absence sets the value to `false`. The Usage property is used for documentation that can be seen on the help screen.

cli.go provides the ability to have a default action when the application is run, to have commands, and to have nested subcommands. We cover commands and subcommands in the next section. Here you set the `Action` property that handles the default action ❸. The value of `Action` is a function that accepts `*cli.Context` as an argument and returns an error. This function contains the application code that should be run. In this case, it obtains the name to say hello to by using `c.GlobalString("name")` before printing hello to the name. If you want the returned error to cause the application to exit with a nonzero exit code, return an error of `cli.ExitError`, which can be created using the `cli.NewExitError` function.

The final step is to run the application that was just set up. To do this, `os.Args`, the arguments passed into the application, are passed into the Run method on the application ❹.

> **TIP** Arguments are available in the `Action` function. In this case, a string slice of arguments can be obtained by calling `c.Args`. For example, the first argument would be `c.Args()[0]`.

COMMANDS AND SUBCOMMANDS

Applications built with `cli.go` often have commands and subcommands, as illustrated in figure 2.2. Think of an application such as Git, in which you can run commands such as `git add`, `git commit`, and `git push`.

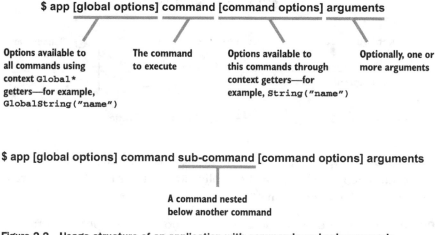

Figure 2.2   Usage structure of an application with commands and subcommands

To illustrate using commands, the following listing is a simple application with commands to count up and count down.

Listing 2.8   Count up and down: `count_cli.go`

```go
package main

import (
    "fmt"
    "os"

    " gopkg.in/urfave/cli.v1"
)

func main() {
    app := cli.NewApp()
    app.Usage = "Count up or down."
    app.Commands = []cli.Command{                    ①  One or more
        {                                                commands is
            Name:       "up",                            defined.
            ShortName: "u",
            Usage:      "Count Up",
            Flags: []cli.Flag{
                cli.IntFlag{
                    Name:  "stop, s",
                    Usage: "Value to count up to",
                    Value: 10,
                },
            },
            Action: func(c *cli.Context) error {    ③  Gets a command-
                start := c.Int("stop")                  specific flag
                if start <= 0 {
                    fmt.Println("Stop cannot be negative.")
                }
                for i := 1; i <= start; i++ {
                    fmt.Println(i)
                }
                return nil
            },
        },
        {
            Name:       "down",
            ShortName: "d",
            Usage:      "Count Down",
            Flags: []cli.Flag{
                cli.IntFlag{
                    Name:  "start, s",
                    Usage: "Start counting down from",
                    Value: 10,
                },
            },
            Action: func(c *cli.Context) error {
                start := c.Int("start")
                if start < 0 {
                    fmt.Println("Start cannot be negative.")
```

② A command-specific option is defined.

```
                                }
                                for i := start; i >= 0; i-- {
                                        fmt.Println(i)
                                }
                                return nil
                        },
                },
        }

        app.Run(os.Args)
}
```

Instead of defining the Action, a slice of cli.Command is defined on the Commands property with details about each command ❶. Action, by default, will be set to show the help screen. That way, if no commands are used with the application, help will be displayed. Each command has a Name and Action along with optional Flags, Usage, and ShortName. Just as the base application can have a Commands property with a list of commands, each command can have a Commands property with a list of subcommands to that command.

Flags defined on a command are similar to those defined globally. The pattern of definition is the same with the Name and Usage, and in some cases, a default Value. Global options, as shown in figure 2.2, are available to every command and come before the command itself. Command-specific options, defined on the command ❷, are placed after the command. Additionally, retrieving them is done from cli .Context by using a function such as String, Int, or Bool ❸. Global flags are similar but have Global prepended to them.

We started off this section by showing how Go command-line programs differ from the UNIX norm. First we presented command-line flags. We introduced libraries that provide UNIX-style command-line flags. Then we introduced a higher-level issue: how do you quickly and repeatedly build command-line applications without rewriting the same old boilerplate code? You looked at a fantastic library for that. Now you're ready to explore a topic relevant to almost all programs: configuration.

2.2   *Handling configuration*

A second foundational area that complements flag handling is persistent application configuration. Examples of this form of configuration include the files in the etc directory on some Linux installations and user-specific configuration files such as .gitconfig or .bashrc files.

Passing configuration to an application is a common need. Virtually every application, including console applications and servers, can benefit from persistent configuration. Operation toolchains such as Ansible, Chef, and Puppet have quite a bit of functionality for managing configuration in a distributed manner. How can configuration information be easily passed into and made available in your applications?

> **Ansible, Chef, and Puppet**
>
> Ansible, Chef, and Puppet are popular ops platforms for managing computers and their configurations. They're commonly used to manage the software installed on clusters of servers and the configuration needed for the applications running in them. For example, take an application connected to a database. The database could be on the same server, a different server, or a cluster of servers. The ops platform would manage the installation and configuration, providing the right connection information to the application.

Whereas the preceding section talked about passing in configuration via command-line options, this section looks at passing in configuration via files, or in the case of 12-factor apps, using environment variables. In this section, we add support for common configuration formats, including JSON, YAML, and INI. Then we present the approach favored in the 12-factor pattern, which passes in configuration through environment variables.

TECHNIQUE 3   Using configuration files

Command-line arguments, like those in the preceding section, are good for many things. But when it comes to one-time configuration of a program installed into a particular environment, command-line arguments aren't the right fit. The most common solution is to store configuration data in a file that the program can load at startup.

In the next few sections, you'll look at the three most popular configuration file formats and how to work with them in Go.

PROBLEM

A program requires configuration above and beyond that which you can provide with a few command-line arguments. And it would be great to use a standard file format.

SOLUTION

One of today's most popular configuration file formats is JavaScript Object Notation (JSON). The Go standard library provides JSON parsing and handling. It should be no surprise that JSON configuration files are common.

DISCUSSION

Consider the JSON file config.json with the following:

```
{
    "enabled": true,
    "path": "/usr/local"
}
```

The following listing showcases a JSON configuration parser.

Listing 2.9   Parsing a JSON configuration file: `json_config.go`

```go
package main

import (
    "encoding/json"
    "fmt"
    "os"
)

type configuration struct {        ❶ A type capable of holding
    Enabled bool                      the JSON values
    Path    string
}

func main() {
    file, _ := os.Open("conf.json")   ◁── ❷ Opens the configuration file
    defer file.Close()

    decoder := json.NewDecoder(file)  ❸ Parses the JSON
    conf := configuration{}             into a variable
    err := decoder.Decode(&conf)        with the variables
    if err != nil {
            fmt.Println("Error:", err)
    }
    fmt.Println(conf.Path)
}
```

This method has only a few parts. First, a type or collection of types needs to be created representing the JSON file ❶. The names and nesting must be defined and map to the structure in the JSON file. The main function begins by opening the configuration file ❷ and decoding the JSON file into an instance of the `configuration` struct ❸. If no errors occur, the values from the JSON file won't be available on the `conf` variable and can be used in your application.

NOTE   JSON parsing and handling has many features and nuances. Chapter 6, which covers working with JSON APIs, presents the JSON features in more detail.

Storing configuration in JSON is useful if you're already familiar with JSON, using a distributed configuration store such as etcd, or want to stick with the Go standard library. JSON files can't contain comments, which can be a common complaint when creating configuration files or generating examples of them. In the following two techniques, comments are available.

etcd

Inspired by Apache ZooKeeper and Doozer, etcd provides distributed shared configuration and service discovery. This highly available store uses the Raft consensus algorithm to manage the replication. etcd is written in Go. For more information, visit https://github.com/coreos/etcd.

SOLUTION

YAML, a recursive acronym meaning *YAML Ain't Markup Language*, is a human-readable data serialization format. YAML is easy to read, can contain comments, and is fairly easy to work with. Using YAML for application configuration is common and a method we, the authors, recommend and practice. Although Go doesn't ship with a YAML processor, several third-party libraries are readily available. You'll look at one here.

DISCUSSION

Consider this simple YAML configuration file:

```
# A comment line
enabled: true
path: /usr/local
```

The following listing is an example of parsing and printing configuration from a YAML file.

Listing 2.10   Parsing a YAML configuration file: `yaml_config.go`

```
package main

import (
    "fmt"
    "github.com/kylelemons/go-gypsy/yaml"     ❶ Imports a third-party YAML
)

func main() {
    config, err := yaml.ReadFile("conf.yaml")   ❷ Reads a YAML file into
if err != nil {                                     a struct parser
            fmt.Println(err)
    }
    fmt.Println(config.Get("path"))            ❸ Prints the values
    fmt.Println(config.GetBool("enabled"))        from the YAML file
}
```

To work with YAML files and content, this listing imports the `github.com/kylelemons/go-gypsy/yaml` package ❶. This package, which we've used and recommend, provides features to read YAML as a string or from a file ❷, deal with different types, and turn configuration into YAML output.

Using the function `ReadFile`, the configuration file is read in and returns a `File` struct from the `yaml` package. This struct provides access to the data in the YAML file. Using the `Get` method, the value of a string can be obtained ❸. For other types, such as a Boolean, you can use methods such as `GetBool`. Each type has its own method to ensure proper handling and return type.

SOLUTION

INI files are a format in wide use and have been around for decades. This is another format your Go applications can potentially use. Although the Go developers didn't include a processor in the language, once again libraries are readily available to meet your needs.

DISCUSSION

Consider the following INI file:

```
; A comment line
[Section]
enabled = true
path = /usr/local # another comment
```

In the following listing, this file is parsed, and you can see how to use the internal data.

Listing 2.11   Parsing an INI configuration file: `ini_config.go`

```
package main

import (
    "fmt"

    "gopkg.in/gcfg.v1"            ❶ Includes third-party
)                                    package to parse INI files

func main() {
    config := struct {           ❷ Creates a structure to
        Section struct {             hold the config values
            Enabled bool
            Path    string
        }
    }{}

    err := gcfg.ReadFileInto(&config, "conf.ini")
    if err != nil {
        fmt.Println("Failed to parse config file: %s", err)
    }
    fmt.Println(config.Section.Enabled)
    fmt.Println(config.Section.Path)      ❹ Uses the INI values
}
```

Parses the INI file into the struct handling errors ❸

In this case, the third-party package `gopkg.in/gcfg.v1` handles parsing the INI file into a data structure ❶. This package provides a means to parse INI files and strings similar to JSON handling in the standard library.

Before the INI file can be parsed, a variable needs to exist to receive the values from the file. As in the JSON technique, the structure of this variable needs to map to the structure in the INI file. In this case, a struct is created, though a new type similar to the JSON example could be used instead, with an internal struct for a section ❷. This struct is where the configuration values will reside after parsing.

The function `ReadFileInto` reads the file into the struct that was created ❸. If an error occurs, it will be available. After this has passed, the configuration from the INI file is available to be used ❹.

The `gopkg.in/gcfg.v1` package has several useful features such as tags and reading strings, files, or anything implementing the `io.Reader` interface. For more information, see the package documentation.

TECHNIQUE 4   **Configuration via environment variables**

The venerable configuration file certainly provides a great vehicle for passing configuration data to programs. But some of today's emerging environments defy some of the assumptions we make when using traditional configuration files. Sometimes the one configuring the application won't have access to the filesystem at the level we assume. Some systems treat configuration files as part of the source codebase (and thus as static pieces of an executable). This removes some of the utility of configuration files.

Nowhere is this trend clearer than in the emerging PaaS cloud services. Deploying into these systems is usually accomplished by pushing a source-code bundle to a control server (like a Git push). But the only runtime configuration you get on such servers is done with environment variables. Let's take a look at a technique for working in such an environment.

PROBLEM

Many PaaS systems don't provide a way to specify per-instance configuration files. Configuration opportunities are limited to a small number of environmental controls, such as environment variables.

SOLUTION

Twelve-factor apps, commonly deployed to Heroku, Cloud Foundry, Deis, and other PaaS or container cluster managers (covered in chapter 11), are becoming more common. One of the factors of a twelve-factor app is storing the configuration in the environment. This provides a way to have a different configuration for each environment an application runs in.

> **Twelve-factor apps**
>
> This popular and widely used methodology for building web applications, software as a service, and similar applications uses the following 12 factors:
>
> 1 Use a single codebase, tracked in revision control, that can be deployed multiple times.
> 2 Explicitly declare dependencies and isolate them from other applications.
> 3 Store application configuration in the environment.
> 4 Attach supporting services.
> 5 Separate the build and run stages.
> 6 Execute the application as one or more stateless processes.
> 7 Export services via TCP port binding.
> 8 Scale horizontally by adding processes.
> 9 Maximize robust applications with fast startup and graceful shutdown.
> 10 Keep development, staging, and production as similar as possible.
> 11 Handle logs as event streams.
> 12 Run admin tasks as separate processes.
>
> More details can be found on these factors at http://12factor.net.

DISCUSSION

Consider, for example, the environment variable PORT containing the port a web server should listen to. The following listing retrieves this piece of configuration and uses it when starting a web server.

> **Listing 2.12 Environment variable–based configuration: env_config.go**

```go
package main

import (
    "fmt"
    "net/http"
    "os"
)

func main() {
    http.HandleFunc("/", homePage)
    http.ListenAndServe(":"+os.Getenv("PORT"), nil)      ⦿ Retrieves the PORT
}                                                           from the environment

func homePage(res http.ResponseWriter, req *http.Request) {
    if req.URL.Path != "/" {
        http.NotFound(res, req)
        return
    }
    fmt.Fprint(res, "The homepage.")
}
```

This example uses the http package from the standard library. You may remember it from the simple Hello World web server in listing 1.16. In the following section, we cover more on web servers.

Retrieving configuration from the environment is fairly straightforward. From the os package, the Getenv function retrieves the value as a string ⦿. When no environment variable is found, an empty string is returned. If you need to convert the string to another type, you can use the strconv package. For example, if the PORT in this example needed to be an integer, you could use the ParseInt function.

> **WARNING** Be careful with the information in environment variables and the processes able to obtain the information in them. For example, a third-party subprocess started by your application could have access to the environment variables.

2.3 *Working with real-world web servers*

Although the Go standard library provides a great foundation for building web servers, it has some options you may want to change and some tolerance you may want to add. Two common areas, which we cover in this section, are matching URL paths to callback functions and starting and stopping servers with an interest in gracefully shutting down.

Web servers are a core feature of the http package. This package uses the foundation for handling TCP connections from the net package. Because web servers are a core part of the standard library and are commonly in use, simple web servers were introduced in chapter 1. This section moves beyond base web servers and covers some practical gotchas that come up when building applications. For more information on the http package, visit http://golang.org/pkg/net/http/.

2.3.1 Starting up and shutting down a server

Starting a server in Go is fairly easy. Using the net or http packages, you can create a server, listen on a TCP port, and start responding to incoming connections and requests. But what happens when you want to shut down that server? What if you shut down the server while users are connected, or before all the data (such as logs or user information) has been written to disk?

The commands used to start and stop a server in the operating system should be handled by an initialization daemon. Using go run on a codebase is handy in development and may be used with some systems based on twelve-factor apps but isn't typical or recommended. Manually starting an application is simple but isn't designed to integrate nicely with operations tools or handle problems such as an unexpected system restart. Initialization daemons were designed for these cases and do them well.

Most systems have a default toolchain used for initialization. For example, systemd (https://freedesktop.org/wiki/Software/systemd/) is common on Linux distributions such as Debian and Ubuntu systems. If a script is used with systemd, you'll be able to use commands like those in the following listing.

Listing 2.13 Start and stop applications with upstart

```
$ systemctl start myapp.service        ◁——— Starts the application myapp
$ systemctl stop myapp.service         ◁——— Stops the running application myapp
```

A wide variety of initialization daemons are available. They vary depending on your flavor of operating system, and numerous ones exist for the various versions of Linux. You may be familiar with some of their names, including upstart, init, and launchd. Because configuration scripts and commands can vary widely among these systems, we don't cover them here. These tools are well documented, and many tutorials and examples are available.

> **NOTE** We recommend that you don't write your applications as daemons but rather use an initialization daemon to manage the execution of the application.

A COMMON ANTIPATTERN: A CALLBACK URL

A simple pattern (or rather antipattern) for development is to have a URL such as /kill or /shutdown, that will shut down the server when called. The following listing showcases a simple version of this method.

Listing 2.14   Callback shutdown URL: `callback_shutdown.go`

```go
package main

import (
    "fmt"
    "net/http"
    "os"
)

func main() {
    http.HandleFunc("/shutdown", shutdown)        ← A special path registered
    http.HandleFunc("/", homePage)                  to shut down the server
    http.ListenAndServe(":8080", nil)
}

func shutdown(res http.ResponseWriter, req *http.Request) {    Tells the
    os.Exit(0)                                                  application
}                                                            ← to exit
                                                               immediately
func homePage(res http.ResponseWriter, req *http.Request) {
    if req.URL.Path != "/" {
        http.NotFound(res, req)
        return
    }
    fmt.Fprint(res, "The homepage.")
}
```

We don't recommend this method, but we share it because it's a pattern easily found on the internet. Although its simplicity is an advantage, the list of disadvantages is problematic and includes the following:

- The URL needs to be blocked in production, or more likely, removed before going to production. Needing to have code differences for development and production is prone to introducing bugs. If this URL were left in for production, anyone who discovered it could easily take down your service.
- When the callback URL receives a request, the server shuts down immediately. Any actions in progress are immediately stopped. Any data not saved to disk is lost because there's no opportunity to save it before exiting.
- Using a URL sidesteps typical operations tooling such as Ansible, Chef, and Puppet or initialization toolchains. More-appropriate tools exist that manage updates and running applications.

We don't recommend using this method. It's most useful for development when the process is in the background or being run as a daemon. Go applications typically shouldn't be daemons, and better methods are available for starting and stopping the server, even for development.

TECHNIQUE 5   **Graceful shutdowns using manners**

When a server shuts down, you'll often want to stop receiving new requests, save any data to disk, and cleanly end connections with existing open connections. The http package in the standard library shuts down immediately and doesn't provide an opportunity to handle any of these situations. In the worst cases, this results in lost or corrupted data.

PROBLEM

To avoid data loss and unexpected behavior, a server may need to do some cleanup on shutdown.

SOLUTION

To handle these, you'll need to implement your own logic or use a package such as github.com/braintree/manners.

DISCUSSION

Braintree, a division of PayPal, created the manners package that gracefully shuts down while maintaining the same interface for ListenAndServe that the core http package uses. Internally, the package uses the core http server while keeping track of connections by using WaitGroup from the sync package. WaitGroup is designed to keep track of goroutines. The following listing takes a look at a simple manners-based server.

> **Listing 2.15   Graceful shutdown using manners: `manners_shutdown.go`**

```go
package main

import (
    "fmt"
    "net/http"
    "os"
    "os/signal"
    "github.com/braintree/manners"
)

func main() {
    handler := newHandler()                           ❶ Gets instance
                                                        of a handler

    ch := make(chan os.Signal)                        ❷ Sets up monitoring of
    signal.Notify(ch, os.Interrupt, os.Kill)            operating system signals
    go listenForShutdown(ch)

    manners.ListenAndServe(":8080", handler)          ❸ Starts the web server
}

func newHandler() *handler {
    return &handler{}
}

type handler struct{}

func (h *handler) ServeHTTP(res http.ResponseWriter, req *http.Request) {
    query := req.URL.Query()
    name := query.Get("name")
    if name == "" {                                   ❹ Handler
        name = "Inigo Montoya"                            responding to
    }                                                    web requests
    fmt.Fprint(res, "Hello, my name is ", name)
}
```

```
func listenForShutdown(ch <-chan os.Signal) {
    <-ch
    manners.Close()
}
```

❺ **Waits for shutdown signal and reacts**

The main function begins by getting an instance of a handler function capable of responding to web requests ❶. This handler is a simple Hello World responder ❹. In its place, a more complex one handling routing rules, such as the path or regular expression handlers covered later in the chapter, could be used.

To gracefully shut down, you need to know when to do so. The signal package provides a means to get signals from the operating system, including signals to interrupt or kill the application. The next step is to set up a channel that receives interrupt and kill signals from the operating system so the code can react to them ❷. ListenAndServe, like its counterpart in the http package, blocks execution. To monitor signals, a goroutine needs to run concurrently. The function listenForShutdown waits until it receives a signal on the channel ❺. After a signal comes in, it sends a message to Shutdown on the server. This tells the server to stop accepting new connections and shut down after all the current requests are completed.

Calling ListenAndServe in the same manner as the http package ❸ starts the server.

> **TIP** The server waits only for request handlers to finish before exiting. If your code has separate goroutines that need to be waited on, that would need to happen separately, using your own implementation of WaitGroup.

This approach has several advantages, including the following:

- Allows current HTTP requests to complete rather than stopping them mid-request.
- Stops listening on the TCP port while completing the existing requests. This opens the opportunity for another application to bind to the same port and start serving requests. If you're updating versions of an application, one version could shut down while completing its requests, and another version of the application could come online and start serving.

A couple of disadvantages also exist under some conditions:

- The manners package works for HTTP connections rather than all TCP connections. If your application isn't a web server, the manners package won't work.
- In some cases, one version of an application will want to hand off exiting socket connections currently in use to another instance of the same application or another application. For example, if you have long-running socket connections between a server and client applications, the manners package will attempt to wait or interrupt the connections rather than hand them off.

2.3.2   *Routing web requests*

One of the fundamental tasks of any HTTP server is to receive a given request and map it to an internal function that can then return a result to the client. This routing of a request to a handler is important; do it well, and you can build web services that are easily maintainable and flexible enough to fit future needs. This section presents various routing scenarios and solutions for each.

We start with simple scenarios and provide simple solutions. But we encourage you to plan ahead. The simple solution we talk about first is great for direct mappings, but may not provide the flexibility that a contemporary web application needs.

TECHNIQUE 6   **Matching paths to content**

Web applications and servers providing a REST API typically execute different functionality for different paths. Figure 2.3 illustrates the path portion of the URL compared to the other components. In the Hello World example from chapter 1, listing 1.16 uses a single function to handle all possible paths. For a simple Hello World application, this works. But a single function doesn't handle multiple paths well and doesn't scale to real-world applications. This section covers multiple techniques to handle differentiating paths and, in some cases, different HTTP methods (sometimes referred to as *verbs*).

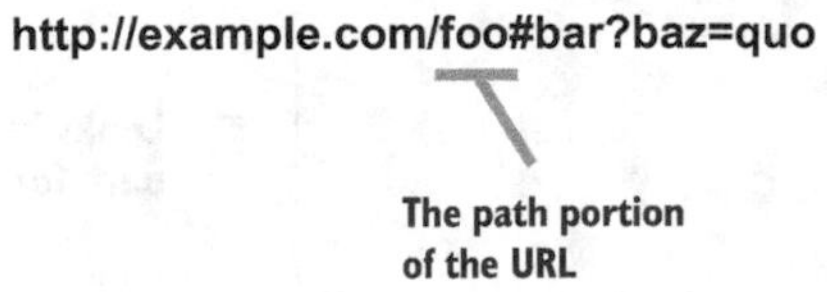

http://example.com/foo#bar?baz=quo

The path portion
of the URL

Figure 2.3   The path portion of
the URL used in routing requests

PROBLEM

To correctly route requests, a web server needs to be able to quickly and efficiently parse the path portion of a URL.

SOLUTION: MULTIPLE HANDLERS

To expand on the method used in listing 1.16, this technique uses a handler function for each path. This technique, presented in the guide "Writing Web Applications" (http://golang.org/doc/articles/wiki/), uses a simple pattern that can be great for web apps with only a few simple paths. This technique has nuances that you'll see in a moment that may make you consider one of the techniques following it.

DISCUSSION

Let's start with a simple program that illustrates using multiple handlers, shown in the following listing.

Listing 2.16 Multiple handler functions: `multiple_handlers.go`

```go
package main

import (
        "fmt"
        "net/http"
        "strings"
)

func main() {
        http.HandleFunc("/hello", hello)
        http.HandleFunc("/goodbye/", goodbye)
        http.HandleFunc("/", homePage)
        http.ListenAndServe(":8080", nil)
}

func hello(res http.ResponseWriter, req *http.Request) {
        query := req.URL.Query()
        name := query.Get("name")
        if name == "" {
                name = "Inigo Montoya"
        }
        fmt.Fprint(res, "Hello, my name is ", name)
}

func goodbye(res http.ResponseWriter, req *http.Request) {
        path := req.URL.Path
        parts := strings.Split(path, "/")
        name := parts[2]
        if name == "" {
                name = "Inigo Montoya"
        }
        fmt.Fprint(res, "Goodbye ", name)
}

func homePage(res http.ResponseWriter, req *http.Request) {
        if req.URL.Path != "/" {
                http.NotFound(res, req)
                return
        }
        fmt.Fprint(res, "The homepage.")
}
```

❶ Registers URL path handlers

Starts the web server on port 8080

Handler function mapped to /hello ❷

❸ Gets the name from the query string

❹ Handler function for /goodbye/

❺ Looks in the path for a name

❻ Home and not found handler function

❼ Checks the path to decide if home page or not found

NOTE Content collected from an end user should be sanitized before using. That includes displaying the content back to a user. This functionality is part of the templating Go package covered in chapter 5.

Here you use three handler functions for three paths or path parts ❶. When a path is resolved, it tries to go from the most specific to the least specific. In this case, any path that isn't resolved prior to the / path will resolve to this one.

It's worth noting that paths ending in / can have redirection issues. In this listing, a user who visits /goodbye will be automatically redirected to /goodbye/. If you have query strings, they may be dropped. For example, /goodbye?foo=bar will redirect to /goodbye/.

The way resolution works by default is important to know as well. The handler registered to /hello will work only for /hello. The handler registered to /goodbye/ will be executed for /goodbye (with a redirect), /goodbye/, /goodbye/foo, /goodbye /foo/bar, and so on.

The handler function hello is mapped to the path /hello ❷. As arguments, the handler functions receive an http.ResponseWriter and an http.Request. Optionally, a name to say hello to can be in a query string with a key of name ❸. The requested URL is a property on http.Request as url.URL. The Query method on the URL returns either the value for the key, or an empty string if no value is available for the key. If the value is empty here, it's set to Inigo Montoya.

> **TIP** The net/url package, which contains the URL type, has many useful functions for working with URLs.

> **NOTE** To differentiate between HTTP methods, check the value of http.Request.Method. This contains the method (for example, GET, POST, and so on).

The goodbye function handles the path /goodbye/, including the case where additional text is appended ❹. In this case, a name can be optionally passed in through the path. For example, a path of /goodbye/Buttercup will set the name to Buttercup ❺. To achieve this, the URL is split by using the strings package to find the part of the path following /goodbye/.

The homePage function handles both the / path and any case where a page isn't found ❻. To decide whether to return a 404 Page Not Found message or home page content, the http.Request.Path needs to be checked ❼. The http package contains a NotFound helper function that can optionally be used to set the response HTTP code to 404 and send the text 404 page not found.

> **TIP** The http package contains the Error function that can be used to set the HTTP error code and respond with a message. The NotFound function takes advantage of this for the 404 case.

Using multiple function handlers is the core way to handle different functions alongside different paths. The pros of this method include the following:

- As the basic method in the http package, it's well documented and tested, and examples are right at hand.
- The paths and their mappings to functions are easy to read and follow.

Alongside the pros are some cons that lead many, including the authors, to use other methods. The cons are as follows:

- You can't use different functions for different HTTP methods on the same path. When creating REST APIs, the verb (for example, GET, POST, or DELETE) can require significantly different functionality.

- Wildcard or named sections to a path, a common feature or feature request for mapping systems, aren't available.
- Virtually every handler function needs to check for paths outside their bounds and handle returning a Page Not Found message. For example, in listing 2.16 the handler /goodbye/ will receive paths prepended with /goodbye. Anything returned by any path is handled here, so if you want to return a Page Not Found message for the path /goodbye/foo/bar/baz, that would need to be handled here.

Using multiple handlers is useful for simple cases. Because it doesn't require packages outside the http package, the external dependencies are kept to a minimum. If an application is going to move beyond simple use cases, one of the following techniques is likely to be a better fit.

TECHNIQUE 7   **Handling complex paths with wildcards**

The previous technique is straightforward, but as you saw, it's decidedly inflexible when it comes to path naming. You must list every single path that you expect to see. For larger applications or for applications that follow the REST recommendations, you need a more flexible solution.

PROBLEM

Instead of specifying exact paths for each callback, an application may need to support wildcards or other simple patterns.

SOLUTION

Go provides the path package with functionality to work with slash-separated paths. This package isn't directly designed to work with URL paths. Instead, it's a generic package intended to work with paths of all sorts. In fact, it works well when coupled with an HTTP handler.

DISCUSSION

The following listing builds a router that uses path matching to map URL paths and HTTP methods to a handler function.

Listing 2.17   Resolve URLs using path package: path_handlers.go

```
package main

import (
    "fmt"
    "net/http"           Imports the path package
    "path"               to handle URL matches
    "strings"
)

func main() {                              ① Gets an instance of a
    pr := newPathResolver()                   path-based router
    pr.Add("GET /hello", hello)
    pr.Add("* /goodbye/*", goodbye)        ③ Sets the HTTP server
    http.ListenAndServe(":8080", pr)          to use your router
}
```

Maps ② functions to paths

```
func newPathResolver() *pathResolver {                      Creates new
    return &pathResolver{make(map[string]http.HandlerFunc)}  initialized
}                                                            pathResolver

type pathResolver struct {
    handlers map[string]http.HandlerFunc
}
                                                             Adds paths
func (p *pathResolver) Add(path string, handler http.HandlerFunc) {   to internal
    p.handlers[path] = handler                                       lookup
}

func (p *pathResolver) ServeHTTP(res http.ResponseWriter, req *http.Request)
{
    check := req.Method + " " + req.URL.Path        <- Constructs our method + path to check
    for pattern, handlerFunc := range p.handlers {   <- 4 Iterates over registered paths
        if ok, err := path.Match(pattern, check); ok && err == nil {   <- 5 Checks whether current path matches a registered one
            handlerFunc(res, req)                    <- 6 Executes the handler function for a matched path
            return
        } else if err != nil {
            fmt.Fprint(res, err)
        }
    }

    http.NotFound(res, req)    <- 7 If no path matches, the page wasn't found.
}

func hello(res http.ResponseWriter, req *http.Request) {
    query := req.URL.Query()
    name := query.Get("name")
    if name == "" {
        name = "Inigo Montoya"
    }
    fmt.Fprint(res, "Hello, my name is ", name)
}

func goodbye(res http.ResponseWriter, req *http.Request) {
    path := req.URL.Path
    parts := strings.Split(path, "/")
    name := parts[2]
    if name == "" {
        name = "Inigo Montoya"
    }
    fmt.Fprint(res, "Goodbye ", name)
}
```

The `main` function starts off quite differently by getting an instance of a `pathResolver` ❶. The `pathResolver`, which you'll look at in a moment, contains the core logic for matching functions to paths. After an instance of the `pathResolver` has been created, two mappings of HTTP verbs and their paths are added to the resolver ❷. The format for these is the HTTP method name followed by a path, with a space separating the two. You can use an asterisk (`*`) as a wildcard character for the HTTP method or in the path.

The `pathResolver` is set as the handler function for the built-in HTTP server when the server is started ❸. For `pathResolver` to work as a handler function, it needs to implement the `ServeHTTP` method and implicitly implement the `HandlerFunc` interface. The `ServeHTTP` method is where path resolving happens.

When a request comes into the server, the `ServeHTTP` method iterates over the paths registered with the `pathResolver` ❹. For each path, it checks the current HTTP method and path to see if a function is mapped to the combination ❺. This is a check you construct because with REST servers you'll often need to handle different HTTP methods (for example, a `DELETE` or `GET` request) with entirely different functions. When a match is found, the handler function registered for that case is executed ❻. If no matched paths are found in the lookup, you default to a 404 Page Not Found error ❼.

You should be aware of the pros and cons of path resolution using the `path` package. Here are the pros:

- Easy to get started with simple path matching.
- Included in the standard library, the `path` package is well traveled and tested.

The cons have a common thread in that the `path` package is generic to paths and not specific to URL paths. The cons are as follows:

- The wildcard abilities of the `path` package are limited. For example, a path of `foo/*` will match `foo/bar` but not `foo/bar/baz`. Using `*` for a wildcard stops at the next `/`. To match `foo/bar/baz`, you'd need to look for a path like `foo/*/*`.
- Because this is a generic path package rather than one specific to URLs, some nice-to-have features are missing. For example, in listing 2.17 the path `/goodbye/*` is registered. Visiting the path `/goodbye` in a browser will display a Page Not Found message, whereas visiting `/goodbye/` works. Although there's a technical path difference (the trailing `/`), the common web use case isn't transparently handled. You'll need to identify and handle cases such as this one.

This method is useful for simple path scenarios and it's one that we, the authors, have successfully used.

TECHNIQUE 8   URL pattern matching

For most REST-style apps, simple pattern matching with regular expressions is more than sufficient. But what if you want to go beyond that and do something fancy with your URLs? The path package isn't well suited for this because it supports only simple POSIX-style pattern matching.

PROBLEM

Simple path-based matching isn't enough for an application that needs to treat a path more like a text string and less like a file path. This is particularly important when matching across a path separator (`/`).

SOLUTION

The built-in `path` package enables simple path-matching schemes, but sometimes you may need to match complex paths or have intimate control over the path. For those cases, you can use regular expressions to match your paths. You'll combine Go's built-in regular expressions with the HTTP handler and build a fast but flexible URL path matcher.

DISCUSSION

In the next listing you'll walk through using paths and a resolver based on regular expressions.

Listing 2.18   Resolve URLs using regular expressions: `regex_handlers.go`

```go
package main

import (
    "fmt"
    "net/http"             Imports the regular
    "regexp"               expression package
    "strings"
)

func main() {
    rr := newPathResolver()
    rr.Add("GET /hello", hello)                               ❶ Registers paths
    rr.Add("(GET|HEAD) /goodbye(/?[A-Za-z0-9]*)?", goodbye)      to functions
    http.ListenAndServe(":8080", rr)}

func newPathResolver() *regexResolver {
    return &regexResolver{
            handlers: make(map[string]http.HandlerFunc),
            cache:    make(map[string]*regexp.Regexp),
    }
}

type regexResolver struct {
    handlers map[string]http.HandlerFunc        Stores compiled regular
    cache    map[string]*regexp.Regexp          expressions for reuse
}

func (r *regexResolver) Add(regex string, handler http.HandlerFunc) {
    r.handlers[regex] = handler
    cache, _ := regexp.Compile(regex)
    r.cache[regex] = cache
}

func (r *regexResolver) ServeHTTP(res http.ResponseWriter, req *http.Request)
    {
    check := req.Method + " " + req.URL.Path                    Looks up and
    for pattern, handlerFunc := range r.handlers {           ❷ executes the
            if r.cache[pattern].MatchString(check) == true {     handler function
                handlerFunc(res, req)
                return
            }
    }
    http.NotFound(res, req)        If no path matches,
}                                  returns a Page Not
                                   Found error
```

```go
func hello(res http.ResponseWriter, req *http.Request) {
    query := req.URL.Query()
    name := query.Get("name")
    if name == "" {
            name = "Inigo Montoya"
    }
    fmt.Fprint(res, "Hello, my name is ", name)
}

func goodbye(res http.ResponseWriter, req *http.Request) {
    path := req.URL.Path
    parts := strings.Split(path, "/")
    name := ""
    if len(parts) > 2 {
            name = parts[2]
    }
    if name == "" {
            name = "Inigo Montoya"
    }
    fmt.Fprint(res, "Goodbye ", name)
}
```

The layout of the regular-expression-based path resolution (listing 2.18) is the same as the path resolution example (listing 2.17). The differences lie in the format of the path patterns registered for a function and in the ServeHTTP method handling the resolution.

Paths are registered as regular expressions ❶. The structure is the same as the path package technique, with an HTTP method followed by the path, separated by a space. Whereas GET /hello showcases a simple path, a more complicated example is (GET|HEAD) /goodbye(/?[A-Za-z0-9]*)?. This more complicated example accepts either a GET or HEAD HTTP method. The regular expression for the path will accept /goodbye, /goodbye/ (the trailing / matters), and /goodbye/ followed by letters and numbers.

In this case, ServeHTTP iterates over the regular expressions looking for a match ❷. When the first match is found, it will execute the handler function registered to that regular expression. If more than one regular expression matches an incoming path, the first one added would be the first one checked and used.

> **NOTE**   Compiled versions of the regular expressions are built and cached at the time they're added. Go provides a Match function in the regexp package that can check for matches. The first step for this function is to compile the regular expression. By compiling and caching the regular expression, you don't need to recompile the regular expressions each time the server handles a request.

Using regular-expression checking for paths provides a significant amount of power, allowing you to finely tune the paths you want to match. This flexibility is paired with the complicated nature of regular expressions that may not be easy to read, and you'll likely want to have tests to make sure your regular expressions are matching the proper paths.

Faster routing (without the work)

One criticism of Go's built-in `http` package is that its routing and multiplexing (muxing) is basic. In the previous sections, we showed some straightforward ways of working with the `http` package, but depending on your needs, you may not be satisfied with the configurability, performance, or capabilities of the built-in HTTP server. Or you may just want to avoid writing boilerplate routing code.

PROBLEM

The built-in `http` package isn't flexible enough, or doesn't perform well in a particular use case.

SOLUTION

Routing URLs to functions is a common problem for web applications. Therefore, numerous packages have been built and tested, and are commonly used to tackle the problem of routing. A common technique is to import an existing request router and use it within your application.

Popular solutions include the following:

- `github.com/julienschmidt/httprouter` is considered a fast routing package with a focus on using a minimal amount of memory and taking as little time as possible to handle routing. It has features such as the ability to have case-insensitive paths, cleaning up `/../` in a path, and dealing with an optional trailing `/`.
- `github.com/gorilla/mux` is part of the Gorilla web toolkit. This loose collection of packages provides components you can use in an application. The `mux` package provides a versatile set of criteria to perform matching against, including host, schemes, HTTP headers, and more.
- `github.com/bmizerany/pat` provides a router inspired by the routing in Sinatra. The registered paths are easy to read and can contain named parameters such as `/user/:name`. It has inspired other packages such as `github.com/gorilla/pat`.

> ### Sinatra web application library
> Sinatra is an open source web application framework written in Ruby. This framework has been used by numerous organizations and has inspired well over 50 comparable frameworks in many other languages, including several in Go.

Each package has a different feature set and API. Numerous other routing packages exist as well. With a little investigation, you can easily find a quality third-party package that meets your needs.

2.4   *Summary*

After the foundational elements for an application are decided on and in place, it's easier to dive into application-specific situations and the elements that will make your application useful. This chapter covered several foundational elements and options:

- Handling command-line options in a comfortable and accessible manner. This ranges from lightweight solutions to a simple framework for building console-based applications and utilities.
- Retrieving configuration information from files and the environment in various ways and data formats.
- Starting and stopping a web server that works with ops tooling and graceful shutdowns to avoid a bad user experience or loss of data.
- Several ways to handle resolving URL paths for an application, and route to handler functions.

In the next chapter, you'll look at concurrency in Go. Concurrency is a cornerstone and building block of Go applications. You'll learn how to effectively use it.

Concurrency in Go 3

This chapter presents Go's concurrency model. Unlike many recent procedural and object-oriented languages, Go doesn't provide a threading model for concurrency. Instead, it uses goroutines and channels. Concurrency is cheap (resource-wise) and much easier to manage than traditional thread pools. This chapter first focuses on goroutines, functions capable of running concurrently. Then it dives into channels, Go's mechanism for communicating between goroutines.

3.1 Understanding Go's concurrency model

Roughly speaking, *concurrency* is a program's ability to do multiple things at the same time. In practice, when we talk about concurrent programs, we mean programs that have two or more tasks that run independently of each other, at about the same time, but remain part of the same program.

Popular programming languages such as Java and Python implement concurrency by using threads. Go takes a different route. Following a model proposed by the renowned computer scientist Tony Hoare, Go uses the concurrency model called *Communicating Sequential Processes* (CSP). This chapter covers the practical aspects of working with Go's concurrency model, though we suggest reading a little about the theory behind CSP and Go at golang.org.

Two crucial concepts make Go's concurrency model work:

- *Goroutines*—A goroutine is a function that runs independently of the function that started it. Sometimes Go developers explain a goroutine as a function that runs as if it were on its own thread.
- *Channels*—A channel is a pipeline for sending and receiving data. Think of it as a socket that runs inside your program. Channels provide a way for one goroutine to send structured data to another.

The techniques in this chapter use goroutines and channels. We won't spend time on the theory or underpinnings of the goroutine and channel systems, but will stick to practical use of these two concepts.

Concurrency in Go is cheap and easy. Therefore, you'll frequently see it used in libraries and tools. In fact, you'll see it used frequently throughout this book. This chapter introduces several concurrency topics, with emphasis on how Go's model differs from that of other popular languages. It also focuses on best practices. Goroutines and channels are one of the few places in the Go language where programmers can introduce memory leaks. You can remedy this situation by following certain patterns, which we introduce in this chapter.

3.2   *Working with goroutines*

When it comes to syntax, a goroutine is any function that's called after the special keyword go. Almost any function could, in theory, be called as a goroutine, though there are plenty of functions you probably wouldn't want to call as goroutines. One of the most frequent uses of goroutines is to run a function "in the background" while the main part of your program goes on to do something else. As an example, let's write a short program that echoes back any text you type in, but only for 30 seconds, as shown in the next listing. After that, it exits on its own.

Listing 3.1   Using a goroutine to run a task

```
package main

import (
    "fmt"
    "io"
    "os"
    "time"
```

```
)
func main() {
    go echo(os.Stdin, os.Stdout)
    time.Sleep(30 * time.Second)
    fmt.Println("Timed out.")
    os.Exit(0)
}
func echo(in io.Reader, out io.Writer) {
    io.Copy(out, in)
}
```

Calls the function echo as a goroutine

Prints out a message saying we're done sleeping

Exits the program. This stops the goroutine.

The echo function is a normal function.

io.Copy copies data to an os.Writer from an os.Reader.

Sleeps for 30 seconds

This program uses a goroutine to run the echoing behavior in the background, while a timer runs in the foreground. If you were to run the program and type in some text, the output would look something like this:

```
$ go run echoback.go
Hello.
Hello.
My name is Inigo Montoya
My name is Inigo Montoya
You killed my father
You killed my father
Prepare to die
Prepare to die
Timed out.
```

Here's how the program works. Each line that you type in is displayed by the shell as you type it, and then echoed back by the program as soon as it reads the line. And it continues this echo loop until the timer runs out. As you can see in the example, there's nothing special about the echo function, but when you call it with the keyword go, it's executed as a goroutine.

The main function starts the goroutine and then waits for 30 seconds. When the main function exits, it terminates the main goroutine, which effectively halts the program.

TECHNIQUE 10   Using goroutine closures

Any function can be executed as a goroutine. And because Go allows you to declare functions inline, you can share variables by declaring one function inside another and closing over the variables you want to share.

PROBLEM

You want to use a one-shot function in a way that doesn't block the calling function, and you'd like to make sure that it runs. This use case frequently arises when you want to, say, read a file in the background, send messages to a remote log server, or save a current state without pausing the program.

SOLUTION

Use a closure function and give the scheduler opportunity to run.

DISCUSSION

In Go, functions are first-class. They can be created inline, passed into other functions, and assigned as values to a variable. You can even declare an anonymous function and call it as a goroutine, all in a compact syntax, as the following listing shows.

Listing 3.2   An anonymous goroutine

```go
package main

import (
    "fmt"
    "runtime"
)

func main() {
    fmt.Println("Outside a goroutine.")
    go func() {
            fmt.Println("Inside a goroutine")     Declares an anonymous
    }()                                           function and executes it
    fmt.Println("Outside again.")                 as a goroutine

    runtime.Gosched()            <——— Yields to the scheduler
}
```

This listing shows how to create the function inline and immediately call it as a goroutine. But if you execute this program, you may be surprised at the output, which may change from run to run. It's not uncommon to see this:

```
$ go run ./simple.go
Outside a goroutine.
Outside again.
Inside a goroutine
```

Goroutines run concurrently, but not necessarily in parallel. When you schedule a goroutine to run by calling go func, you're asking the Go runtime to execute that function for you as soon as it can. But that's likely not immediately. In fact, if your Go program can use only one processor, you can almost be sure that it won't run immediately. Instead, the scheduler will continue executing the outer function until a circumstance arises that causes it to switch to another task. This leads us to another facet of this example.

You may have noticed the last line of the function, runtime.Gosched(). This is a way to indicate to the Go runtime that you're at a point where you could pause and yield to the scheduler. If the scheduler has other tasks queued up (other goroutines), it may then run one or more of them before coming back to this function.

If you were to omit this line and rerun the example, your output would likely look like this:

```
$ go run ./simple.go
Outside a goroutine.
Outside again.
```

The goroutine never executes. Why? The main function returns (terminating the program) before the scheduler has a chance to run the goroutine. When you run `runtime.Gosched`, though, you give the runtime an opportunity to execute other goroutines before it exits.

There are other ways of yielding to the scheduler; perhaps the most common is to call `time.Sleep`. But none gives you the explicit ability to tell the scheduler what to do when you yield. At best, you can indicate to the scheduler only that the present goroutine is at a point where it can or should pause. Most of the time, the outcome of yielding to the scheduler is predictable. But keep in mind that other goroutines may also hit points at which they pause, and in such cases, the scheduler may again continue running your function.

For example, if you execute a goroutine that runs a database query, running `runtime.Gosched` may not be enough to ensure that the other goroutine has completed its query. It may end up paused, waiting for the database, in which case the scheduler may continue running your function. Thus, although calling the Go scheduler may guarantee that the scheduler has a chance to check for other goroutines, you shouldn't rely on it as a tool for ensuring that other goroutines have a chance to complete.

There's a better way of doing that. The solution to this complex situation is shown next.

TECHNIQUE 11   **Waiting for goroutines**

Sometimes you'll want to start multiple goroutines but not continue working until those goroutines have completed their objective. *Go wait groups* are a simple way to achieve this.

PROBLEM
One goroutine needs to start one or more other goroutines, and then wait for them to finish. In this practical example, you'll focus on a more specific problem: you want to compress multiple files as fast as possible and then display a summary.

SOLUTION
Run individual tasks inside goroutines. Use `sync.WaitGroup` to signal the outer process that the goroutines are done and it can safely continue. Figure 3.1 illustrates this general design: several workers are started, and work is delegated to the workers. One process delegates the tasks to the workers and then waits for them to complete.

DISCUSSION
Go's standard library provides several useful tools for working with synchronization. One that frequently comes in handy is `sync.WaitGroup`, a tool for telling one goroutine to wait until other goroutines complete.

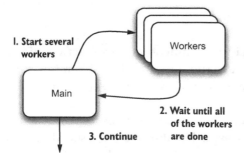

Figure 3.1   Start multiple workers and wait for completion.

Let's begin with a simple tool that compresses an arbitrary number of individual files. In the following listing you'll use the built-in Gzip compression library (compress /gzip) to take each individual file and compress it.

Listing 3.3   Simple Gzip compression tool

```
package main

import (
    "compress/gzip"
    "io"
    "os"
)

func main() {
    for _, file := range os.Args[1:] {         Collects a list of files
        compress(file)                          passed in on the
    }                                           command line
}

func compress(filename string) error {
    in, err := os.Open(filename)        ◄─────── Opens the source file for reading
    if err != nil {
        return err
    }
    defer in.Close()
                                                Opens a destination file,
                                                with the .gz extension added
    out, err := os.Create(filename + ".gz")  ◄─ to the source file's name
    if err != nil {
        return err
    }
    defer out.Close()
                                        The gzip.Writer compresses
                                        data and then writes it to
    gzout := gzip.NewWriter(out)    ◄── the underlying file.
    _, err = io.Copy(gzout, in)     ◄──
    gzout.Close()                       The io.Copy function does all
                                        the copying for you.
    return err
}
```

This tool takes a list of files on the command line and then compresses each file, creating a file with the same name as the original, but with .gz appended as an extension. Say you have a directory that looks like this:

```
$ ls -1 exampledata
example1.txt
example2.txt
example3.txt
```

You have three text files in your exampledata directory. Using your tool, you can compress them:

```
$ go run simple_gz.go exampledata/*
$ ls -1 exampledata
example1.txt
example1.txt.gz
example2.txt
example2.txt.gz
example3.txt
example3.txt.gz
```

In that example run, you can see that your `simple_gz.go` program created a Gzipped version of each file.

Now let's talk about performance. As written, the preceding program uses only one goroutine (and thus uses only one CPU core). It's unlikely that this program is going to make good use of all of the disk I/O bandwidth, too. Although the code runs just fine, it's nowhere near as fast as it could be. And because each file can be compressed individually, it's conceptually simple to break out your single thread of execution into something parallelized.

You can rewrite a program like this to compress each file in its own goroutine. Although this would be a suboptimal solution for compressing thousands of files (you'd probably overwhelm the I/O capacity of the system), it works well when dealing with a few hundred files or less.

Now here's the trick: you want to compress a bunch of files in parallel, but have the parent goroutine (`main`) wait around until all of the workers are done. You can easily accomplish this with a wait group. In listing 3.4 you'll modify the code in such a way that you don't change the `compress` function at all. This is generally considered better design because it doesn't require your worker function (`compress`) to use a wait group in cases where files need to be compressed serially.

> **Listing 3.4   Compressing files in parallel with a wait group**

```
package main

import (
    "compress/gzip"
    "fmt"
    "io"
    "os"
    "sync"
)

func main() {
    var wg sync.WaitGroup          ◁──── A WaitGroup doesn't need
                                          to be initialized.
```

```
var i int = -1
var file string
for i, file = range os.Args[1:] {
        wg.Add(1)
        go func(filename string) {
                compress(filename)
                wg.Done()
        }(file)
}
wg.Wait()

fmt.Printf("Compressed %d files\n", i+1)
}

func compress(filename string) error {
    // Unchanged from above
}
```

Because you want to reference i outside the for loop you declare the variables here.

The outer goroutine (main) waits until all the compressing goroutines have called wg.Done.

Because you're calling a goroutine in a for loop, you need to do a little trickery with the parameter passing.

This function calls compress and then notifies the wait group that it's done.

For every file you add, you tell the wait group that you're waiting for one more compress operation.

In this revised compression tool, you've changed the main function in significant ways. First, you've added a wait group.

A *wait group* is a message-passing facility that signals a waiting goroutine when it's safe to proceed. To use it, you tell the wait group when you want it to wait for something, and then you signal it again when that thing is done. A wait group doesn't need to know more about the things it's waiting for other than (a) the number of things it's waiting for, and (b) when each thing is done. You increment the first with `wg.Add`, and as your task completes, you signal this with `wg.Done`. The `wg.Wait` function blocks until all tasks that were added are done. Figure 3.2 illustrates the process.

In this program, you call `wg.Done` inside a goroutine. That goroutine accepts a filename and then runs your `compress` function on it. Notice that you've done something that at first blush appears redundant. Instead of closing over `file` inside the closure,

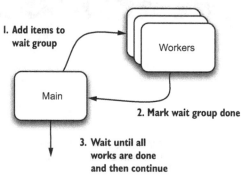

I. Add items to wait group

Workers

Main

2. Mark wait group done

3. Wait until all works are done and then continue

Figure 3.2   Wait groups in action

you pass the file into the program as `filename`. You do this for a reason related to the Go scheduler.

The variable file is scoped to the `for` loop, which means that its value will change on each iteration of the loop. But as you saw earlier in the chapter, declaring a goroutine doesn't result in its immediate execution. If your loop runs five times, you'll have five goroutines scheduled, but possibly none of them executed. And on each of those five iterations, the value of `file` will change. By the time the goroutines execute, they may all have the same (fifth) version of the `file` string. That isn't what you want. You want each to be scheduled with that iteration's value of `file`, so you pass it as a function parameter, which ensures that the value of `file` is passed to each goroutine as it's scheduled.

Although this might at first seem an esoteric problem, it's not uncommon. Anytime a loop executes goroutines, you need to be extra careful that the variables the goroutine uses aren't changed by the loop. The easiest way to accomplish this is to make copies of the variables inside the loop.

TECHNIQUE 12 **Locking with a mutex**

Anytime two or more goroutines are working with the same piece of data, and that data may change, you have the potential for a race condition. In a *race condition*, two things are "racing" to use the same piece of information. Problems arise when both are working with the same data at around the same time. One goroutine may be only partway through modifying a value when another goroutine tries to use it. And that situation can have unintended consequences.

PROBLEM

Multiple goroutines need to access or modify the same piece of data.

SOLUTION

One simple way to avoid this situation is for each goroutine to place a "lock" on a resource that it's using, and then unlock the resource when it's done. For all other goroutines, when they see the lock, they wait until the lock is removed before attempting to lock that resource on their own. Use `sync.Mutex` to lock and unlock the object.

DISCUSSION

The built-in sync package provides a `sync.Locker` interface as well as a couple of lock implementations. These provide essential locking behavior.

> **Don't reimplement locks**
>
> For a while now, a rumor has been circulating that Go locks perform so poorly that you're better off implementing your own. This has led many Go developers to build their own lock libraries. In the best case, this is unnecessary work. In the worst case, developers build broken or slower locking systems.
>
> Unless you have a proven use case and performance-sensitive code, you should refrain from reimplementing locks on your own. The built-in package is simple to use, battle-tested, and meets the performance needs of most applications.

> *(continued)*
>
> Later in the chapter, you'll work with channels. On occasion, you may find that code already using channels can better handle locking with channels. This is fine (we'll show you how to do it). But in general, there's no practical reason for implementing your own locking library.

The following listing is an example of a program with a race condition. This simple program reads any number of files and tallies the number of occurrences for each word it finds. At the end of its execution, it prints a list of words that appear more than once.

Listing 3.5   Word counter with race condition

```go
package main

import (
    "bufio"
    "fmt"
    "os"
    "strings"
    "sync"
)

func main() {
    var wg sync.WaitGroup          // Again, you'll use a wait
                                   // group to monitor a
                                   // group of goroutines.
    w := newWords()
    for _, f := range os.Args[1:] {       // The main loop
        wg.Add(1)                         // uses the pattern
        go func(file string) {            // in technique 12.
            if err := tallyWords(file, w); err != nil {
                fmt.Println(err.Error())
            }
            wg.Done()
        }(f)
    }
    wg.Wait()

    fmt.Println("Words that appear more than once:")
    for word, count := range w.found {       // At the end of the
        if count > 1 {                       // program, you print
            fmt.Printf("%s: %d\n", word, count)  // what you found.
        }
    }
}

type words struct {         // You track words in a struct. You could
    found map[string]int    // use a map type, but using a struct
}                           // here makes the next refactor easier.

func newWords() *words {                        // Creates a new words instance
    return &words{found: map[string]int{}}
}
```

```
func (w *words) add(word string, n int) {          ◄──┐   Tracks the number of times
    count, ok := w.found[word]                              you've seen this word
    if !ok {                                           If the word isn't
        w.found[word] = n                              already tracked, add
        return                                         it. Otherwise,
    }                                                  increment the count.
    w.found[word] = count + n
}

func tallyWords(filename string, dict *words) error {   ◄──   Open a file, parse its
    file, err := os.Open(filename)                            contents, and count
    if err != nil {                                           the words that appear.
        return err                                            Copy function does all
    }                                                         the copying for you.
    defer file.Close()

    scanner := bufio.NewScanner(file)                   Scanner is a useful tool
    scanner.Split(bufio.ScanWords)                      for parsing files like this.
    for scanner.Scan() {
        word := strings.ToLower(scanner.Text())
        dict.add(word, 1)
    }
    return scanner.Err()
}
```

The main function loops over all the files you supply on the command line, generating statistics for each as it goes. What you expect, when you run the preceding code, is for the tool to read text files and print out a list of the words that it finds. Let's try it on a single file:

```
$ go run race.go 1.txt
Words that appear more than once:
had: 2
down: 2
the: 5
have: 2
that: 3
would: 3
...
```

That's what you'd expect the output to look like. Now, if you pass in more than one filename, the tool will process each file in its own goroutine. Let's try that:

```
$ go run race.go *.txt
fatal error: concurrent map writes

goroutine 8 [running]:
runtime.throw(0x115890, 0xd)
    /usr/local/go/src/runtime/panic.go:527 +0x90 fp=0x82029cbf0
    sp=0x82029cbd8
runtime.evacuate(0xca600, 0x8202142d0, 0x16)
    /usr/local/go/src/runtime/hashmap.go:825 +0x3b0 fp=0x82029ccb0
    sp=0x82029cbf0
```

```
runtime.growWork(0xca600, 0x8202142d0, 0x31)
     /usr/local/go/src/runtime/hashmap.go:795 +0x8a fp=0x82029ccd0
     sp=0x82029ccb0
runtime.mapassign1(0xca600, 0x8202142d0, 0x82029ce70, 0x82029cdb0)
     /usr/local/go/src/runtime/hashmap.go:433 +0x175 fp=0x82029cd78
     sp=0x82029ccd0
...
```

At least some of the time, this will fail. Why? The error gives a hint: concurrent map writes. If you rerun the command with the --race flag, you'll get an even better idea:

```
go run --race race.go *.txt
==================
WARNING: DATA RACE
Read by goroutine 8:
  runtime.mapaccess2_faststr()
      /tmp/workdir/go/src/runtime/hashmap_fast.go:281 +0x0
  main.tallyWords()
      /Users/mbutcher/Code/go-in-practice/chapter3/race/race.go:62 +0x3ed
  main.main.func1()
      /Users/mbutcher/Code/go-in-practice/chapter3/race/race.go:18 +0x66

Previous write by goroutine 6:
  runtime.mapassign1()
      /tmp/workdir/go/src/runtime/hashmap.go:411 +0x0
  main.tallyWords()
      /Users/mbutcher/Code/go-in-practice/chapter3/race/race.go:62 +0x48a
  main.main.func1()
      /Users/mbutcher/Code/go-in-practice/chapter3/race/race.go:18 +0x66

Goroutine 8 (running) created at:
  main.main()
      /Users/mbutcher/Code/go-in-practice/chapter3/race/race.go:22 +0x238

Goroutine 6 (running) created at:
  main.main()
      /Users/mbutcher/Code/go-in-practice/chapter3/race/race.go:22 +0x238
==================
```

The call to words.add has a problem. Multiple goroutines are accessing the same bit of memory, the words.found map, at the same time (note the bold lines). This causes a race condition to modify the map.

Go includes built-in race detection

Many of the Go tools, including go run and go test, accept a --race flag, which enables race detection. Race detection substantially slows execution, but it's useful for detecting race conditions during the development cycle.

If you look back at the original program, you can quickly find the problem. If add is called by multiple goroutines at around the same time, multiple simultaneous operations may occur on the same map. This is a recipe for corrupting the map.

One simple solution is to lock the map before you modify it, and then unlock it afterward. You can accomplish this with a few changes to the code, as shown in the next listing.

Listing 3.6 Word counter with locks

```go
package main

import (
    // Same as before…
    "sync"
)

func main() {
    var wg sync.WaitGroup

    w := newWords()
    for _, f := range os.Args[1:] {
        wg.Add(1)
        go func(file string) {
            if err := tallyWords(file, w); err != nil {
                fmt.Println(err.Error())
            }
            wg.Done()
        }(f)
    }
    wg.Wait()

    fmt.Println("Words that appear more than once:")
    w.Lock()
    for word, count := range w.found {
        if count > 1 {
            fmt.Printf("%s: %d\n", word, count)
        }
    }
    w.Unlock()
}

type words struct {
    sync.Mutex
    found map[string]int
}

func newWords() *words {
    return &words{found: map[string]int{}}
}

func (w *words) add(word string, n int) {
    w.Lock()
    defer w.Unlock()
    count, ok := w.found[word]
    if !ok {
        w.found[word] = n
        return
    }
    w.found[word] = count + n
}
```

> Locks and unlocks the map when you iterate at the end. Strictly speaking, this isn't necessary because you know that this section won't happen until all files are processed.

> The words struct now inherits the mutex lock.

> Locks the object, modifies the map, and then unlocks the object

```
func tallyWords(filename string, dict *words) error {
    // Unchanged from before
}
```

In this revised version, the `words` struct declares an anonymous field referencing `sync.Mutex`, basically granting the `words.Lock` and `words.Unlock` methods. This is a common way of exposing a lock on a struct. (You used these methods when looping over the words at the end of `main`.)

Now, inside the `add` method, you lock the object, modify the map, and then unlock the object. When multiple goroutines enter the `add` method, the first will get the lock, and the others will wait until the lock is released. This will prevent multiple goroutines from modifying the map at the same time.

It's important to note that locks work only when all access to the data is managed by the same lock. If some data is accessed with locks, and others without, a race condition can still occur.

Sometimes it's useful to allow multiple read operations on a piece of data, but to allow only one write (and no reads) during a write operation. The `sync.RWLock` provides this functionality. The `sync` package has several other useful tools that simplify coordination across goroutines. But at this point, let's turn our attention to another core concept in Go's concurrency model: channels.

3.3   *Working with channels*

Channels provide a way to send messages from one goroutine to another. This section covers several ways of using channels to accomplish common tasks and solve common problems.

The easiest way to understand channels is to compare them to network sockets. Two applications can connect over a network socket. Depending on how these applications were written, network traffic can flow in a single direction or bidirectionally. Sometimes network connections are short-lived, and sometimes they stick around for a long time. Smart applications may even use multiple network connections, each sending and receiving different kinds of data. Just about any data can be sent over a network socket, but there's a drawback: that data has to be marshaled into raw bytes.

Go channels work like sockets between goroutines within a single application. Like network sockets, they can be unidirectional or bidirectional. Channels can be short-lived or long-lived. And it's common to use more than one channel in an app, having different channels send different kinds of data. But unlike network connections, channels are typed and can send structured data. There's generally no need to marshal data onto a channel.

Let's dive into channels by refactoring an earlier code sample to use channels.

> ## Don't overuse channels
>
> Channels are a fantastic tool for communicating between goroutines. They're simple to use, as you'll see, and make concurrent programming much easier than the threading models of other popular languages.
>
> But be wary of overuse. Channels carry overhead and have a performance impact. They introduce complexity into a program. And most important, channels are the single biggest source of memory management issues in Go programs. As with any tool, use channels when the need arises, but resist the temptation to polish your new hammer and then go looking for nails.

TECHNIQUE 13 Using multiple channels

Go developers are fond of pointing out that channels are communication tools. They enable one goroutine to communicate information to another goroutine. Sometimes the best way to solve concurrency problems in Go is to communicate more information. And that often translates into using more channels.

PROBLEM

You want to use channels to send data from one goroutine to another, and be able to interrupt that process to exit.

SOLUTION

Use `select` and multiple channels. It's a common practice in Go to use channels to signal when something is done or ready to close.

DISCUSSION

To introduce channels, let's revisit the first code example in this chapter. That program echoed user input for 30 seconds. It accomplished this by using a goroutine to echo the information, and a `time.Sleep` call to wait. Let's rewrite that program to use channels in addition to goroutines.

You're not looking to add new functionality or even to vastly improve the initial example. You're interested in taking a different approach to solving the same problem. In so doing, you'll see several idiomatic uses of channels.

Before looking at the code in listing 3.7, consider the following concepts that you'll see come into play here:

- Channels are created with `make`, just like maps and slices.
- The arrow operator (`<-`) is used both to signify the direction of a channel (`out chan<- []byte`) and to send or receive data over a channel (`buf := <-echo`).
- The `select` statement can watch multiple channels (zero or more). Until something happens, it'll wait (or execute a `default` statement, if supplied). When a channel has an event, the `select` statement will execute that event. You'll see more on channels later in this chapter.

Listing 3.7   Using multiple channels

```
package main

import (
        "fmt"
        "os"
        "time"
)

func main() {
        done := time.After(30 * time.Second)
        echo := make(chan []byte)
        go readStdin(echo)
        for {
                select {
                case buf := <-echo:
                        os.Stdout.Write(buf)
                case <-done:
                        fmt.Println("Timed out")
                        os.Exit(0)
                }
        }
}

func readStdin(out chan<- []byte) {
        for {
                data := make([]byte, 1024)
                l, _ := os.Stdin.Read(data)
                if l > 0 {
                        out <- data
                }
        }
}
```

Creates a channel that will receive a message when 30 seconds have elapsed

Makes a new channel for passing bytes from Stdin to Stdout. Because you haven't specified a size, this channel can hold only one message at a time.

Starts a goroutine to read Stdin, passes it our new channel for communicating

Uses a select statement to pass data from Stdin to Stdout when received, or to shut down when the time-out event occurs

Takes a write-only channel (chan<-) and sends any received input to that channel

Copies some data from Stdin into data. Note that File.Read blocks until it receives data.

Sends the buffered data over the channel

Running the preceding code results in the following:

```
$ go run echoredux.go
test 1
test 1
test 2
test 2
test 3
test 3
Timed out
```

As you saw with the previous implementation, if you type test 1, that text is echoed back. After 30 seconds, the program halts itself.

Rewriting the echo example has introduced new concepts regarding channels. The first channel in the preceding code is created by the time package. The time.After function builds a channel that will send a message (a time.Time) when the given duration has elapsed. Calling time.After(30 * time.Second) returns a <-chan time.Time (receive-only channel that receives time.Time objects) that, after 30 seconds, will receive a message. Thus, practically speaking, the two methods of pausing in the following listing are operationally equivalent.

Listing 3.8   Pausing with Sleep and After

```
package main

import (
    "time"
)

func main() {
    time.Sleep(5 * time.Second)          ◁─── Blocks for five seconds

    sleep := time.After(5 * time.Second)
    <-sleep
}
```

Blocks for five seconds

Creates a channel that will get notified in five seconds, then block until that channel receives a notification

Some functions (for example, time.After) create and initialize channels for you. But to create a new channel, you can use the built-in make function.

Channels are bidirectional by default. But as you saw in the preceding example, you can specify a "direction" for the channel when passing it into a function (or during any other assignment). The readStdin function can only write to the out channel. Any attempt to read from it will result in a compile-time error. Generally, it's considered good programming practice to indicate in a function signature whether the function receives or sends on a channel.

The last important facet of this program is select. A select statement is syntactically similar to a switch statement. It can take any number of case statements, as well as a single optional default statement.

The select statement checks each case condition to see whether any of them have a send or receive operation that needs to be performed. If exactly one of the case statements can send or receive, select will execute that case. If more than one can send or receive, select randomly picks one. If none of the case statements can send or receive, select falls through to a default (if specified). And if no default is specified, select blocks until one of the case statements can send or receive.

In this example, select is waiting to receive on two channels. If a message comes over the echo channel, the string that's sent is stored in buf (buf := <-echo), and then written to standard output. This illustrates that a receive operation can assign the received value to a variable.

But the second case that your select is waiting for is a message on the done channel. Because you don't particularly care about the contents of the message, you don't assign the received value to a variable. You just read it off the channel, and the select discards the value (<-done).

There's no default value on your select, so it'll block until either a message is received on <-echo or a message is received on <-done. When the message is received, select will run the case block and then return control. You've wrapped your select in a for loop, so the select will be run repeatedly until the <-done channel receives a message and the program exits.

One thing we didn't cover in this technique is closing channels when you're done with them. In our example app, the program is too short-lived to require this, and you rely on the runtime to clean up after you. In the next technique, you'll look at a strategy for closing channels.

TECHNIQUE 14   Closing channels

In Go, developers rely on the memory manager to clean up after themselves. When a variable drops out of scope, the associated memory is scrubbed. But you have to be careful when working with goroutines and channels. What happens if you have a sender and receiver goroutine, and the sender finishes sending data? Are the receiver and channel automatically cleaned up? Nope. The memory manager will only clean up values that it can ensure won't be used again, and in our example, an open channel and a goroutine can't be safely cleaned.

Imagine for a moment that this code was part of a larger program, and that the function main was a regular function called repeatedly throughout the lifetime of the app. Each time it's called, it creates a new channel and a new goroutine. But the channel is never closed, nor does the goroutine ever return. That program would leak both channels and goroutines.

The question arises: how can you correctly and safely clean up when you're using goroutines and channels? Failing to clean up can cause memory leaks or channel/goroutine leaks, where unneeded goroutines and channels consume system resources but do nothing.

PROBLEM

You don't want leftover channels and goroutines to consume resources and cause leaky applications. You want to safely close channels and exit goroutines.

SOLUTION

The straightforward answer to the question "How do I avoid leaking channels and goroutines?" is "Close your channels and return from your goroutines." Although that answer is correct, it's also incomplete. Closing channels the wrong way will cause your program to panic or leak goroutines.

The predominant method for avoiding unsafe channel closing is to use additional channels to notify goroutines when it's safe to close a channel.

DISCUSSION

You can use a few idiomatic techniques for safely shutting down channels.

Let's start, though, with a negative example, shown in the following listing. Beginning with the general idea of the program from listing 3.7, let's construct a program that incorrectly manages its channel.

Listing 3.9 Improper channel close

```
package main

import (
    "fmt"
    "time"
)

func main() {
    msg := make(chan string)
    until := time.After(5 * time.Second)

    go send(msg)

    for {
        select {
        case m := <-msg:
            fmt.Println(m)
        case <-until:
            close(msg)
            time.Sleep(500 * time.Millisecond)
            return
        }
    }
}

func send(ch chan string) {
    for {
        ch <- "hello"
        time.Sleep(500 * time.Millisecond)
    }
}
```

Starts a send goroutine
with a sending channel

Loops over a select that
watches for messages from
send, or for a time-out

If a message
arrives from
send, prints it

When the time-out
occurs, shuts things
down. You pause to
ensure that you see
the failure before the
main goroutine exits.

Sends "Hello" to the
channel every half-second

This example code is contrived to illustrate a problem that's more likely to occur in a server or another long-running program. You'd expect this program to print 10 or so hello strings and then exit. But if you run it, you get this:

```
$ go run bad.go
hello
hello
hello
hello
hello
hello
hello
hello
hello
hello
panic: send on closed channel

goroutine 20 [running]:
main.send(0x82024c060)
    /Users/mbutcher/Code/go-in-practice/chapter3/closing/bad.go:28 +0x4c
created by main.main
    /Users/mbutcher/Code/go-in-practice/chapter3/closing/bad.go:12 +0x90
```

```
goroutine 1 [sleep]:
time.Sleep(0x1dcd6500)
        /usr/local/go/src/runtime/time.go:59 +0xf9
main.main()
        /Users/mbutcher/Code/go-in-practice/chapter3/closing/bad.go:20 +0x24f
exit status 2
```

At the end, the program panics because main closes the msg channel while send is still sending messages to it. A send on a closed channel panics. In Go, the close function should be closed only by a sender, and in general it should be done with some protective guards around it.

What happens if you close the channel from the sender? No panic will happen, but something interesting does. Take a look at the quick example in the next listing.

Listing 3.10   Close from sender

```
package main

import "time"

func main() {
        ch := make(chan bool)
        timeout := time.After(600 * time.Millisecond)          Loops over a select
        go send(ch)                                            with two channels and
        for {                                                  a default
                select {
                case <-ch:                          If you get a message over your
                        println("Got message.")     main channel, prints something
                case <-timeout:
                        println("Time out")
                        return
                default:                                      By default, sleeps for
                        println("*yawn*")                     a bit. This makes the
                        time.Sleep(100 * time.Millisecond)    example easier to
                }                                             work with.
        }
}

func send(ch chan bool) {                   Sends a single
        time.Sleep(120 * time.Millisecond)  message over the
        ch <- true                          channel and then
        close(ch)                           closes the channel
        println("Sent and closed")
}
```

If a time-out occurs, terminates the program

After running this code, you'd expect that the main loop would do the following: hit the default clause a couple of times, get a single message from send, and then hit the default clause a few more times before the time-out happens and the program exits.

Instead, you'll see this:

```
$ go run sendclose.go
*yawn*
*yawn*
*yawn*
```

```
*yawn*
Got message.
Got message.
Sent and closed
*yawn*
Sent and closed
*yawn*
Got message.
Got message.
Got message.
Got message.
… #thousands more
Time out
```

This occurs because a closed channel always returns the channel's `nil` value, so send sends one `true` value and then closes the channel. Each time the `select` examines `ch` after `ch` is closed, it'll receive a `false` value (the `nil` value on a `bool` channel).

You could work around this issue. For example, you could break out of the `for`/`select` loop as soon as you see `false` on `ch`. Sometimes that's necessary. But the better solution is to explicitly indicate that you're finished with the channel and then close it.

The best way to rewrite listing 3.9 is to use one additional channel to indicate that you're done with the channel. This gives both sides the opportunity to cleanly handle the closing of the channel, as shown in the next listing.

Listing 3.11   Using a close channel

```go
package main

import (
    "fmt"
    "time"
)

func main() {
    msg := make(chan string)       // Adds an additional Boolean
    done := make(chan bool)        // channel that indicates when
    until := time.After(5 * time.Second)   // you're finished

    go send(msg, done)             // Passes two channels into send

    for {
        select {
        case m := <-msg:
            fmt.Println(m)
        case <-until:
            done <- true           // When you time-out,
            time.Sleep(500 * time.Millisecond)   // lets send know the
            return                 // process is done
        }
    }
}

func send(ch chan<- string, done <-chan bool) {   // ch is a receiving
                                                   // channel, while done is
                                                   // a sending channel.
```

```
for {
        select {
        case <-done:
                println("Done")
                close(ch)
                return
        default:
                ch <- "hello"
                time.Sleep(500 * time.Millisecond)
        }
    }
}
```

> When done has a message, shuts things down

This example demonstrates a pattern that you'll frequently observe in Go: using a channel (often called done) to send a signal between goroutines. In this pattern, you usually have one goroutine whose primary task is to receive messages, and another whose job is to send messages. If the receiver hits a stopping condition, it must let the sender know.

In listing 3.11, the main function is the one that knows when to stop processing. But it's also the receiver. And as you saw before, the receiver shouldn't ever close a receiving channel. Instead, it sends a message on the done channel indicating that it's done with its work. Now, the send function knows when it receives a message on done that it can (and should) close the channel and return.

TECHNIQUE 15   Locking with buffered channels

Thus far, you've looked at channels that contain one value at a time and are created like this: make(chan TYPE). This is called an *unbuffered channel*. If such a channel has received a value, and is then sent another one before the channel can be read, the second send operation will block. Moreover, the sender will also block until the channel is read.

Sometimes you'll want to alter those blocking behaviors. And you can do so by creating buffered channels.

PROBLEM

In a particularly sensitive portion of code, you need to lock certain resources. Given the frequent use of channels in your code, you'd like to do this with channels instead of the sync package.

SOLUTION

Use a channel with a buffer size of 1, and share the channel among the goroutines you want to synchronize.

DISCUSSION

Technique 12 introduced sync.Locker and sync.Mutex for locking sensitive areas of code. The sync package is part of Go's core, and is thus well tested and maintained. But sometimes (especially in code that already uses channels), it's desirable to implement locks with channels instead of the mutex. Often this is a stylistic preference: it's prudent to keep your code as uniform as possible.

When talking about using a channel as a lock, you want this kind of behavior:

1 A function acquires a lock by sending a message on a channel.
2 The function proceeds to do its sensitive operations.
3 The function releases the lock by reading the message back off the channel.
4 Any function that tries to acquire the lock before it's been released will pause when it tries to acquire the (already locked) lock.

You couldn't implement this scenario with an unbuffered channel. The first step in this process would cause the function to block because an unbuffered channel blocks on send. In other words, the sender waits until something receives the message it puts on the channel.

But one of the features of a buffered channel is that it doesn't block on send provided that buffer space still exists. A sender can send a message into the buffer and then move on. But if a buffer is full, the sender will block until there's room in the buffer for it to write its message.

This is exactly the behavior you want in a lock. You create a channel with only one empty buffer space. One function can send a message, do its thing, and then read the message off the buffer (thus unlocking it). The next listing shows a simple implementation.

Listing 3.12 Simple locking with channels

```
package main

import (
        "fmt"
        "time"
)

func main() {
        lock := make(chan bool, 1)          ◁   Creates a buffered
        for i := 1; i < 7; i++ {                channel with one space
                go worker(i, lock)
        }                                       Starts up to six goroutines
        time.Sleep(10 * time.Second)            sharing the locking channel
}

func worker(id int, lock chan bool) {       A worker acquires the lock by sending
        fmt.Printf("%d wants the lock\n", id)   it a message. The first worker to hit
        lock <- true                        ◁   this will get the one space, and thus
        fmt.Printf("%d has the lock\n", id)     own the lock. The rest will block.
        time.Sleep(500 * time.Millisecond)
        fmt.Printf("%d is releasing the lock\n", id)   ◁
        <-lock                              ◁       The space between the
}                                                   lock <- true and the <-
                                                    lock is "locked."
```

Releases the lock by reading a value, which then opens that one space on the buffer again so that the next function can lock it

This pattern is simple: there's one step to lock and one to unlock. If you run this program, the output will look like this:

```
$ go run lock.go
2 wants the lock
1 wants the lock
2 has the lock
5 wants the lock
6 wants the lock
4 wants the lock
3 wants the lock
2 is releasing the lock
1 has the lock
1 is releasing the lock
5 has the lock
5 is releasing the lock
6 has the lock
6 is releasing the lock
3 has the lock
3 is releasing the lock
4 has the lock
4 is releasing the lock
```

In this output, you can see how your six goroutines sequentially acquire and release the lock. Within the first few milliseconds of starting the program, all six goroutines have tried to get the lock. But only goroutine 2 gets it. A few hundred milliseconds later, 2 releases the lock and 1 gets it. And the lock trading continues until the last goroutine (4) acquires and releases the lock. (Note that in this code, you can rely on the memory manager to clean up the locking channel. After all references to the channel are gone, it'll clean up the channel for you.)

Listing 3.12 illustrates one advantage of using buffered queues: preventing send operations from blocking while there's room in the queue. Specifying a queue length also allows you to specify just how much buffering you want to do. You might be able to imagine needing a lock that can be claimed by up to two goroutines, and you could accomplish this with a channel of length 2. Buffered queues are also employed for constructing message queues and pipelines.

3.4   Summary

This chapter introduced Go's concurrency system. You first looked at goroutines and the useful packages that Go provides for synchronizing across goroutines. Then you looked at Go's powerful channel system, which allows multiple goroutines to communicate with each other over typed pipes. You covered several important idioms and patterns, including the following:

- Go's CSP-based concurrency model
- Concurrent processing with goroutines
- Using the sync package for waiting and locking

- Communicating between goroutines with channels
- Closing channels properly

In the coming chapters, you'll see goroutines and channels in practice. You'll see how Go's web server starts a new goroutine for each request, and how patterns such as fan-out work for distributing a workload among multiple channels. If there's one feature that makes Go a standout system language, it's Go's concurrency model.

Next, we turn to error handling. Although it's not a glamorous topic, Go's method of handling errors is one of its exceptional features.

Part 2

Well-rounded applications

The second part covers when things don't go as planned. What happens if an application panics? How do you have tests that help catch problems before they occur in production? Chapter 4 focuses on errors and panics—how things can be handled well when they go wrong. This is especially true when handling panics and errors on goroutines. Chapter 5 shifts gears into debugging and testing. This includes logging problems so that you can debug when situations arise in production.

Handling errors and panics

This chapter covers

- Learning the Go idioms for errors
- Providing meaningful data with errors
- Adding your own error types the Go way
- Working with panics
- Transforming panics into errors
- Working with panics on goroutines

As Robert Burns famously expressed in his poem "To a Mouse," "The best-laid schemes o' mice an' men / Gang aft agley." Our best plans often still go wrong. No other profession knows this truth as thoroughly as software developers. This chapter focuses on handling those situations when things go awry.

Go distinguishes between errors and panics—two types of bad things that can happen during program execution. An *error* indicates that a particular task couldn't be completed successfully. A *panic* indicates that a severe event occurred, probably as a result of a programmer error. This chapter presents a thorough look at each category.

We start with errors. After briefly revisiting the error-handling idioms for Go, we dive into best practices. Errors can inform developers about something that has gone wrong, and if you do it right, they can also assist in recovering and moving on. Go's way of working with errors differs from the techniques used in languages such as Python, Java, and Ruby. But when you correctly use these techniques, you can write robust code.

The panic system in Go signals abnormal conditions that may threaten the integrity of a program. Our experience has been that it's used sporadically, and often reactively, so our focus in this chapter is on making the most of the panic system, especially when it comes to recovering from a panic. You'll learn when to use panics, how (and when) to recover from them, and how Go's error and panic mechanisms differ from other languages.

Although Go is occasionally criticized for having a verbose error system, this chapter illustrates why this system is conducive to building better software. By keeping errors at the forefront of the developer's mind, Go fights against our own cognitive overconfidence bias. We may be disposed to believe that we write bug-free code. But when we always keep error handling front and center, Go gets us used to the idea that we have to code defensively, regardless of how good we think we are.

4.1 Error handling

One of Go's idioms that often trips up newcomers is its error handling. Many popular languages, including Python, Java, and Ruby, involve a theory of exception handling that includes throwing and catching special exception objects. Others, like C, often use the return value for error handling, and manage the mutated data through pointers.

In lieu of adding exception handlers, the Go creators exploited Go's ability to return multiple values. The most commonly used Go technique for issuing errors is to return the error as the last value in a return, as shown in the following listing.

Listing 4.1   Returning an error

```go
package main

import (
    "errors"            Useful error and
    "strings"           string utilities
)
                                              Concat returns a string
                                              and an error.
func Concat(parts ...string) (string, error) {  ◄─┘
    if len(parts) == 0 {
        return "", errors.New("No strings supplied")
    }                                                Returns an error if
                                                     nothing was passed in

    return strings.Join(parts, " "), nil  ◄─┐
}                                           │
                                            Returns the new
                                            string and nil
```

The Concat function takes any number of strings, concatenates them together (separating the strings with a space character), and then returns the newly joined string. But if no strings are passed into the function, it returns an error.

Variable-length arguments

As Concat illustrates, Go supports variable-length argument lists (varargs). By using the … prefix before a type, you can tell Go that any number of that type of argument is allowed. Go collapses these into a slice of that type. In listing 4.1, parts will be treated as a [] string.

The declaration of the Concat function illustrates the typical pattern for returning errors. In idiomatic Go, the error is always the last return value.

Because errors are always the last value returned, error handling in Go follows a specific pattern. A function that returns an error is wrapped in an if/else statement that checks whether the error value is something other than nil, and handles it if so. The next listing shows a simple program that takes a list of arguments from the command line and concatenates them.

Listing 4.2   Handling an error

```
func main() {

    args := os.Args[1:]                                  Uses just the args after Args[0].
                                                         You don't want the program name.
    if result, err := Concat(args...); err != nil {   ⟵────  Handles the error
        fmt.Printf("Error: %s\n", err)
    } else {
        fmt.Printf("Concatenated string: '%s'\n", result)   ⟵  Prints the
    }                                                           result in a non-
                                                                error case
}
```

If you were to run this code, you'd see output like this:

```
$ go run error_example.go hello world
Concatenated string: 'hello world'
```

Or, if you didn't pass any arguments, you'd see the error message:

```
$ go run error_example.go
Error: No strings supplied
```

Listing 4.2 shows how to use the Concat function you made already, and it illustrates a common Go idiom. As you no doubt recall, Go's if statement has an optional assignment clause before the expression. The intent is to provide a place to get ready for the evaluation, but stay in the if/else scope. You could read it like this: if GET READY; EVALUATE SOMETHING.

Listing 4.2 shows this technique in action. First, you run `Concat(args…)`, which expands the `args` array as if you'd called `Concat(arg[0], arg[1],…)`. You assign the two return values to `result` and `err`. Then, still on that line, you check to see if `err` isn't `nil`. If `err` is set to something, you know an error occurred, so you print the error message.

It's important to note that when you use this two-part `if` statement, the assignments stay in scope for any `else` and `else if` statements, so `result` is still in scope when you go to print it.

This scoping illustrates why the two-clause `if` is a nice feature to have. It encourages good memory-management practices while simultaneously preventing that pattern that haunts our debugging nightmares: if a = b.

In listing 4.1, you saw the `Concat` function, and in listing 4.2 you've seen how it's used. But there's a technique already present in this example that you should look at explicitly.

TECHNIQUE 10 **Minimize the nils**

Nils are annoying for several reasons. They're a frequent cause of bugs in the system, and we as developers are often forced into a practice of checking values to protect against nils.

In some parts of Go, nils are used to indicate something specific. As you saw in the preceding code, anytime an error return value is `nil`, you ought to construe that as meaning, specifically, "There were no errors when this function executed." But in many other cases, the meaning of a `nil` is unclear. And in perhaps the most annoying cases, nils are treated as placeholders anytime a developer doesn't feel like returning a value. That's where this technique comes in.

PROBLEM

Returning `nil` results along with errors isn't always the best practice. It puts more work on your library's users, provides little useful information, and makes recovery harder.

SOLUTION

When it makes sense, avail yourself of Go's powerful multiple returns and send back not just an error, but also a usable value.

DISCUSSION

This pattern is illustrated in the `Concat` function you saw previously. Let's take a second look, focusing on the line where an error is returned.

Listing 4.3 Returning useful data with an error

```
func Concat(parts ...string) (string, error) {
    if len(parts) == 0 {
            return "", errors.New("No strings supplied")    ⟵ Returns both an
    }                                                           empty string and
    return strings.Join(parts, " "), nil                        an error
}
```

When an error occurs, both an empty string and an error message are returned. A savvy library user can carefully use the preceding code without having to add a lot of explicit error handling. In our contrived Concat case, returning an empty string makes sense. If you have no data to concatenate, but the return value's contract says you'll return a string, an empty string is the kind of thing that one would expect.

> **TIP** When you're creating errors, Go has two useful assistive functions. The errors.New function from the errors package is great for creating simple new errors. The fmt.Errorf function in the fmt package gives you the option of using a formatting string on the error message. Go developers use these two functions frequently.

By constructing Concat this way, you've done your library users a favor. The savvy library user who doesn't particularly care about the error case can now streamline the code, as shown in the next listing.

Listing 4.4 Relying on good error handling

```
func main() {
    args := os.Args[1:]
    result, _ := Concat(args...)              ◁——————  Passes the values of batch
    fmt.Printf("Concatenated string: '%s'\n", result)

}
```

Just as before, you take the command-line arguments and pass them to Concat. But when you call Concat, you don't wrap it in an if statement to handle the error. Because Concat is authored in such a way that it returns a usable value even when an error occurs, and because the presence or absence of the error doesn't impact the task at hand, you can avoid having to do an extra error check. Instead of wrapping the code in an if/else block, you ignore the error and work with result as a string.

When your context requires you to detect that an error occurred and respond accordingly, this pattern still facilitates that. You can still capture the error value and figure out what went wrong and why, so the pattern of returning both an error and a usable value makes it easier for your library users to write code that best fits their use case.

It's not always desirable, or even possible, to return non-nil values with every error. If no useful data can be constructed under a failure condition, returning nil may be preferable. The rule of thumb is that if a function can return a useful result when it errs, then it should return one. But if it has nothing useful to return, it should send back nil.

Finally, it's important for you to make your code's behavior easily understood by other developers. Go rightly emphasizes writing concise but useful comments atop every shared function. Documenting how your Concat function behaves should look something like the following listing.

Listing 4.5   Documenting returns under error conditions

```
// Concat concatenates a bunch of strings, separated by spaces.
// It returns an empty string and an error if no strings were passed in.
func Concat(parts ...string) (string, error) {
    //…
}
```

This brief comment follows the Go convention for commenting and makes it clear what happens under normal operation as well as what happens under an error condition.

If you're coming from a background that involves languages like Java or Python, the error system may at first seem primitive. There are no special try/catch blocks. Instead, convention suggests using if/else statements. Most errors that are returned are often of type error. Developers new to Go sometimes express concern that error handling seems clunky.

Such concerns vanish as developers get used to the Go way of doing things. Go's favoring of convention over language syntax pays off, as code is simpler to read and write. But we've noticed a surprising pattern with Go: whereas languages such as Java and Python favor developing specific error or exception types, Go developers rarely create specific error types.

This is no doubt related to the fact that many Go core libraries use the error type as is. As Go developers see it, most errors have no special attributes that would be better conveyed by a specific error type. Consequently, returning a generic error is the simplest way to handle things. Take, for example, the Concat function. Creating a ConcatError type for that function has no compelling benefit. Instead, you use the built-in errors package to construct a new error.

This simple error handling is often the best practice. But sometimes it can be useful to create and use specific error types.

TECHNIQUE 17   Custom error types

Go's error type is an interface that looks like the following listing.

Listing 4.6   The error interface

```
type error interface {
    Error() string
}
```

Anything that has an Error function returning a string satisfies this interface's contract. Most of the time, Go developers are satisfied working with errors as the error type. But in some cases, you may want your errors to contain more information than a simple string. In such cases, you may choose to create a custom error type.

PROBLEM

Your function returns an error. Important details regarding this error might lead users of this function to code differently, depending on these details.

SOLUTION

Create a type that implements the error interface but provides additional functionality.

DISCUSSION

Imagine you're writing a file parser. When the parser encounters a syntax error, it generates an error. Along with having an error message, it's generally useful to have information about where in the file the error occurred. You could build such an error as shown in the following listing.

Listing 4.7 Parse error

```
type ParseError struct {                          The error message without
    Message     string         ◄──────┐           location information
    Line, Char int             ◄────── The location information
}

func (p *ParseError) Error() string {
    format := "%s oln Line %d, Char %d"                      Implements the
    return fmt.Sprintf(format, p.Message, p.Line, p.Char)    Error interface
}
```

This new `ParseError` struct has three properties: `Message`, `Line`, and `Char`. You implement the `Error` function by formatting all three of those pieces of information into one string. But imagine that you want to return to the source of the parse error and display that entire line, perhaps with the trouble-causing character highlighted. The `ParseError` struct makes that easy to do.

   This technique is great when you need to return additional information. But what if you need one function to return different kinds of errors?

TECHNIQUE 18 **Error variables**

Sometimes you have a function that performs a complex task and may break in a couple of different, but meaningful, ways. The previous technique showed one way of implementing the error interface, but that method may be a little heavy-handed if each error doesn't also need additional information. Let's look at another idiomatic use of Go errors.

PROBLEM

One complex function may encounter more than one kind of error. And it's useful to users to indicate which kind of error was returned so that the ensuing applications can appropriately handle each error case. But although distinct error conditions may occur, none of them needs extra information (as in technique 17).

SOLUTION

One convention that's considered good practice in Go (although not in certain other languages) is to create package-scoped error variables that can be returned whenever a certain error occurs. The best example of this in the Go standard library comes in the `io` package, which contains errors such as `io.EOF` and `io.ErrNoProgress`.

DISCUSSION

Before diving into the details of using error variables, let's consider the problem and one obvious, but not particularly good, solution.

The problem you'd like to solve is being able to tell the difference between two errors. Let's build a small program in the next listing that simulates sending a simple message to a receiver.

Listing 4.8   Handling two different errors

```go
package main

import (
        "errors"
        "fmt"
        "math/rand"
)

var ErrTimeout = errors.New("The request timed out")
var ErrRejected = errors.New("The request was rejected")
var random = rand.New(rand.NewSource(35))

func main() {
    response, err := SendRequest("Hello")
    for err == ErrTimeout {
            fmt.Println("Timeout. Retrying.")
            response, err = SendRequest("Hello")
    }
    if err != nil {
            fmt.Println(err)
    } else {
            fmt.Println(response)
    }
}

func SendRequest(req string) (string, error) {
    switch random.Int() % 3 {
    case 0:
            return "Success", nil
    case 1:
            return "", ErrRejected
    default:
            return "", ErrTimeout
    }
}
```

The time-out error instance

The rejection error instance

A random number generator with a fixed source

Calls the stubbed-out SendRequest function

Handles the time-out condition with retries

Handles any other error as a failure

If there's no error, prints the result

Defines a function that superficially behaves like a message sender

Handles the time-out condition with retries

Instead of sending a message, randomly generates behavior

Instead of sending a message, randomly generates behavior

This listing exemplifies using variables as fixed errors. The code is designed to simulate the basics of a sending function. But instead of sending anything anywhere, the SendRequest function randomly generates a response. The response could be a success or it could be one of our two errors, ErrTimeout or ErrRejected.

> **Not so random**
>
> One interesting detail of listing 4.7 is found in the randomizer. Because you initialize the randomizer to a fixed value, it'll always return the same sequence of "random" numbers. This is great for us because you can illustrate a known sequence. But in production applications, you shouldn't use fixed integers to seed a source. One simple alternative is to use `time.Now` as a seed source.

Running the preceding program results in the following output:

```
$ go run two_errors.go
Timeout. Retrying.
The request was rejected
```

The first request to `SendRequest` returns a time-out, and the second call returns a rejection. If the second call had instead returned a time-out too, the program would have continued running until a call to `SendRequest` returned either a success or a rejection. It's common to see patterns like this in network servers.

Software developers working in a language such as Java or Python would be likely to implement `ErrTimeout` and `ErrRejected` as classes, and then throw new instances of each class. The `try/catch` pattern used by many languages is built for dealing with error information encapsulated in error types. But as you've seen previously, Go doesn't provide a `try/catch` block. You could use type matching (especially with a type `switch` statement) to provide the same functionality. But that's not the Go way. Instead, idiomatic Go uses a method that's both more efficient and simpler: create errors as package-scoped variables and reference those variables.

You can see in the preceding code that handling error variables is as simple as checking for equality. If the error is a time-out, you can retry sending the message repeatedly. But when the error is a rejection, you stop processing. And as before, returning a `nil` indicates that neither error occurs, and you handle that case accordingly. With a pattern like this, the same error variables are used repeatedly. This is efficient because errors are instantiated only once. It's also conceptually simple. As long as your error doesn't have special properties (as you saw in technique 16), you can create variables and then work with them as such.

There's one more facet of error handling that you should look at, and that's the Go panic.

4.2 The panic system

In addition to the preceding error handling, Go provides a second way of indicating that something is wrong: the panic system. As the name indicates, a panic tells you that something has gone seriously awry. It should be used sparingly and intelligently. In this section, we explain how and when panics should be used and along the way tell you about some of our own failures.

4.2.1   *Differentiating panics from errors*

The first thing to understand about panics is how they differ conceptually from errors. An error indicates that an event occurred that might violate expectations about what should have happened. A panic, in contrast, indicates that something has gone wrong in such a way that the system (or the immediate subsystem) can't continue to function.

Go assumes that errors will be handled by you, the programmer. If an error occurs and you ignore it, Go doesn't do anything your behalf. Not so with panics. When a panic occurs, Go unwinds the stack, looking for handlers for that panic. If no handler is found, Go eventually unwinds all the way to the top of the function stack and stops the program. An unhandled panic will kill your application.

Let's look at an example that illustrates this difference in the following listing.

Listing 4.9   Error and panic

```go
package main

import (
    "errors"
    "fmt"
)

var ErrDivideByZero = errors.New("Can't divide by zero")

func main() {
    fmt.Println("Divide 1 by 0")
    _, err := precheckDivide(1, 0)        First you divide using the
    if err != nil {                        precheckDivide function,
            fmt.Printf("Error: %s\n", err) which returns an error.
    }

    fmt.Println("Divide 2 by 0")           Then you run a similar division,
    divide(2, 0)                           but with the divide function.
}

func precheckDivide(a, b int) (int, error) {   The precheckDivide
    if b == 0 {                                 function returns an error
            return 0, ErrDivideByZero           if the divisor is 0.
    }
    return divide(a, b), nil          The regular divide function
}                                     wraps the division operator
                                      with no checks.
func divide(a, b int) int {
    return a / b
}
```

Here, you define two functions. The `divide` function performs a division operation. But it doesn't handle that one well-known case of dividing by 0. In contrast, the `precheckDivide` function explicitly checks the divisor and returns an error if the divisor is 0. You're interested in seeing how Go behaves under these two conditions, so in `main` you test first with the `precheckDivide` function and then again with the plain old `divide` function.

Running this program provides this output:

```
go run zero_divider.go
Divide 1 by 0
Error: Can't divide by zero
Divide 2 by 0
panic: runtime error: integer divide by zero
[signal 0x8 code=0x7 addr=0x22d8 pc=0x22d8]

goroutine 1 [running]:
main.main()
    /Users/mbutcher/Code/go-in-practice/chapter4/zero_divider.go:18 +0x2d8
```

The first division using `precheckDivide` returns an error, and the second division causes a panic because you never checked the divisor. Conceptually speaking, the reasons for this are important:

- When you checked the value before dividing, you never introduced the situation where the program was asked to do something it couldn't.
- When you divided, you caused the system to encounter a state that it couldn't handle. This is when a panic should occur.

Practically speaking, errors are something that we as developers ought to expect to go wrong. After all, they're documented in the code. You can glance at the definition of `precheckDivide` and see an error condition that you need to handle when you call the function. Although an error might represent something outside the norm, we can't really say that they're *unexpected*.

Panics, on the other hand, are unexpected. They occur when a constraint or limitation is unpredictably surpassed. When it comes to declaring a panic in your code, the general rule of thumb is don't panic unless there's no clear way to handle the condition within the present context. When possible, return errors instead.

4.2.2 Working with panics

Go developers have expectations about how to correctly panic, though those expectations aren't always clearly laid out. Before diving into the proper handling of panics, you'll look at a technique that all Go developers should know when it comes to issuing panics.

TECHNIQUE 19 **Issuing panics**

The definition of Go's panic function can be expressed like this: `panic(interface{})`. When you call `panic`, you can give it almost anything as an argument. You can, should you so desire, call `panic(nil)`, as shown in the following listing.

Listing 4.10 Panic with nil

```
package main

func main() {
    panic(nil)          ⟵─────  Panic about nothing!
}
```

The defer statement is a great way to close files or sockets when you're finished, free up resources such as database handles, or handle panics. Technique 19 showed the appropriate strategy for emitting a panic. Now you can take what you know about defer and concentrate for a moment on recovering from panics.

TECHNIQUE 20   Recovering from panics

Capturing a panic in a deferred function is standard practice in Go. We cover it here for two reasons. First, this discussion is a building block to another technique. Second, it provides the opportunity to take a step from the pattern into the mechanics so you can see what's happening instead of viewing panics as a formula to be followed.

PROBLEM

A function your application calls is panicking, and as a result your program is crashing.

SOLUTION

Use a deferred function and call recover to find out what happened and handle the panic.

The left side of figure 4.1 illustrates how an unhandled panic will crash your program. The right side illustrates how the recover function can stop the function stack from unwinding and allow the program to continue running.

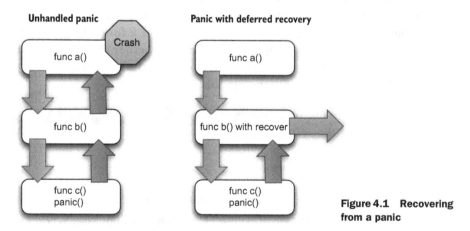

Figure 4.1   Recovering from a panic

DISCUSSION

Go provides a way of capturing information from a panic and, in so doing, stopping the panic from unwinding the function stack further. The recover function retrieves the data.

Let's take a look at a small example in the next listing that shows both emitting and handling a panic.

Listing 4.13   Recovering from a panic

```
package main

import (
    "errors"
    "fmt"
)                                              Provides a deferred closure to
                                                 handle panic recovery
func main() {
    defer func() {
        if err := recover(); err != nil {
            fmt.Printf("Trapped panic: %s (%T)\n", err, err)
        }
    }()

    yikes()                    ◁────── Calls a function that panics
}

func yikes() {                         Emits a panic with an
    panic(errors.New("Something bad happened."))  ◁─ error for a body
}
```

This program illustrates what's probably the most common pattern for panic recovery. To catch the panic that yikes raises, you write a deferred closure function that checks for a panic and recovers if it finds one.

In Go, when you defer a closure, you're defining a function and then marking it to be called (in this case, with an empty argument list). The general form is defer func(){ /* body */ }(). Note that although it looks like it's defined and called at once, Go's runtime won't call the function until it's appropriate for a deferred function to execute. In a moment, you'll see how the separation between defining the closure and then executing it later impacts the scope of the closure in a useful way.

The recover function in Go returns a value (interface{}) if a panic has been raised, but in all other cases it returns nil. The value returned is whatever value was passed into the panic. Running the preceding code returns this:

```
$ go run recover_panic.go
Trapped panic: Something bad happened. (*errors.errorString)
```

Notice that because you add the %T to the formatting string, you also get information about the type of err, which is the error type created by errors.New.

Now you can take things one step further and look at how to use this closure/recover combination to recover from a panic. Closures inherit the scope of their parent. Deferred closures, like the preceding one, inherit whatever is in scope before they're declared. For instance, the following listing works fine.

Listing 4.14   Scope for deferred closures

```
package main

import "fmt"

func main() {                       Defines the variable
    var msg string                  outside the closure
    defer func() {           ←┐
            fmt.Println(msg)        Prints the variable in the
    }()                      ←┘     deferred closure
msg = "Hello world"          ←────  Sets the value of the variable

}
```

Because `msg` is defined before the closure, the closure may reference it. And as expected, the value of the message will reflect whatever the state of `msg` is when the deferred function executes. The preceding code prints `Hello world`.

But even though `defer` is executed after the rest of the function, a closure doesn't have access to variables that are declared after the closure is declared. The closure is evaluated in order, but not executed until the function returns. For that reason, the following listing causes a compile error.

Listing 4.15   `msg` out of scope

```
package main

import "fmt"

func main() {
    defer func() {
            fmt.Println(msg)    ←────  Prints a variable
    }()
    msg := "Hello world"    ←┐  Declares and sets the variable. Compiles will fail
}                            └  because the declaration is after the function.
```

Because `msg` isn't declared prior to the deferred function, when the code is evaluated, `msg` is undefined.

Bringing together the details, you can take one final step in this technique. Let's look at a slightly more sophisticated use of a deferred function. This one handles a panic and cleans up before returning, and is a good representative sample of how to use deferred functions and recover in practice.

Imagine that you're writing a piece of code that preprocesses a CSV file, removing empty lines from the beginning. For the sake of boiling this code down to an example, `RemoveEmptyLines` isn't fully implemented. Instead, it always returns a panic. With this bad behavior, we can illustrate how to recover from a panic, close the problematic file, and then return an error, as shown in the following listing.

Listing 4.16   Cleanup

```
package main

import (
    "errors"
    "fmt"
    "io"
    "os"
)

func main() {
    var file io.ReadCloser
file, err := OpenCSV("data.csv")
    if err != nil {
            fmt.Printf("Error: %s", err)
            return
    }
    defer file.Close()


    // Do something with file.

}
func OpenCSV(filename string) (file *os.File, err error) {
    defer func() {
            if r := recover(); r != nil {
                    file.Close()
                    err = r.(error)
            }
    }()

    file, err = os.Open(filename)
    if err != nil {
            fmt.Printf("Failed to open file\n")
            return file, err
    }

    RemoveEmptyLines(file)

    return file, err
}

func RemoveEmptyLines(f *os.File) {
    panic(errors.New("Failed parse"))
}
```

Runs OpenCSV and handles any errors. This implementation always returns an error.

Uses a deferred function to ensure that a file gets closed

Normally, you'd do more with the file here.

OpenCSV opens and preprocesses your file. Note the named return values.

The main deferred error handling happens here.

Opens the data file and handles any errors (such as file not found)

Runs our intentionally broken RemoveEmptyLines function

Instead of stripping empty lines, you always fail here.

Again, the problem in the preceding code is that your RemoveEmptyLines function always panics. If you were to implement this function, it would check to see whether the leading lines of the file were empty, and if they were, it would advance the reader past those lines.

Listing 4.16 uses deferred functions in two places. In the main function, you use a deferred function to ensure that your file is closed. This is considered good practice when you're working with files, network connections, database handles, and other resources that need to be closed to prevent side effects or leaks. The second deferred function appears inside the OpenCSV function. This deferred function is designed to do three things:

- Trap any panics.
- Make sure that if a panic occurs, the file is closed. This is considered good practice even though in this context it may be redundant.
- Get the error from the panic and pass it back by using the regular error-handling mechanism.

One detail of the declaration of OpenCSV is worth mentioning: we label the return values in the function declaration. That makes it possible to refer to the file and err variables inside the closure, and ensures that when err is set to the panic's error, the correct value is returned.

As we've shown, defer is a powerful and useful way of dealing with panics, as well as reliably cleaning up. As we close out this technique, here are a few useful guidelines for working with deferred functions:

- Put deferred functions as close to the top of a function declaration as possible.
- Simple declarations such as foo := 1 are often placed before deferred functions.
- More-complex variables are declared before deferred functions (var myFile io.Reader), but not initialized until after.
- Although it's possible to declare multiple deferred functions inside a function, this practice is generally frowned upon.
- Best practices suggest closing files, network connections, and other similar resources inside a defer clause. This ensures that even when errors or panics occur, system resources will be freed.

In the next technique, you'll take one more step in handling panics and learn how to reliably prevent panics on goroutines from halting a program.

4.2.4 Panics and goroutines

So far, we haven't talked much about one of Go's most powerful features: goroutines. You start goroutines by using the go keyword; if you have a function called run, you can start it as a goroutine like this: go run. To quote the Go Programming Language Specification, the go statement "starts the execution of a function call as an independent concurrent thread of control, or *goroutine*, within the same address space" (http://golang.org/ref/spec#Go_statements). More simply, you can think of it as running a function on its own thread, but without having access to that thread.

> **Goroutines beneath the hood**
> The implementation of goroutines is a little more sophisticated than just running a function on its own thread. The Go Concurrency Wiki page (https://github.com/golang/go/wiki/LearnConcurrency) provides a big list of articles that dive into various aspects of Go's CSP-based concurrency model.

To illustrate this idea, imagine that you have a simple server. The server functions as follows:

- The main function runs start to start a new server.
- The start function processes configuration data and then runs the listen function.
- The listen function opens a network port and listens for new requests. When it gets a request, instead of handling the request itself, it calls go handle, passing on any necessary information to the handle function.
- The handle function processes the request and then calls response.
- The response function sends data back to the client and terminates the connection.

The listener function uses goroutines to handle multiple client connections at once. As it receives requests, it can push the workload onto a number of handle functions, each running in its own space. Variations of this powerful pattern are used frequently in Go server applications. Figure 4.2 illustrates this application and its function stacks when you use goroutines.

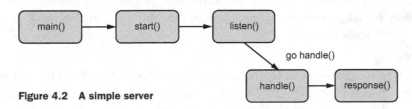

Figure 4.2   A simple server

Each row represents a function stack, and each call to go starts a new function stack. Each time listen receives a new request, a new function stack is created for the ensuing handle instance. And whenever handle finishes (for example, when response returns), that spawned goroutine is cleaned up.

Goroutines are powerful and elegant. Because they're both simple to write and cheap to use (they incur little overhead on your program), Go developers use them frequently. But in one specific (and unfortunately common) situation, the combination of goroutines and panics can result in a program crash.

TECHNIQUE 21   Trapping panics on goroutines

When handling a panic, the Go runtime unwinds the function stack until a recover occurs. But if it gets to the top of a function stack and recover is never called, the program dies. Recall figure 4.2, which showed how a goroutine gets its own function call stack. What happens when a panic occurs on that goroutine? Take a look at figure 4.3. Imagine that during a request, the response function encounters an unforeseen fatal error and panics. As a good server developer, you've added all kinds of error-handling logic to listen. But if you haven't added anything to handle, the program will crash. Why? Because when a panic is unhandled at the top of a function stack, it causes Go to

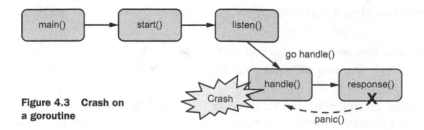

**Figure 4.3   Crash on
a goroutine**

terminate in an error state. A panic on a goroutine can't jump to the call stack of the
function that initiated the goroutine. There's no path for a panic to go from `handle`
to `listen` in this example. This is the problem our current technique focuses on.

PROBLEM

If a panic on a goroutine goes unhandled on that goroutine's call stack, it crashes
the entire program. Sometimes this is acceptable, but often the desired behavior is
recovery.

SOLUTION

Simply stated, `handle` panics on any goroutine that might panic. Our solution will
make it easier to design servers that handle panics without relying on panic handling
in every single handle function.

DISCUSSION

The interesting thing about this particular problem is that although it's trivially easy to
solve, the solution is repetitive, and often the burden of implementing it is pushed to
developers outside your control. First, you'll look at a basic implementation of the
code outlined previously in figure 4.3. From there, you'll explore the trivial solution
and will discover how Go's idioms make this solution troublesome. Then you'll see a
pattern for solving it more conveniently.

The next listing shows a basic implementation of the kind of server illustrated in
figure 4.3. It functions as a basic echo server. When you run it, you can connect to it
on port 1026 and send a plain line of text. The remote server will echo that text back
to you.

Listing 4.17   An echo server

```
package main

import (
    "bufio"
    "fmt"
    "net"
)

func main() {
    listen()
}

func listen() {
```

```go
listener, err := net.Listen("tcp", ":1026")
if err != nil {
        fmt.Println("Failed to open port on 1026")
        return
}
for {
        conn, err := listener.Accept()
        if err != nil {
                fmt.Println("Error accepting connection")
                continue
        }

        go handle(conn)
}
}

func handle(conn net.Conn) {
        reader := bufio.NewReader(conn)

        data, err := reader.ReadBytes('\n')
        if err != nil {
                fmt.Println("Failed to read from socket.")
                conn.Close()
        }

        response(data, conn)
}

func response(data []byte, conn net.Conn) {
        defer func() {
                conn.Close()
        }()
        conn.Write(data)
}
```

Starts a new server listening on port 1026

Listens for new client connections and handles any connection errors

When a connection is accepted, passes it to the handle function

Tries to read a line of data from the connection

If you fail to read a line, prints an error and closes the connection

Once you get a line of text, passes it to response

Writes the data back out to the socket, echoing it to the client; then closes the connection.

If you ran this code, it would start a server. You could then interact with the server like this:

```
$ telnet localhost 1026
Trying ::1...
Connected to localhost.
Escape character is '^]'.
test
test
Connection closed by foreign host.
```

When you type test (indicated in bold in the preceding code), the server echoes back that same text and then closes the connection.

This simple server works by listening for new client connections on port 1026. Each time a new connection comes in, the server starts a new goroutine that runs the handle function. Because each request is handled on a separate goroutine, this server can effectively handle numerous concurrent connections.

The `handle` function reads a line of text (raw bytes) and then passes that line and the connection to the `response` function. The `response` function echoes the text back to the client and then closes the connection.

This isn't exactly an ideal server, but it illustrates the basics. It also shows some pitfalls. Imagine that `response` could panic. Say you replace the preceding code with the following listing to simulate that situation.

Listing 4.18   Panic in the response

```
func response(data []byte, conn net.Conn) {
    panic(errors.New("Failure in response!"))    ◁—  Instead of doing something
}                                                     useful, simulates a panic
```

It might immediately stand out to you that even though the connection is never closed in this situation, things are more worrisome: this panic will crash the server. Servers shouldn't be so fragile that they crash when one particular request fails. Adding recovery handling to the `listen` function seems like a natural move. But that won't help because the goroutine is operating on a separate function stack.

From here, let's refactor our first pass at a server and make it tolerant. This time you'll add the panic handling in the `handle` function. The following listing presents only the `handle` and `response` functions; the rest of the code is the same as in listing 4.17.

Listing 4.19   Handle panics on a goroutine

```
func handle(conn net.Conn) {
    defer func() {
            if err := recover(); err != nil {                    The deferred function
                    fmt.Printf("Fatal error: %s", err)           handles the panic and
            }                                                     makes sure that in all
            conn.Close()                                          cases the connection is
    }()                                                           closed.
    reader := bufio.NewReader(conn)

    data, err := reader.ReadBytes('\n')
    if err != nil {
            fmt.Println("Failed to read from socket.")
    }

    response(data, conn)
}

func response(data []byte, conn net.Conn) {              Again, you issue a
    conn.Write(data)                                     panic to simulate
    panic(errors.New("Pretend I'm a real error"))   ◁—  a failure.
}
```

Your new `handle` function now includes a deferred function that uses `recover` to see whether a panic has occurred. This stops the panic from propagating up the stack. Notice that you've also slightly improved the connection management: you use `defer` to ensure that in all cases, no matter what happens, the connection is closed when `handle` is done. With this new revision, the server no longer crashes when `response` panics.

So far, so good. But you can take this example another step with the Go `handler` server idiom. It's common in Go to create a server library that provides a flexible method of handling responses. The `"net/http"`.`Server` library is a fantastic example of this. As shown earlier in the book, creating an HTTP server in Go is as simple as giving the HTTP system a `handler` function and starting a server (see the following listing).

Listing 4.20   A small HTTP server

```go
package main

import (
    "errors"
    "net/http"
)

func main() {
    http.HandleFunc("/", handler)              // Gives the HTTP system a handler function
    http.ListenAndServe(":8080", nil)          // Starts up a server
}
```

All of the logic for starting and managing a server is within the `net/http` package. But the package leaves it up to you, the developer, to tell it how to handle a request. In the preceding code, you have an opportunity to pass in a handler function. This is any function that satisfies the following type:

```go
type HandlerFunc func(ResponseWriter, *Request)
```

Upon receiving a request, the server does much the same as what you did in the earlier echo server architecture: it starts a goroutine and executes the handler function on that thread. What do you suppose would happen if you wrote a handler that panics?

Listing 4.21   A panicky handler

```go
func handler(res http.ResponseWriter, req *http.Request) {
    panic(errors.New("Fake panic!"))
}
```

If you run the server with that code, you'll find that the server dumps the panic information to the console, but the server keeps running:

```
2015/04/08 07:57:31 http: panic serving [::1]:51178: Fake panic!
goroutine 5 [running]:
net/http.func·011()
    /usr/local/Cellar/go/1.4.1/libexec/src/net/http/server.go:1130 +0xbb
main.handler(0x494fd0, 0xc208044000, 0xc208032410)
    /Users/mbutcher/Code/go-in-practice/chapter4/http_server.go:13 +0xdd
net/http.HandlerFunc.ServeHTTP(0x3191e0, 0x494fd0, 0xc208044000,
    0xc208032410)
...
```

But your handler function didn't do anything to handle the panic! That safety net is provided by the library. With this in mind, if you were to take the echo service and turn it into a well-behaving library, you'd slightly modify your architecture so that panics were handled inside the library.

When we began working with Go in earnest, we wrote a trivial little library (now part of github.com/Masterminds/cookoo) to protect us from accidentally unhandled panics on goroutines. The following listing shows a simplified version of that library.

Listing 4.22 `safely.Go`

```
package safely

import (
        "log"
)

type GoDoer func()                        ←── GoDoer is a simple
                                              parameterless
                                              function.
func Go(todo GoDoer) {                     ←──── safely.Go runs a function
        go func() {                              as a goroutine and
                defer func() {             ←──── handles any panics.
                        if err := recover(); err != nil {   ←── First you run an anonymous function.
                                log.Printf("Panic in safely.Go: %s", err)
                        }
                }()
                todo()                     ──── The anonymous function handles
        }()                                     panics, following the usual pattern
}                                               of deferring a recovery.
```

The function then calls the
GoDoer that was passed in.

This simple library provides panic handling, so you don't have to remember to do it on your own. The next listing shows an example of `safely.Go` in action.

Listing 4.23 Using `safely.Go` to trap panics

```
package main

import (
        "github.com/Masterminds/cookoo/safely"   ←── Imports the
        "errors"                                     safely package
        "time"
)

func message() {                           ←── Defines a callback that
        println("Inside goroutine")            matches the GoDoer type
        panic(errors.New("Oops!"))
}

func main() {
        safely.Go(message)                 ←── Instead of go message,
        println("Outside goroutine")           you use this.
        time.Sleep(1000)                   ←── Make sure the goroutine has a chance
}                                              to execute before the program exits.
```

In this example, you define a simple function that satisfies the GoDoer type (it has no parameters and no return value). Then when you call safely.Go(message), it executes your message function in a new goroutine, but with the added benefit of trapping any panics. Because message does panic, running this program provides the following output:

```
$ go run safely_example.go
Outside goroutine
Inside goroutine
2015/04/08 08:28:00 Panic in safely.Go: Oops!
```

Instead of the panic stopping the program execution, safely.Go traps and logs the panic message.

> **Closures help here**
>
> Instead of using a named function such as message, you could use a closure. A closure allows you to access variables that are in scope, and can be used to sidestep the fact that GoDoer doesn't accept any parameters. But if you do this, beware of race conditions and other concurrency issues!

This particular library might not suit your exact needs, but it illustrates a good practice: construct libraries so that a panic on a goroutine doesn't have the surprising or unintended result of halting your program.

Go's provision of both an error-handling system and a runtime panic system is elegant. But as you've seen in this section, panics tend to arise in surprising situations. If you forget to plan for them, you can find yourself mired in difficult debugging situations. That's why we've spent so much time discussing remedial techniques here—and why we suggest preventative no-brainer techniques like safely.Go instead of relying on developers to remember to do the right thing.

4.3 Summary

Let's be honest: there's nothing glamorous about error handling. But we firmly believe that one of the traits that distinguishes a good programmer from a great programmer is the way the developer writes error-handling code. Great programmers are mindful of protecting the system against bugs and failures.

That's why we spent an entire chapter covering the details of the error and panic systems in Go, and providing techniques for handling common situations. We showed you best practices for providing meaningful data with errors and how such techniques extend to issuing panics. And we wrapped up with a long look at panics and goroutines. We covered these topics:

- Understanding Go's patterns for error handling
- Using error variables

- Adding custom error types
- Properly using and handling panics
- Using error handling on goroutines

As you move into the next chapters, you'll visit other code-quality topics such as logging and writing tests. Taken together, we believe that these tools equip you to be a highly successful (dare we say, *great*) Go developer.

Debugging and testing 5

One of the advantages of working with a modern language is tooling. Over the years, developers have created fantastic tools that streamline the development process. Go is designed as a language for system developers, and it's loaded with tools designed to make your job easier. This chapter focuses on those tools and strategies for building resilient software. We talk about logging, debugging, and different sorts of testing.

In the preceding chapter, we talked about errors and panics. It seems fitting that we begin this chapter with techniques for finding the sorts of bugs that lead to unexpected errors and panics. We'll begin with debugging.

5.1 Locating bugs

Sometimes you see a bug and know immediately what caused it. More often, you need to spend a short amount of time in the code hunting for the problem. And every once in a while, you hit those frustrating beasts that take hours or even days to track down.

That third category of bug usually warrants the use of special tools or tactics to track down the issue. This section covers some of those tools and tactics.

5.1.1 Wait, where is my debugger?

The go-to debugging tool of choice for many software developers is (surprise!) the *debugger.* This magnificent tool executes your code and walks you through each step of the way at whatever pace you desire.

Before we dive headlong into the discussion, there's one thing worth noting. Despite the plethora of developer-oriented features in Go, it doesn't yet have a fully functional debugger. The core team has focused on other things, and the closest thing to an official Go debugger is the GNU Debugger (GDB) plugin. You can use the venerable old GDB to do some debugging, but it's not as reliable as many developers desire.

> **TIP** If you'd like to get GDB configured for debugging Go, the golang website has a great introduction (http://golang.org/doc/gdb).

The Go community has also stepped in, and one project in particular looks good to us. Delve (https://github.com/derekparker/delve) is a new Go debugger under active development. As of this writing, the Delve installation process is tricky, especially on a Mac. But if you're looking for a full-featured debugger that does an admirable job of tracing goroutines, Delve is a sound bet. Our guess is that Delve will supplant GDB as the choice debugger for the Go community.

Another alternative is the slightly less traditional Godebug tool (https://github.com/mailgun/godebug). Although breakpoints have to be coded into your source, Godebug instruments your code and allows you to get a deeper view into what's going on.

With all of that said, maybe we're a little bit old-school, but we haven't found the debugger situation to be much of a drawback. Go provides great libraries and tools that have gotten us out of even our most sticky situations. With that caveat behind us, let's dive into some good code-quality practices in Go.

5.2 Logging

It has long been the accepted practice that long-running processes write status information to a log file or subsystem. If you take a look at any popular programming language, you'll find libraries that provide common logging features. Go is no exception. In fact, the Go designers decided to include logging in the core libraries.

Typically, logs are intended to capture certain pieces of valuable information that developers, system administrators, and other programs can use to learn about an application's running lifetime. For example, a quick peek at a web server's log file should reveal when the server was last started, whether it has encountered any abnormal conditions, and whether it's handling requests.

5.2.1 Using Go's logger

Go provides two built-in packages for logging: `log` and `log/syslog`. We'll talk about the main package first, and in section 5.2.2 we'll turn to the `syslog` package.

The `log` package provides basic support (mainly in the form of formatting) for writing log messages. In its simplest usage, it formats messages and sends them to Standard Error, as shown in the following listing.

Listing 5.1 Simple log usage

```
package main

import (
    "log"
)

func main() {
    log.Println("This is a regular message.")       ← Writes a message to os.Stderr
    log.Fatalln("This is a fatal error.")           ← Writes a message to os.Stderr and then exits with an error code
    log.Println("This is the end of the function.") ← This never gets executed.
}
```

If you were to run this code, the output would look something like this:

```
$ go run simple.go
2015/04/27 08:18:36 This is a regular message.
2015/04/27 08:18:36 This is a fatal error.
exit status 1
```

We have a few things to point out about this example. The first is that the error messages are all sent to Standard Error, regardless of whether the message is an actual error or an informational message. If you glance at the godocs for the `log` package, you'll notice that it doesn't distinguish between message types. But it does make a second distinction, and that leads us to our other point.

When you call `log.Fatalln` or any of the other "fatal" calls, the library prints the error message and then calls `os.Exit(1)`, forcing the program to quit. Additionally, `log.Panic` calls log an error message and then issue a panic.

The log functions all have `printf`-style variants so that you can insert information into your log message string: `log.Printf("The value of i is %s", i)`.

Practically speaking, we haven't found the basic logging functions to be all that useful. Although some momentum exists in the Docker/container world behind logging to Standard Out and Standard Error, the prevailing wisdom seems to be that log messages should be sent to either a logging service or a designated file. To that end, we've gotten a lot more use out of the `log.Logger` type that's also in the package.

TECHNIQUE 22   **Logging to an arbitrary writer**

Sending messages to Standard Error is useful for simple tools. When you're building servers, applications, or system services, you need a better place to send your log messages. Later in the chapter, you'll look at writing directly to the system log, but here you'll look at using the `log` package to write to any `io.Writer`.

PROBLEM

You want to send logging messages to a file or to a network service without having to write your own logging system.

SOLUTION

Initialize a new `log.Logger` and send log messages to that.

DISCUSSION

The `log.Logger` provides features for sending log data to any `io.Writer`, which includes things like file handles and network connections (`net.Conn`). The next listing shows a brief example that illustrates setting up a log file and sending messages.

Listing 5.2   Logging to a file

```
package main

import (
        "log"
        "os"
)

func main() {                                                          Creates a log file
        logfile, _ := os.Create("./log.txt")          ←─────┘
        defer      logfile.Close()                                ←─────┘  Makes sure it
                                                                                      gets closed
        logger := log.New(logfile, "example ", log.LstdFlags|log.Lshortfile)

        logger.Println("This is a regular message.")
        logger.Fatalln("This is a fatal error.")
        logger.Println("This is the end of the function.")    ←─┘ As before, this will
}                                                                                    never get called.
```

Creates a log file (annotation pointing to `os.Create` line)
Makes sure it gets closed (annotation pointing to `logfile.Close()` line)
Creates a logger (annotation pointing to `logger := log.New` line)
Sends it some messages (annotation pointing to the three logger lines)
As before, this will never get called. (annotation pointing to last Println line)

This example begins by creating a log file and then using it as a destination for log messages.

> **NOTE**   The way we set up this example, the log file will get overwritten every time because we used `os.Create`. This is nice for our example, but you may want to open an existing log file instead of clobbering it.

When creating a new `log.Logger`, you can pass three pieces of information to it. The first is the `io.Writer` where you want to send messages. The second is a prefix for log messages, and the third is a list of flags that determines the format of the log message. To understand the second and third, let's take a look at some sample log data from the log.txt file generated by the preceding program:

```
$ cat log.txt
example 2015/05/12 08:42:51 outfile.go:16: This is a regular message.
example 2015/05/12 08:42:51 outfile.go:17: This is a fatal error.
```

As before, only two of the three `logger.Log` calls succeed because the second one also generates a fatal error. But you can see from the file how the Go logger logs the data. Roughly speaking, you can break a log message into three parts: the prefix, the automatically generated information, and the log message itself, as shown in figure 5.1.

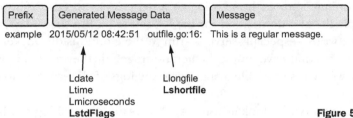

Figure 5.1   Components of a log file

You can control the prefix field with the second argument to `log.New`. As you may have noticed, when we created our logger, the prefix had a trailing whitespace (after `example`). That wasn't an accident. By default, the logger doesn't put any space between the prefix and the generated data.

When it comes to the generated information, you don't have direct control over the information, but you have some degree of indirect control. For example, although you can't format the date and time fields exactly as you'd like, you can set flags that determine how specific the log message is. When creating the `log.Logger`, the third argument is a bitmask of flags. As you saw in this example, we passed in the flags `log.LstdFlags | log.Lshortfile`. This sets the date format and then instructs the logger to show the file and line info. (You might notice that those are also highlighted bold in figure 5.1.)

For the most part, only two pieces of information are automatically generated for you: information about when the event happened and information about where it happened. With the date and time information, you can set the precision of the timestamp:

- `Ldate` controls printing the date.
- `Ltime` prints the timestamp.
- `Lmicrosends` adds microsecond precision to the time. This automatically results in the time being printed, even if `Ltime` isn't set.
- `LstdFlags` turns on both `Ldate` and `Ltime`.

Then a pair of flags deals with the location information:

- `Llongfile` shows a full file path and then the line number: `/foo/bar/baz.go:123`.
- `Lshortifle` shows just the filename and the line number: `baz.go:123`.

Although you can combine flags with a Boolean OR, some combinations are obviously incompatible (namely, Llongfile and Lshortfile).

Logging to files is usually straightforward, but sometimes logging to different sources can introduce complexity. We'll start with one of the more difficult cases—working with network-based loggers—and then return to more straightforward cases in which existing logging tools cover our needs.

TECHNIQUE 23   Logging to a network resource

The previous technique showed how to log to a generic io.Writer. The code we wrote used a simple file as a destination for the log message. But these days, many of the applications we write—especially servers—run in the cloud inside Docker images, VMs, or other resources that have only ephemeral storage. Furthermore, we often run servers in clusters, where it's desirable to aggregate the logs of all servers onto one logging service.

Later in this chapter, you'll look at using syslog as an external logger. But right now you'll look at another option: logging onto a network resource.

Many popular logging services, including Logstash (http://logstash.net/) and Heka (http://hekad.readthedocs.org/en/v0.9.2/), aggregate logs. These services typically expose a port to which you can connect and stream log messages. This style of logging has been popularized in the influential Twelve-Factor App paradigm (http://12factor.net/), whose eleventh factor is "Treat logs as event streams." As simple as all that sounds, some bugaboos arise in sending log messages as streams.

PROBLEM

Streaming logs to a network service is error-prone, but you don't want to lose log messages if you can avoid it.

SOLUTION

By using Go's channels and some buffering, you can vastly improve reliability.

DISCUSSION

Before you can get going on the code, you need something that can simulate a log server. Although existing services such as Logstash and Heka are available, you'll avail yourself of a simple UNIX tool called Netcat (nc). Netcat ships standard on most UNIX and Linux flavors, including OS X. A Windows version is also available.

You want to start a simple TCP server that accepts simple text messages and writes them to the console. This is a simple Netcat command:

```
nc -lk 1902
```

Now you have a listener (-l) listening continuously (-k) on port 1902. (Some versions of Netcat may also need the –p flag.) This little command will do a fine job of simulating a log server.

Now you can get some code running by adapting listing 5.2 to write to a network socket, as shown in the following listing.

Listing 5.3 Network log client

```
package main

import (
    "log"
    "net"
)

func main() {
    conn, err := net.Dial("tcp", "localhost:1902")      ◁─┐  Connects to
    if err != nil {                                         the log server
            panic("Failed to connect to localhost:1902")
    }                                                       Makes sure you clean
    defer conn.Close()                                  ◁─┐ up by closing the
                                                            connection, even on
    f := log.Ldate | log.Lshortfile                         panic
    logger := log.New(conn, "example ", f)              ◁─┐ Sends log messages to
                                                            the network connection
    logger.Println("This is a regular message.")        Logs a message and then
    logger.Panicln("This is a panic.")                  ◁─┐ panics—don't use Fatalln here.
}
```

Surprisingly, little needs to be changed to write to a network connection instead of a file. Go's network library is convenient and simple. You create a new TCP connection with net.Dial, connecting it to the port you opened with Netcat. It's always recommended to close a network connection in a defer block. If nothing else, when a panic occurs (as it will in this demo code), the network buffer will be flushed on close, and you're less likely to lose critical log messages telling you why the code panicked.

Again, you use the log package to log to the remote server. Using the logging package here gives you a few advantages. The first is that you get a timestamp for free, and when logging to a network server, it's always a good idea to log the host time and not rely solely on the log server's timestamp. This helps you reconstruct a record of events even if the log messages are delayed on their way to the log server. Second, as you can see by comparing listings 5.2 and 5.3, when you stick with the logging system, it's trivially easy to swap out the underlying log storage mechanism. This is great for testing and running developer environments.

Did you notice that we also changed log.Fatalln to a log.Panicln in this example? There's a simple reason for this; the log.Fatal* functions have an unfortunate side effect: the deferred function isn't called. Why not? Because log.Fatal* calls os.Exit, which immediately terminates the program without unwinding the function stack. We covered this topic in the preceding chapter. Because the deferred function is skipped, your network connection is never properly flushed and closed. Panics, on the other hand, are easier to capture. In reality, production code for anything but simple command-line clients should avoid using fatal errors. And as you saw in the previous chapter, there are specific cases in which you should call a panic.

With all of this in mind, when you execute the preceding code, your nc instance should receive some log messages:

```
$ nc -lk 1902
example 2015/05/27 log_client.go:23: This is a regular message.
example 2015/05/27 log_client.go:24: This is a panic.
```

These messages made their way from the example client to the simple server you're running on nc. You have a nice, simple network logging utility. But you may also have a problem here in the form of a culprit commonly known as *back pressure*.

TECHNIQUE 24 Handling back pressure in network logging

In the previous technique, you saw how to log messages to a network server. Logging to a network offers compelling advantages:

- Logs from many services can be aggregated to one central location.
- In the cloud, servers with only ephemeral storage can still have logs preserved.
- Security and auditability are improved.
- You can tune log servers and app servers differently.

But there's one major drawback to sending your log messages to a remote logging server: you're dependent on the network. In this technique, you'll see how to deal with network-based issues in logging.

PROBLEM

Network log services are prone to connection failures and back pressure. This leads to lost log messages and sometimes even service failures.

SOLUTION

Build a more resilient logger that buffers data.

DISCUSSION

You're likely to run into two major networking issues:

- The logger's network connection drops (either because the network is down or because the remote logger is down).
- The connection over which the logs are sent slows down.

The first problem is familiar to us all and is clearly a problem to be addressed. The second is a little less obvious.

Listing 5.3 detailed a rough sequence of events. Let's trace it out at a high level, as shown in figure 5.2. (The network mechanics are a little more complicated, but you don't need to know them to understand the situation.)

Your application first opens a TCP connection, then sends messages, then closes the connection. But something you don't see in your code is the response from the logger. This is because things are going on at the TCP layer that don't bubble up into the application code.

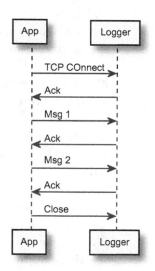

Figure 5.2 Sending messages over TCP

Specifically, when a message is sent as a TCP/IP packet, the receiver is obligated to respond to the packet by acknowledging (ACK) that the message was received. It's possible (and even likely) that one log message may become more than one packet sent across the network. Say a log message is split into two separate packets. The remote logger would then receive the first part and send an ACK. Then the client would send the second half, to which the logger would also send an ACK. With this system, the client gains some assurance that the data it sent was indeed received by the remote host.

That's all well and good until the remote host slows down. Imagine a log server that's receiving thousands of messages from many clients at once. With all of that data coming in, it may slow down. But while it slows, the quantity of logs coming in doesn't diminish. And with TCP, the log server must send an ACK for each new message that comes in. When it delays sending the ACK, the client sits waiting. The client must slow down too, as its resources are tied up waiting for log messages to send. This is the scenario known as back pressure.

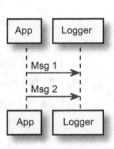

One solution to the back-pressure problem is to switch from TCP to UDP. By doing this, you get rid of connection overhead at the protocol level. And most significantly, the application doesn't need to wait for ACK messages from the log server. Figure 5.3 illustrates this method.

UDP requires no network connection maintenance. The client sends information to the server whenever it's ready. And altering the Go code from listing 5.3 is simple, as you can see in the next listing.

Figure 5.3　UDP log messages

Listing 5.4　UDP-based logging

```go
package main

import (
    "log"
    "net"
    "time"
)

func main() {
    timeout := 30 * time.Second            // Adds an explicit timeout
    conn, err := net.DialTimeout("udp", "localhost:1902", timeout)  // Dials a UDP connection instead of a TCP one
    if err != nil {
        panic("Failed to connect to localhost:1902")
    }
    defer    conn.Close()

    f := log.Ldate | log.Lshortfile
    logger := log.New(conn, "example ", f)

    logger.Println("This is a regular message.")
    logger.Panicln("This is a panic.")
}
```

The changes to the code are minimal. Instead of using the regular net.Dial, this code has net.DialTimeout, which adds a nicety to the regular net.Dial call: it specifies how long it'll wait for the connection before giving up. You set this to 30 seconds. With TCP, the timeout includes time to send the message and receive the ACK. But with UDP, you set the timeout largely for just how long it takes your app to resolve the address and send the message. Setting a timeout gives you a little bit of a safety net when the network isn't functioning as expected.

To run the preceding code, you also need to restart your nc server as a UDP server: nc -luk 1902.

Using UDP for logging has distinct advantages:

- The app is resistant to back pressure and log server outages. If the log server hiccups, it may lose some UDP packets, but the client won't be impacted.
- Sending logs is faster even without back pressure.
- The code is simple.

But this route also has some major disadvantages. Depending on your needs, these drawbacks may indicate that this is the wrong route for you:

- Log messages can get lost easily. UDP doesn't equip you to know whether a message was received correctly.
- Log messages can be received out of order. Large log messages may be packetized and then get jumbled in transition. Adding a timestamp to the message (as you've done) can help with this, but not totally resolve it.
- Sending the remote server lots of UDP messages may turn out to be more likely to overwhelm the remote server, because it can't manage its connections and slow down the data intake. Although your app may be immune to back pressure, your log server may be worse off.

Based on our own experiences, UDP-based logging definitely has a time and a place. It's quick and efficient. If you can predict with relative accuracy how much work your log server needs to do, this method provides a useful and simple path to network logging.

But a few cases might definitively tilt your decision away from UDP logging. You may not want to use UDP logging when you can't accurately predict how much logging data will go from the app server to the log server, or when losing occasional log messages is unacceptable.

TCP logging is prone to back pressure, but UDP logging won't guarantee data accuracy. It's a conundrum that we're used to dealing with from image encoding: do you want precise images at the expense of large file sizes (GIF, PNG), or compact images that lose some data (JPEG)? With logging, you may need to make a similar choice. This isn't to say that nothing can be done to make things better. For example, back-pressure stress can be delayed by creating a large buffer for logs to be temporarily stored in case of network saturation.

5.2.2   *Working with system loggers*

In the previous sections, we took it upon ourselves to write a logging system. In many cases, though, existing system loggers may be adequate for the task at hand. In this section, you'll look at system loggers.

> **NOTE**   Powerful third-party logging packages are available for Go. Logrus (https://github.com/Sirupsen/logrus) and Glog (https://github.com/golang/glog) are two popular examples.

The ideas behind logging have solidified over the decades, and one idea that's now firmly entrenched in our code is the concept of assigning a log level to a message. The level indicates the importance of the information in the log message and at the same time often indicates the kind of message being logged. Typical log levels include Trace, Debug, Info, Warn, Error, and Critical, though you'll sometimes see others including Notice, Alert, and Emergency.

Although applications may deviate from the norm, the following list represents common types of log messages that applications write, together with the typical name or names of the log level:

- *Informational message*—These tend to include information on the application's current status, when it started, and when it stopped. Metrics are usually logged as informational messages too. The Info log level is designated for this kind of message.
- *Problems*—When an application encounters an error, the error message (and supporting information) is sent to a log. Typically, log levels are Warn, Error, and Critical, depending on severity.
- *Debugging information*—As developers write code, it's often convenient to send debugging information into the log. This information is targeted specifically to the programmers (not usually the operators or sys admins). It's assigned to the Debug log level.
- *Stack dumps or deep info*—Sometimes you need to get at extremely detailed information about a program. For a particularly complex portion of code, you may want to dump a stack trace or information about the goroutine. The Trace level is used for this.

Many systems, including all modern UNIX-like systems, support these log levels in the system logger. Go itself also provides a system logging library. We'll look at that now.

TECHNIQUE 25   **Logging to the syslog**

Logging is a well understood problem, and over the decades, standard facilities have emerged for system-wide logging. Unsurprisingly, Go includes out-of-the-box support for such facilities.

Syslogs provide some major advantages to creating your own. First, they're mature and stable products that are optimized for dealing with latency, redundant messages, and archiving. Most contemporary system loggers handle periodic log rotation, compression, and deduplication. These things make your life easier. Additionally, system administrators are adept at using these log files for analysis, and many tools and utilities are available for working with the log files. These are compelling reasons to log to the standard facility rather than creating your own.

PROBLEM

You want to send application log messages into the system logger.

SOLUTION

Configure Go's `syslog` package and use it.

DISCUSSION

Go's logging package includes support for syslogs. In fact, a dedicated package is available for this: `log/syslog`. The `syslog` package gives you two ways of working with the system log. First, you can use it as a logging back end to the logger you've looked at already. This is a great way of taking code that you already have and redirecting it into the syslog.

Second, you can use all of the defined log levels and facilities directly in a syslog-specific style. This second route isn't as portable, but it's closer to what `syslog` expects.

Although we'll focus on this second method of doing things, the following listing is a quick example of generating a Go logger that's backed to `syslog`.

Listing 5.5   A logger directed to syslog

```go
package main

import (
    "fmt"
    "log"
    "log/syslog"                                    Tells the logger how to
)                                                   appear to syslog

func main() {
    priority := syslog.LOG_LOCAL3 | syslog.LOG_NOTICE    Sets the flags,
    flags := log.Ldate | log.Lshortfile                  as you've
    logger, err := syslog.NewLogger(priority, flags)     done before
    if err != nil {
        fmt.Printf("Can't attach to syslog: %s", err)
        return
    }
    logger.Println("This is a test log message.")        Sends a
}                                                        simple message
```

Creates a new syslog logger → `logger, err := syslog.NewLogger(priority, flags)`

When you run this code, your syslog should have a message that looks something like this:

```
Jun 30 08:34:03 technosophos syslog_logger[76564]: 2015/06/30
    syslog_logger.go:18: This is a test log message.
```

This message formatting is less than ideal, but it captures what you need to know. Let's walk through the highlights of the code.

When you map a Go logger's front end to a syslog back end, you need to make some simplifications. Syslog's rich notion of facilities and priorities isn't adequately represented in Go's logger, so you have to specifically tell the Go logger how to set facility and severity. And unfortunately, you get to do this only once, at creation time. In this example, you tell Go where to log the messages (the LOG_LOCAL3 facility), and how important the log message is. Because you can set this only once, you set it to LOG_NOTICE, which is important enough to get it logged by default, but not important enough to trigger any alarms.

UNIX-like sysloggers (including those in Linux and OS X) rely on configuration files to indicate where the logs will be written. On a Mac, for example, the preceding messages are written to /var/log/system.log, whereas some flavors of Linux write it to /var/log/messages.

When you first create the Go logger, not only do you have to set the priority (the combination of facility and severity), but you also pass it the formatting flags that other instances of the Go logger use. For simplicity, you've used the same flags used in previous examples.

Now, any messages you send to the logger—regardless of their severity—will be written to the log file as notices.

Using Go's logger is convenient, but setting the severity correctly and using more of syslog's capabilities would be more useful. You can do that by using the log/syslog logging functions directly, as shown in the next listing.

Listing 5.6 Logging to the system log

```
package main

import (
    "log/syslog"
)

func main() {
    logger, err := syslog.New(syslog.LOG_LOCAL3, "narwhal")    ⟵  Creates a new syslog client
    if err != nil {
            panic("Cannot attach to syslog")
    }
    defer logger.Close()

    logger.Debug("Debug message.")
    logger.Notice("Notice message.")        Sends the logger a
    logger.Warning("Warning message.")      variety of messages
    logger.Alert("Alert message.")
}
```

This code sets up a system logger and then sends it messages with a variety of severity levels. Setting up the logger is straightforward. Logging locally requires you to provide two pieces of information: the facility that you want to log to (LOG_LOCAL3) and the prefix you want every message to begin with (narwhal). Normally, the prefix is the name of the service or application that's running.

> **Logging to a remote syslog**
>
> Go also provides a `syslog.Dial` function that allows you to connect to a remote syslog daemon. Network-attached syslog daemons are useful for aggregating logs across a variety of servers. Many times, the local syslog is proxied to such a remote server. But the `syslog.Dial` function is there for the occasions when you need to connect directly to a remote logging server.

The Go syslog library comes with various logging functions, most of them mapping to severity. Each call to a logging function sends the message to the system logger, which can then decide (based on its own rules) what to do with the message.

If you run the preceding example and then look at the syslog file, you should see something like this:

```
Jun 30 08:52:06 technosophos narwhal[76635]: Notice message.
Jun 30 08:52:06 technosophos narwhal[76635]: Warning message.
Jun 30 08:52:06 technosophos narwhal[76635]: Alert message.
```

The first few fields are the timestamp and hostname. Those are generated by the syslog. Next comes the label, which you set as `narwhal`. After that, the system adds the process ID (PID). Finally, it sends your message. The order and format of the syslog-generated fields vary depending on the configuration of the logger.

You logged four messages, but only three are displayed. The call to `syslog.Debug` isn't present. The reason is that the system log used to run the example is configured to not send debug messages to the log file. If you wanted to see debug messages, you'd need to alter the configuration of your system's syslog facility. The nice thing about this setup is that you, as the developer, don't have to make decisions about what's displayed and under what circumstances. You can leave that choice up to those who use the application.

This section has covered many of the common log message types, but there remains one common tool we programmers often value for debugging. Sometimes it's handy to log a stack trace.

5.3   *Accessing stack traces*

Many languages provide access to the call stack. A *stack trace* (or *stack dump*) provides a human-readable list of the functions being used at the time the stack is captured. For example, imagine a program in which `main` calls `foo`, which then calls `bar`. The `bar` function then dumps a stack trace. The trace would be three calls deep, showing how `bar` is the current function, called by `foo`, which is in turn called by `main`.

TECHNIQUE 26   **Capturing stack traces**

Stack traces can give developers critical insight into what's happening on the system. They're useful for logging and debugging. Go makes it possible to access the stack trace at any given point in program execution.

PROBLEM

You want to fetch a stack trace at a critical point in the application.

SOLUTION

Use the `runtime` package, which has several tools.

DESCRIPTION

Generating stack dumps in Go isn't a particularly difficult exercise when you know how to do it. But how to get one seems to be a commonly asked question. If all you need is a trace for debugging, you can easily send one to Standard Output by using the `runtime/debug` function `PrintStack`, as the next listing shows.

Listing 5.7 Print stack to Standard Output

```go
package main

import (
    "runtime/debug"
)

func main() {
    foo()
}

func foo() {
    bar()
}

func bar() {
    debug.PrintStack()
}
```

Defines a few functions so you have something to trace

Prints the trace

Running the code prints a stack trace like this:

```
$ go run trace.go
/Users/mbutcher/Code/go-in-practice/chapter5/stack/trace.go:20 (0x205b)
    bar: debug.PrintStack()
/Users/mbutcher/Code/go-in-practice/chapter5/stack/trace.go:13 (0x203b)
    foo: bar()
/Users/mbutcher/Code/go-in-practice/chapter5/stack/trace.go:9 (0x201b)
    main: foo()
/usr/local/Cellar/go/1.4.2/libexec/src/runtime/proc.go:63 (0x12983)
    main: main_main()
/usr/local/Cellar/go/1.4.2/libexec/src/runtime/asm_amd64.s:2232 (0x37711)
    goexit:
```

This can be helpful for simple debugging cases. But if you want to capture the trace to send it somewhere else, you need to do something slightly more sophisticated. You can use the `runtime` package's `Stack` function, shown in the next listing.

Listing 5.8 Using the `Stack` function

```go
package main

import (
```

```
        "fmt"
        "runtime"
)

func main() {
        foo()
}

func foo() {
        bar()
}

func bar() {
        buf := make([]byte, 1024)           ◁———— Makes a buffer
        runtime.Stack(buf, false)           ◁———— Writes the stack into the buffer
        fmt.Printf("Trace:\n %s\n", buf)          ◁———— Prints the results
}
```

In this example, you send the stack to Standard Output, but you could just as easily log or store it. Running this code produces output like this:

```
$ go run trace.go
Trace:
 goroutine 1 [running]:
main.bar()
        /Users/mbutcher/Code/go-in-practice/chapter5/stack/trace.go:18 +0x7a
main.foo()
        /Users/mbutcher/Code/go-in-practice/chapter5/stack/trace.go:13 +0x1b
main.main()
```

You may notice that this version is shorter than the other. The lower-level system calls are left out of `Stack`'s data. We have a few quick things to point out about this code.

First, with `Stack`, you must supply a presized buffer. But there's no convenient way to determine how big the buffer needs to be to capture all of the output. (And in some cases, the output is so big that you might not want to capture it all.) You need to decide ahead of time how much space you'd like to allocate.

Second, `Stack` takes two arguments. The second is a Boolean flag, which is set to `false` in this example. Setting it to `true` will cause `Stack` to also print out stacks for all running goroutines. This can be tremendously useful when debugging concurrency problems, but it substantially increases the amount of output. The trace of the preceding code, for example, runs an entire printed page.

If all of this isn't sufficient, you can use the `runtime` package's `Caller` and `Callers` functions to get programmatic access to the details of the call stack. Although it's quite a bit of work to retrieve and format the data, these functions give you the flexibility to discover the details of a particular call stack. Both the `runtime` and the `runtime/debug` packages contain numerous other functions for analyzing memory usage, goroutines, threading, and other aspects of your program's resource usage.

In the last part of this chapter, we switch from debugging to testing.

5.4 Testing

Testing and debugging are exercises that require learning the details about a program. But whereas debugging is reactive, testing is proactive. This section covers a few strategies for making the most of Go's testing tools.

5.4.1 Unit testing

Writing tests alongside your code has become a standard software development practice. Some software development strategies (such as test-driven development) even hinge on the authoring of test cases.

Most introductions to the Go language explain how to write tests by

> **Testing code goes with source code**
>
> We see two common mistakes when programmers are learning to test Go code. The first is to try to put the test files in their own directory. Popular testing tools in other languages do this, but Go doesn't. Test files belong in the same directory as the code they test.
>
> The second mistake is to try to put the tests in a different package (`package hello_test` or something similar). Tests should go in the same package as the code they test. This makes it possible to test unexported code as well as just the public API.

using the built-in tools. Go was designed with testing in mind, and includes tooling for running tests inside projects. Any Go source file that ends with _test.go is treated as a test file. The tool `go test` is used to run these tests.

Within _test.go files, you can write functions that begin with `Test` and that take a single parameter of type `*testing.T`. Each function will be executed as a unit test. Say you have a source file called hello.go. This file contains a single function, `Hello`, that returns the string `hello`, as shown in the following listing.

Listing 5.9   A Simple hello

```
package hello

func Hello() string {
    return "hello"
}
```

To write a test for this simple function, create a file called hello_test.go and add tests there, as shown in the next listing.

Listing 5.10   A hello test

```
package hello          ← The test is always in the same
                         package as the code it's testing.
import "testing"       ← The testing package contains
                         Go's built-in testing tools.
func TestHello(t *testing.T) {          ← TestHello follows the
    if v := Hello(); v != "hello" {       pattern of a test function.
        t.Errorf("Expected 'hello', but got '%s'", v)   ←
    }
}                      Reports errors through the *testing.T object
```

This example points out the earmarks of a typical Go test. Go doesn't include a lot of assertion tools like other testing frameworks (though libraries are available for this). But the `testing.T` object supplies functions for reporting unexpected conditions. The most frequently used functions on `testing.T` are as follows:

- `T.Error(args …interface{})` or `T.Errorf(msg string, args interface{})` — These log a message and then mark the test as failed. The second version allows formatting strings, as shown in listing 5.10.
- `T.Fatal(args …interface{})` or `T.Fatalf(msg string, args interface{})` — These log a message, mark the test as failed, and then stop the testing. You should do this whenever one failed test indicates that no others will pass.

Various other functions are available as well, designed to make it possible to skip tests, to fail immediately, and so on. With this in mind, let's look at a few techniques for testing.

TECHNIQUE 27   Using interfaces for mocking or stubbing

Go's type system focuses on composition rather than inheritance. Instead of building large trees of object types, the Go developer creates interfaces that describe desired behavior. Anything that fulfills the interface type can be considered to be of that type. For example, one of the most commonly used interfaces is called `io.Writer`. It looks like the following listing.

Listing 5.11   The stringer interface

```
type Writer interface {
        Write(p []byte) (n int, err error)
}
```

The `io.Writer` interface applies to anything that can write a sequence of bytes according to the preceding signature. The `os.File` type and the `net.Conn` type both implement `io.Writer`, as do many other types. One of the best parts of Go's type system is that the implementing type doesn't need to explicitly declare which interfaces it satisfies (though documenting these isn't a bad idea). You may even choose to declare an interface that matches some properties of an existing type, and thereby create a useful abstraction. Nowhere is this more useful than when testing.

PROBLEM

You're writing code that depends on types defined in external libraries, and you want to write test code that can verify that those libraries are correctly used.

SOLUTION

Create interfaces to describe the types you need to test. Use those interfaces in your code, and then write stub or mock implementations for your tests.

DISCUSSION

Say you're writing software that uses a third-party library that looks like the following listing.

Listing 5.12   The message struct

```go
type Message struct {
    // ...
}

func (m *Message) Send(email, subject string, body []byte) error {
    // ...
    return nil
}
```

This describes some kind of message-sending system. In your code, you use that library to send a message from your application. In the course of writing your tests, you want to ensure that the code that sends the message is being called, but you don't want to send the message. One way to gracefully deal with this is to write your own interface that describes the methods shown in listing 5.12, and have your code use that interface in its declarations instead of directly using the `Message` type, as the following listing shows.

Listing 5.13   Use an interface

```go
type Messager interface {                                      ◁── Defines an interface that
    Send(email, subject string, body []byte) error                describes the methods
}                                                                 you use on Message

func Alert(m Messager, problem []byte) error {                 ◁──
    return m.Send("noc@example.com", "Critical Error", problem)
}
```
                                            **Passes that interface instead
                                                of the Message type**

Because you've created an abstraction from `Message` to `Messager`, you can easily write a mock and use that for your testing, as shown in the next listing.

Listing 5.14   Testing with a mock

```go
package msg

import (
    "testing"
)
                                                        The MockMessage
                                                     implements Messager.
type MockMessage struct {                          ◁──
    email, subject string
    body           []byte
}

func (m *MockMessage) Send(email, subject string, body []byte) error  ◁──
    m.email = email
```

```
        m.subject = subject
        m.body = body
        return nil
}

func TestAlert(t *testing.T) {
        msgr := new(MockMessage)                          Creates a new
        body := []byte("Critical Error")                  MockMessage

        Alert(msgr, body)                                 Runs the Alert method
                                                          with your mock
        if msgr.subject != "Critical Error" {
                t.Errorf("Expected 'Critical Error', Got '%s'", msgr.subject)
        }
        // ...                                            Accesses the MockMessage
}                                                         properties to verify results
```

You implement the `Messager` interface with the `MockMessage` type. That type provides the same functions that your production code uses, but instead of sending the message, it stores the data. You can then conveniently test that the information sent to the `Messager` is indeed what you expect.

This is a simple and powerful technique for writing good tests. As an additional bonus, abstracting with interfaces in this way makes it easier to later change implementations. The pattern lends itself to modular programming.

TECHNIQUE 28   Verifying interfaces with canary tests

The preceding example illustrated a technique that relies on using interfaces to describe an existing set of functions. Sometimes, though, subtle errors in interface definitions may cause runtime headaches. This is especially true when you're either relying on type assertions or using external libraries whose function signatures change often. One trivially simple testing technique can save you some needless headaches.

> **Interfaces change infrequently**
>
> Ideally, after an interface is exported and made public, it shouldn't be changed. But in the world of software development, this expectation isn't always met. Library authors do occasionally change interfaces to fix poor design or to add new features. These days, it's considered okay to change interfaces as long as you indicate this by increasing the major version number of your program (for example, 1.2.3 becomes 2.0.0). Be aware, though, that many projects—including some major ones—don't follow this recommendation.

PROBLEM

You want to make sure that the interfaces you're defining describe the things that you're intending to describe. This is useful in four cases:

- When you're exporting types that implement external interfaces.
- When you create interface types that describe external types.

- When you rely on external interfaces, and those interfaces change (even though by convention, they shouldn't).
- When use of that interface is restricted to type assertions. (We give an example of this next.)

SOLUTION

Write type-assertion "canary" tests that will fail quickly if you made a mistake on your interface definition.

DISCUSSION

When you're writing interfaces or implementations of interfaces—especially in cases where type information is resolved at runtime—it's helpful to write simple type-assertion canary tests that will explode at compile time.

Say you're writing a customer writer that implements io.Writer. You're exporting this in your library so that other code may use it. Your implementation looks like the following listing.

Listing 5.15   MyWriter

```
type MyWriter struct{
    // …
}

func (m *MyWriter) Write([]byte) error {
    // Write data somewhere…
    return nil
}
```

This code looks pretty straightforward, and at a quick glance, it looks like it implements io.Writer. Now imagine using this code with a type assertion, as shown in the next listing.

Listing 5.16   Asserting a writer

```
func main() {
    m := map[string]interface{}{
        "w": &MyWriter{},
    }
}

func doSomething(m map[string]interface{}) {
    w := m["w"].(io.Writer)
}
```

This generates a
runtime exception.

This code compiles just fine. And if your test coverage is thorough, it might even pass that, too. But something is wrong.

You can write a quick canary test to see this. A canary test (deriving its name from the "canary in the coal mine" story) is a test designed to alert you of basic failures in your assumptions. The next listing shows a canary test for whether MyWriter is an io.Writer.

Listing 5.17   Canary test of `MyWriter`

```
func TestWriter(t *testing.T) {
    var _ io.Writer = &MyWriter{}
}
```

Have the compiler do a
type assertion for you.

This is a simple test. You don't even have to run the test to cause it to fail. The compiler will fail before the binary can ever be built:

```
$ go test
# _/Users/mbutcher/Code/go-in-practice/chapter5/tests/canary
./canary_test.go:15: cannot use MyWriter literal (type *MyWriter)
    as type io.Writer in assignment:
    *MyWriter does not implement io.Writer (wrong type for Write method)
            have Write([]byte) error
            want Write([]byte) (int, error)
FAIL _/Users/mbutcher/Code/go-in-practice/chapter5/tests/canary
[build failed]
```

The test fails because your `Write` method doesn't match the signature of `io.Writer`'s `Write([]byte) (int, error)`. The compilation error tells you exactly how to fix your writer to match the interface you intended to match. Some interfaces are more complex than `io.Writer`, and it's with these that you tend to benefit most when writing canary tests.

The last technique showed how to create interfaces to describe existing types. That strategy is great for generalizing testing. But creating an interface to match an existing type is another example of a case where a canary test might be useful. By canary testing your interfaces, you'll catch cases where the external library author changes a function signature.

5.4.2   *Generative testing*

Generative testing is a large and complex topic. But in its most basic form, generative testing refers to the strategy of automatically generating test data in order to both broaden the information tested and overcome our biases when we choose our test data.

PROBLEM

You want to bulletproof your code against surprising edge cases.

SOLUTION

Use Go's `testing/quick` package to generate testing data.

DISCUSSION

Go has a testing package that's frequently overlooked. The `testing/quick` package provides several helpers for rapidly building tests that are more exhaustive than usual. These tools aren't useful in all cases, but sometimes they can help you make your testing process more reliable.

Say you have a simple function that pads a given string to a given length (or truncates the string if it's greater than that length). The function looks like the next listing.

Listing 5.18 A padding function

```
func Pad(s string, max uint) string {
    log.Printf("Testing Len: %d, Str: %s\n", max, s)    ⟵— Logs the output just
    ln := uint(len(s))                                         for your convenience
    if ln > max {                                              here
            return s[:max-1]                          ⟵ If the string is longer than
    }                                                     the max, truncates it.
    s += strings.Repeat(" ", int(max-ln))      ⟵———— Pads the string until
    return s                                                 it's the max length
}
```

Normally, you'd be inclined to write some simple tests for this function, perhaps like the following listing.

Listing 5.19 Simple pad unit test

```
func TestPad(t *testing.T) {
    if r := Pad("test", 6); len(r) != 6 {
            t.Errorf("Expected 6, got %d", len(r))
    }
}
```

Unsurprisingly, this test passes. But this is a great function to test with a generator. You know that regardless of the string that's passed in, you always want a string of exactly the given length. Using the testing/quick function called Check(), you can test a much broader range of strings (including those that use characters you might not have thought to test), as shown in the next listing.

Listing 5.20 Generative test for pad

```
func TestPadGenerative(t *testing.T) {
    fn := func(s string, max uint8) bool {
            p := Pad(s, uint(max))                ⟵ fn takes a string and a uint8,
            return len(p) == int(max)                runs Pad(), and checks that
    }                                                the returned length is right.

    if err := quick.Check(fn, &quick.Config{MaxCount: 200}); err != nil {  ⟵┐
            t.Error(err)                          ⟵——┐                        │
    }                                                 │           Using testing/quick, you tell it
}                          You report any errors through          to run no more than 200
                           the normal testing package.            randomly generated tests of fn.
```

The "testing/quick".Check function is the heart of your test. It takes a function that you've defined and an optional configuration, and then constructs numerous tests. It does this by introspecting the function's parameters and then generating random test data of the right parameter type. If you wanted to test longer strings, for example, you could change your fn function to take a uint16 instead of a uint8.

If you run this test, you'll discover a bug in the original code:

```
$ go test
2015/07/21 09:20:15 Testing Len: 6, Str: test
2015/07/21 09:06:09 Testing Len: 32, Str: XXXXXXXXXXXXXXXXXXXXXXXXXXXXXXXX
--- FAIL: TestPadGenerative (0.00s)
    generative_test.go:39: #1: failed on input
    "\U000305ea\U000664e9\U000cbd92\U00091bbf\U0010b40d\U000fd581...", 0x20
FAIL
exit status 1
FAIL    _/Users/mbutcher/Code/go-in-practice/chapter5/tests/generative
0.005s
```

What happened? One of the strings that was generated was longer than its maximum length, which kicked off the truncation code (listing 5.17) that your previous test didn't account for. You accidentally sliced incorrectly—s[:max-1] should be s[:max] because you're giving it a length, not an index. After you've fixed that, rerunning the test should show many tests using randomly generated values.

> ### Go's random generator
>
> If the values are randomly generated, why do you get the same strings when you run the test repeatedly? Go doesn't automatically seed the "math/rand".Rand generator each time it runs. If you want different data each run, you can pass a seeded random generator by using "testing/quick".Config. This is a good way to increase test data coverage, but it comes at the cost of repeatability. If you do hit a failure, you'll need to make note of the data that caused the error because it may not come up again for a long time.

Go's quick testing package comes with other utilities. Most of these are designed to help you quickly generate test data, as in the preceding example. Go's generator is good enough that it can extend beyond simple types like integers and strings, and even generate random struct instances.

5.5   *Using performance tests and benchmarks*

Which is faster: the path-matching package or a custom-written regular expression to patch paths? How is that fan-out pattern working in practice? Why is my HTTP server so slow? One of the frequent tasks of the seasoned programmer is to identify and fix performance issues with code. Once again, Go provides some useful tools.

Nestled inside Go's testing package are some performance-testing features designed to repeatedly run pieces of code and then report on their efficiency.

| TECHNIQUE 29 | **Benchmarking Go code** |

In this technique, you'll learn how to use the `testing.B` benchmarking tool to test the efficiency of a piece of code.

PROBLEM

You have code paths for accomplishing something, and you want to know which way is faster. Is it faster to use `text/template` for formatting text, or just stick with `fmt`?

SOLUTION

Use the benchmarking feature, `testing.B`, to compare the two.

DISCUSSION

Benchmarks are treated similarly to tests. They go in the same _test files that unit tests and examples go in, and they're executed with the go test command. But their construction differs.

In the next listing, let's write a benchmark designed to zero in on the average time it takes to compile and run a simple text template.

| Listing 5.21 | **Benchmark template compile and run** |

```
package main

import (
    "bytes"
    "testing"
    "text/template"
)

func BenchmarkTemplates(b *testing.B) {         ◁──── BenchmarkTemplates
                                                       gets a *testing.B.
    b.Logf("b.N is %d\n", b.N)                  ◁
    tpl := "Hello {{.Name}}"                        Prints the value of b.N
    data := &map[string]string{
        "Name": "World",
    }                                               Runs the core of your
    var buf bytes.Buffer                            test b.N times
    for i := 0; i < b.N; i++ {                  ◁
Parses the template  ──▷   t, _ := template.New("test").Parse(tpl)
            t.Execute(&buf, data)               ◁─────── Executes the template
            buf.Reset()                         ◁
    }                                               Clears the buffer to avoid
}                                                   memory-allocation issues
```

Just as tests are prefixed with Test, benchmarks should be prefixed with Benchmark. And instead of receiving a *testing.T, a benchmark receives a *testing.B. Although the *testing.B instance has many of the same methods as a *testing.T, it also has several properties specific to benchmarking. The most important is the N struct member. This is used in the preceding code as the upper limit on a loop. This is the key to benchmarking. Every benchmark should iterate to the *b.N point. The benchmarking tool repeatedly runs the same test and attempts to gain meaningful insight into the performance of the code by varying the number of times the test is run.

If you run this code, you'll see this:

```
$ go test -bench .
testing: warning: no tests to run
PASS
BenchmarkTemplates        100000              10102 ns/op
--- BENCH: BenchmarkTemplates
    bench_test.go:10: b.N is 1
    bench_test.go:10: b.N is 100
    bench_test.go:10: b.N is 10000
    bench_test.go:10: b.N is 100000
ok      /Users/mbutcher/Code/go-in-practice/chapter5/tests/bench     1.145s
```

To run benchmarks, use the go test tool, but pass it –bench PATTERN, where PATTERN is a regular expression that matches the benchmarking functions you want to run. The dot (.) tells the benchmarker to run all of the benchmarks.

The preceding output tells you that the test was run with a maximum number of 100,000 iterations and that each run through the loop averaged 10,102 nanoseconds. Because you included Printf, you get a little extra visibility into how the benchmarking works. It begins with a low value for b.N: 1. Then it raises the value of b.N (not always exponentially) until the algorithms in the benchmarking suite settle in on an average.

Listing 5.20 runs only one benchmark, and on some code that you might be able to easily optimize. Let's expand and add an extra test in the following listing.

Listing 5.22 Two template benchmarks

```
func BenchmarkTemplates(b *testing.B) {
    b.Logf("b.N is %d\n", b.N)
    tpl := "Hello {{.Name}}"
    data := &map[string]string{
        "Name": "World",
    }
    var buf bytes.Buffer
    for i := 0; i < b.N; i++ {
        t, _ := template.New("test").Parse(tpl)
        t.Execute(&buf, data)
        buf.Reset()
    }
}
func BenchmarkCompiledTemplates(b *testing.B) {
    b.Logf("b.N is %d\n", b.N)
    tpl := "Hello {{.Name}}"
    t, _ := template.New("test").Parse(tpl)          ← Moves the template compilation out of the loop
    data := &map[string]string{
        "Name": "World",
    }
    var buf bytes.Buffer
    for i := 0; i < b.N; i++ {
        t.Execute(&buf, data)
        buf.Reset()
    }
}
```

The second benchmark, BenchmarkCompiledTemplates, compiles the template once and then executes it multiple times. You can guess that this optimization reduces runtime, but how much?

```
$ go test -bench .
testing: warning: no tests to run
PASS
BenchmarkTemplates          200000              10167 ns/op
--- BENCH: BenchmarkTemplates
    bench_test.go:10: b.N is 1
    bench_test.go:10: b.N is 100
    bench_test.go:10: b.N is 10000
    bench_test.go:10: b.N is 200000
BenchmarkCompiledTemplates          1000000              1318 ns/op
--- BENCH: BenchmarkCompiledTemplates
    bench_test.go:23: b.N is 1
    bench_test.go:23: b.N is 100
    bench_test.go:23: b.N is 10000
    bench_test.go:23: b.N is 1000000
ok        _/Users/mbutcher/Code/go-in-practice/chapter5/tests/bench        3.483s
```

These results show that reusing the compiled template shaves almost 9,000 nanoseconds off the average loop iteration. It runs in one-tenth the original time! The benchmarking package provides other features that can assist in creating good benchmarks. Here you'll look at another benchmarking technique for testing concurrency.

TECHNIQUE 30 Parallel benchmarks

One of Go's strongest points is its goroutine model of concurrent programming. But for any given piece of code, how can you tell how well it will perform when spread out over multiple goroutines? Again, the benchmarking tool can help you here.

PROBLEM

You want to test how a given piece of code performs when spread over goroutines. Ideally, you want to test this with a variable number of CPUs.

SOLUTION

A *testing.B instance provides a RunParallel method for exactly this purpose. Combined with command-line flags, you can test how well goroutines parallelize.

DISCUSSION

Beginning with listing 5.21, you can fashion the template test into a parallel test. Instead of executing the body of a loop, the testing framework executes a function repeatedly, but as separate goroutines, as shown in the following listing.

Listing 5.23 Parallel benchmarking

```go
func BenchmarkParallelTemplates(b *testing.B) {
    tpl := "Hello {{.Name}}"
    t, _ := template.New("test").Parse(tpl)
    data := &map[string]string{
        "Name": "World",
```

```
        }
    b.RunParallel(func(pb *testing.PB) {                    Instead of a for loop, passes
        var buf bytes.Buffer                    ◄──┘       a closure into RunParallel
        for pb.Next() {
                t.Execute(&buf, data)
                buf.Reset()
        }
    })
}
```

Most of our testing code remains unchanged. But instead of looping over a call to
t.Execute(), you segment the code a little further. Running RunParallel runs the
closure on multiple goroutines. Each one receives an indication, through pb.Next(),
as to whether it should continue iterating. (Again, the looping feature is required.)
This code example is almost the same as the one included with the Go documentation.

Now you need to run it. First, you'll run it alongside our other two examples
(though with the Logf() functions removed). And you'll run it on only one CPU,
which is the default:

```
$ go test -bench .
testing: warning: no tests to run
PASS
BenchmarkTemplates                    200000              10695 ns/op
BenchmarkCompiledTemplates            1000000              1406 ns/op
BenchmarkParallelTemplates            1000000              1404 ns/op
ok      _/Users/mbutcher/Code/go-in-practice/chapter5/tests/bench      5.097s
```

Your parallel version didn't outperform the regular version. Why? Because the goroutines were all run on the same processor. Let's specify that you want to see the testing
tool run several versions of the same code, using a different number of CPUs each
time:

```
$ go test -bench . -cpu=1,2,4
testing: warning: no tests to run
PASS
BenchmarkTemplates                    200000              10019 ns/op
BenchmarkTemplates-2                  100000              14033 ns/op
BenchmarkTemplates-4                  100000              14971 ns/op
BenchmarkCompiledTemplates            1000000              1217 ns/op
BenchmarkCompiledTemplates-2          1000000              1137 ns/op
BenchmarkCompiledTemplates-4          1000000              1307 ns/op
BenchmarkParallelTemplates            1000000              1249 ns/op
BenchmarkParallelTemplates-2          2000000               784 ns/op
BenchmarkParallelTemplates-4          2000000               829 ns/op
ok    _/Users/mbutcher/Code/go-in-practice/chapter5/tests/bench   14.993s
```

In this run, you specify –cpu=1,2,4, which tells go test to run the tests with one, two,
and then four CPUs, respectively. It runs each test this way and prints the results,
appending –N to indicate when more than one processor was used.

Unsurprisingly, your earlier nonparallel tests don't perform any better when using more CPUs. With only one main goroutine running, there's no optimization to be had. A noticeable hit occurs, due to the higher accounting overhead of multiple CPUs, but that disappears when you look at the results of BenchmarkParallelTemplates. There, you drop about a third of the time off when you spread processing over multiple CPU cores. The slightly higher time for the four cores, compared to two, may indicate that locking slows you down ever so slightly.

What if you make a naïve mistake, though, and try a quick optimization?

TECHNIQUE 31 **Detecting race conditions**

When attempting to parallelize processing with multiple goroutines and multiple CPUs, you run the possibility of accidentally accessing things in the wrong order. A *race condition* occurs when two or more goroutines attempt to modify the same piece of information at about the same time. If the execution order differs from what you intend, the result may be surprising. And these conditions are often hard to diagnose. But Go includes a race detection tool, and the preceding parallel benchmark technique provides an opportunity to try it.

PROBLEM

In programs with many goroutines, race conditions could occur. Being able to test for this possibility is desirable.

SOLUTION

Use the –race flag (sometimes called *go race* or *grace*).

DISCUSSION

Let's begin with listing 5.22 and make an ill-conceived performance optimization. Instead of declaring a new buffer for each goroutine, let's share one in the following listing. This will reduce the allocations your tested code has to perform.

Listing 5.24 Benchmarks and race conditions

```
func BenchmarkParallelOops(b *testing.B) {
    tpl := "Hello {{.Name}}"
    t, _ := template.New("test").Parse(tpl)
    data := &map[string]string{
        "Name": "World",
    }
    var buf bytes.Buffer            ◁──── Moved out of
    b.RunParallel(func(pb *testing.PB) {      the closure
        for pb.Next() {
            t.Execute(&buf, data)
            buf.Reset()
        }
    })
}
```

Now let's run that code sample. It's likely that the parallel benchmark will fail:

```
$ go test -bench Oops -cpu=1,2,4
testing: warning: no tests to run
PASS
BenchmarkParallelOops          1000000              1371 ns/op
BenchmarkParallelOops-2        panic: runtime error: slice bounds out of
      range [recovered]
      panic: runtime error: slice bounds out of range

goroutine 26 [running]:
text/template.errRecover(0x208355f40)
      /usr/local/Cellar/go/1.4.2/libexec/src/text/template/exec.go:100 +0xbc
bytes.(*Buffer).Write(0x2082e2070…, 0x0)
…
```

A look through the stack trace gives a few clues about what happened, but the real underlying cause isn't clear. If you add the –race flag onto the testing call, Go instruments for race conditions, and the information you receive is much more helpful:

```
$ go test -bench Oops -race -cpu=1,2,4
testing: warning: no tests to run
PASS
BenchmarkParallelOops          200000               5675 ns/op
BenchmarkParallelOops-2        ==================
WARNING: DATA RACE
Write by goroutine 20:
  bytes.(*Buffer).Write()
      /usr/local/Cellar/go/1.4.2/libexec/src/bytes/buffer.go:126 +0x53
      text/template.(*state).walk()
      /usr/local/Cellar/go/1.4.2/libexec/src/text/template/exec.go:182 +0x401
      text/template.(*state).walk()
…
```

Now the cause is much clearer: more than one thing tried to use the bytes.Buffer at once. Reading through more of the special race condition stack trace will even show where the race occurs. Multiple goroutines are writing at the same time. From here, you have the options of stepping back to the older method or using a sync.Mutex to lock and unlock access around the buffer.

This illustration is a good example of a race failure. It's easy to reproduce. But many other race conditions are less predictable. The race may manifest negatively only on occasion, which makes detecting and debugging difficult. That's where using the –race flag becomes handy. You can use it not only on benchmarks (which is a great place), but also with go run and all calls to go test.

5.6 *Summary*

This chapter has covered techniques for debugging and testing your Go programs. You've looked at logging tools, stack tracing, unit testing, and benchmarking. All of these are fundamental tools for writing production-grade Go code.

The chapter covered the following topics:

- Logging over the network
- Working with the Go log package
- Capturing stack traces
- Using Go's pattern for writing unit tests
- Benchmarking with Go's testing tools
- Performing basic generative testing
- Detecting race conditions

In the coming chapters, the techniques you learned here will shape the way you write your code.

Part 3

An interface
for your applications

Applications often interact with the outside world through APIs and user interfaces. This is the focus of part 3.

Quite often, user interfaces are built using web technologies. Go provides numerous features out of the box that help you build and operate them. But these base features don't provide the more complex capabilities available in other platforms. Chapter 6 powers up HTML and email templates, going beyond what you can do with the standard library. Chapter 7 builds on this and covers serving assets and dealing with submissions that come from forms.

REST APIs provide a common means of interaction. These APIs enable Java-Script, mobile, and desktop applications to interact with your application. REST APIs are also the way to expose web services. Chapter 8 covers working with and exposing web service APIs.

HTML and email template patterns

This chapter covers

- Adding functionality inside templates
- Nesting templates
- Using template inheritance
- Rendering objects to HTML
- Using email templates

When you're programmatically creating text or HTML responses in many programming environments, you need to seek out the right library to handle the HTML. Go handles this a little differently. In the standard library, Go provides template handling for both text and HTML. The HTML handling is built on top of the text template engine to add HTML-aware intelligence.

Although the standard library enables you to work with HTML templates, it stops short of having too many opinions. Instead, it provides a foundation along with the ability to extend and combine templates. For example, you could nest templates or have a template inherit from another one. This simple and extensible design allows you to use many common template patterns.

In this chapter, you'll learn how to extend the functionality inside HTML templates and techniques to use templates together. Along the way, we offer tips, including some related to performance, that can speed up applications. For example, you'll learn where you can parse a template that can save overall processing time. You'll then learn how to use text templates when you send email messages.

6.1 Working with HTML templates

The `html` and `html/template` packages in the standard library provide the foundation for working with HTML. This includes the ability to work with variables and functions in the templates. The `html/template` package is built on the `text/template` package, which provides general text template handling. HTML, being text, can use the text handling. The advantage of the `html/template` package over the `text/template` package for HTML is the context-aware intelligence that saves developers work.

Although these packages provide the groundwork to working with HTML, they stop short of having many opinions. What you can do and how you should structure your HTML templates is left to the application authors. In the next couple of techniques, you'll look at patterns that will be helpful in extending the template packages for your own applications.

6.1.1 Standard library HTML package overview

Before you look at those patterns, you need to look at how the packages in the standard library work. Whereas the `html` package provides only a couple of functions to escape and unescape strings for HTML, the `html/template` package provides a good foundation for working with templates. First, let's look at a basic HTML template in the next listing.

> **Listing 6.1   A simple HTML template: simple.html**

```
<!DOCTYPE HTML>
<html>
  <head>
    <meta charset="utf-8">
    <title>{{.Title}}</title>          Title based on
  </head>                              Title property
  <body>
    <h1>{{.Title}}</h1>                The title and content
    <p>{{.Content}}</p>                being displayed
  </body>
</html>
```

This listing illustrates the basics of a template. Aside from the actions (also called *directives*), which are enclosed in double curly brackets, the template looks like a normal HTML file. Here the directives are to print a value passed into the template, such as printing the passed-in title. The next step is to call this template from code and pass it the values to fill in for {{.Title}} and {{.Content}}, as shown in the next listing.

Listing 6.2   Using a simple HTML template: simple_template.go

```go
package main

import (
    "html/template"        Uses html instead of
    "net/http"             text template package
)

type Page struct {
    Title, Content string
}

func displayPage(w http.ResponseWriter, r *http.Request) {
    p := &Page{
        Title:   "An Example",            Data object to pass to
        Content: "Have fun stormin' da castle.",   template containing
    }                                      properties to print
    t := template.Must(template.ParseFiles("templates/simple.html"))
    t.Execute(w, p)
                                    Writes to HTTP output using
}                                   template and dataset

func main() {
    http.HandleFunc("/", displayPage)         Serves the output via
    http.ListenAndServe(":8080", nil)         simple web server
}
```

Parses a template for later use → (annotation pointing to `t := template.Must(...)`)

This simple application takes some data and displays it via a simple web server, using the template from listing 6.1. The `html/template` package is used here instead of the `text/template` package because it's context-aware and handles some operations for you.

Being context-aware is more than knowing that these are HTML templates. The package understands what's happening inside the templates. Take the following template snippet:

```
<a href="/user?id={{.Id}}">{{.Content}}</a>
```

The `html/template` package expands this intelligently. For escaping purposes, it adds context-appropriate functionality. The preceding snippet is automatically expanded to look like this:

```
<a href="/user?id={{.Id | urlquery}}">{{.Content | html}}</a>
```

The variables (in this case, `.Id` and `.Content`) are piped through appropriate functions to escape their content before turning it into the final output. Escaping turns characters that could be seen as markup and that alter the page structure or meaning into references that display properly but don't alter the structure or meaning. If you were using the `text/template` package, you would need to add the escaping yourself.

The context-aware escaping is built around a security model in which template developers are considered trusted, and user data, injected via variables, is considered untrusted and should be escaped. For example, if an application user input the string `<script>alert('busted pwned')</script>`, and you displayed that string through the HTML template system, it would be escaped and <script>alert('busted pwned')</script> would be rendered in the template. This is safe to display to users and avoids a potential cross-site scripting (XSS) vulnerability.

When you want a variable to be rendered as is, without being escaped, you can use the HTML type in the html/template package. Technique 35 provides an example that uses the HTML type to inject data into a template and avoid escaping.

The following four techniques look at ways to extend the built-in template system, allowing you to use common template patterns.

6.1.2 *Adding functionality inside templates*

Templates in Go have functions that can and will be called from within them. As you just saw, the intelligence in the HTML templates adds escaping functions in the right place for you. These functions are where complex functionality is handled in the templates. Out of the box, the template packages provide fewer than 20 functions, and several are to support this intelligence.

For example, consider one of the built-in functions, whose implementation is provided by fmt.Sprintf, is printf. The following code shows its use inside a template:

```
{{"output" | printf "%q"}}
```

The snippet takes the string output and passes it into printf by using the format string %q. The output is the quoted string output.

TECHNIQUE 32   **Extending templates with functions**

Although templates provide quite a few features, often you need to extend them with your own functionality. The need to add features isn't uncommon or uncalled for. For example, we've often seen the need to display a date and time in an easy-to-read format. This common request could easily be implemented as part of the template system. This is just one common example, and template systems can be extended in many cases.

PROBLEM

The built-in functions in the templates don't provide all the functionality you need.

SOLUTION

Just as Go makes functions available in templates (such as fmt.Sprintf being available in templates as printf), make your own functions available.

DISCUSSION

You can display information in templates in various ways. Although the way data is generated should be kept in the application logic, the way it's formatted and displayed should cleanly happen in a template. Presenting date and time information is a good example. In an application, the time information should be stored in a type, such as time.Time. When displayed to users, it could be displayed in a myriad of ways.

Go actions, the data and commands enclosed in double curly brackets, can have commands that act on the data. These commands can be chained into pipelines separated by a `|`. This is the same idea as using pipes from a UNIX-based command-line interface (CLI). Go provides an API to add commands to the set available to a template. The limited set of commands that comes out of the box doesn't need to be the only set available to your templates. The following listing takes a template and adds the capability to display formatted dates.

Listing 6.3 Add template functions: date_command.go

```go
package main

import (
    "html/template"
    "net/http"
    "time"
)

var tpl = `<!DOCTYPE HTML>                          // An HTML template as a string
<html>
  <head>
    <meta charset="utf-8">
    <title>Date Example</title>
  </head>
  <body>
      <p>{{.Date | dateFormat "Jan 2, 2006"}}</p>    // Pipes Date through the dateFormat command
  </body>
</html>`

var funcMap = template.FuncMap{                    // Maps Go functions to template functions
    "dateFormat": dateFormat,
}

func dateFormat(layout string, d time.Time) string {   // Function to convert a time to a formatted string
    return d.Format(layout)
}

func serveTemplate(res http.ResponseWriter, req *http.Request) {
    t := template.New("date")                      // Creates a new template.Template instance
    t.Funcs(funcMap)                               // Passes additional functions in map into template engine
    t.Parse(tpl)                                   // Parses the template string into the template engine
    data := struct{ Date time.Time }{              // Creates a dataset to pass into template to display
        Date: time.Now(),
    }
    t.Execute(res, data)                           // Sends template with data to output response
}

func main() {
    http.HandleFunc("/", serveTemplate)            // Serves the template and dataset using a web server
    http.ListenAndServe(":8080", nil)
}
```

Rather than referencing an external file, this HTML template is stored as a string in a variable. Inside the template, the data in Date is passed through the template function dateFormat with a specified format string before becoming part of the output. It's important to know that the piping mechanism passes the output from one item in the pipeline into the next item in the pipeline as the last argument.

Because dateFormat isn't one of the core template functions, it needs to be made available to the template. Making custom functions available in templates requires two steps. First, a map needs to be created in which names to be used inside the template are mapped to functions in Go. Here the function dateFormat is mapped to the name dateFormat. Although the same name is used for both the Go function and name available inside the template, that doesn't have to be the case. They can be different names.

When a new template.Template instance is created, the function map (here, named funcMap) needs to be passed into Funcs to make the new function mapping available to templates. After this happens, templates can use the functions. Before using the template, the final step is to parse the template into template.Template.

From here, the template instance is used normally. The data structure is defined, in this case, by an anonymous struct, with the data to pass in as a key-value mapping. The data structure is passed into Execute along with the io.Writer to output the rendered template. In this case, when dateFormat is encountered in the template, the format of Jan 2, 2006 is passed in, followed by the time.Time instance. The instance of time.Time is converted to a string following this format.

> **NOTE** The date and time used in format strings needs to be specific and is detailed in the package documentation at http://golang.org/pkg/time/#Time.Format.

If you're going to apply the same function set to numerous templates, you can use a Go function to create your templates and add your template functions each time:

```
func parseTemplateString(name, tpl string) *template.Template {
    t:= template.New(name)
    t.Funcs(funcMap)
    t = template.Must(t.Parse(tpl))
    return t
}
```

This function could be repeatedly used to create a new template object from a template string with your custom template functions included. In listing 6.3, this could be used inside the serveTemplate function instead of parsing the template and adding the template functions there. Using a Go function to configure your templates for you could be done with files as well.

6.1.3   *Limiting template parsing*

Parsing templates that were originally in text into type instances is a bit of work for a Go application. Parsing a template turns a string of characters into an object model with a variety of nodes and node types that Go knows how to use. The parser in the text/template/parser package sits behind functions in the template packages such as Parse and ParseFiles. Unless you work directly with the parser, which isn't recommended, it's easy to miss all the work going on behind the functions you use.

Methods such as the following technique allow you to avoid extra work by using a parser that can speed up your application.

TECHNIQUE 33 Caching parsed templates

Go applications, as servers that respond to multiple requests, can generate many responses to requests from many different clients. If for each response the application has to parse a template, a lot of duplicate work is going on. If you can eliminate some of that work at response time, you can speed up your application's performance.

PROBLEM

You want to avoid repeatedly parsing the same template while an application is running.

SOLUTION

Parse the template, store the ready-to-use template in a variable, and repeatedly use the same template each time you need to generate the output.

DISCUSSION

Instead of parsing the template in the http handler function, which means parsing the template each time the handler function runs, you can move the parsing out of the handler. Then you can repeatedly execute the template against different datasets without parsing it each time. The following listing is a modified version of listing 6.2 that caches the parsed template.

Listing 6.4 Caching a parsed template: cache_template.go

```go
package main

import (
    "html/template"
    "net/http"
)

var t = template.Must(template.ParseFiles("templates/simple.html"))

type Page struct {
    Title, Content string
}

func diaplayPage(w http.ResponseWriter, r *http.Request) {
    p := &Page{
            Title:   "An Example",
            Content: "Have fun stormin' da castle.",
    }
    t.Execute(w, p)
}

func main() {
    http.HandleFunc("/", diaplayPage)
    http.ListenAndServe(":8080", nil)
}
```

Parses the template when the package is initialized

Executes the template in the http handler function

Instead of parsing the template in the handler function, as listing 6.2 does, the template is parsed once when the package is initialized. When the `http` handler function is executed, the template is executed normally.

As the benchmark test examples from chapter 5 showed, parsing a template and reusing the parsed template is faster than parsing each time. This is a subtle, simple way to speed up application responses.

6.1.4   *When template execution breaks*

All software has the potential to fail. Template execution is no exception. When template execution fails, an error is returned. But in some cases, template execution can fail and partial output is displayed to the end user. This can provide an experience you want to avoid.

<hr>

TECHNIQUE 34   **Handling template execution failures**

<hr>

When templates are executed, the output is written as it walks through the template. If a function is called, causing an error midway through the template, an error will be returned and execution will stop. But the part of the template before the error would already be displayed to end users.

PROBLEM

When an error happens while executing a template, you want to catch the error before anything is displayed to the user. Instead of displaying the partially broken pages, display something more appropriate, such as an error page.

SOLUTION

Write the output of the template to a buffer. If no errors occur, write the output of the buffer to end users. Otherwise, handle the error.

DISCUSSION

Templates should be fairly unintelligent. They display data, and functions can be used to format the data. Any errors in the data should be handled before templates are used with the data, and the functions called within the templates should be for display purposes. This keeps the separation of concerns in place and limits failures when templates are executed, which is important for streaming.

Streaming responses is useful. When you execute a template to a response writer, end users start to receive the page more quickly. When you buffer a response, there's a delay in end users receiving it. End users expect native desktop performance out of web applications, and streaming responses helps achieve that. When possible, write to output.

But at times, the optimal case doesn't work out. If executing templates carries a potential for errors, you can write the output of the template to a buffer. If errors occur, they can be handled before displaying anything to the end users. The following listing builds on listing 6.4 to introduce a buffered output.

Listing 6.5   Buffering a template response: buffered_template.go

```go
package main

import (
    "bytes"
    "fmt"
    "html/template"
    "io"
    "net/http"
)

var t *template.Template

func init() {
    t = template.Must(template.ParseFiles("./templates/simple.html"))
}

type Page struct {
    Title, Content string
}

func diaplayPage(w http.ResponseWriter, r *http.Request) {
    p := &Page{
        Title:   "An Example",
        Content: "Have fun stormin' da castle.",
    }
    var b bytes.Buffer
    err := t.Execute(&b, p)
    if err != nil {
        fmt.Fprint(w, "A error occured.")
        return
    }
    b.WriteTo(w)
}

func main() {
    http.HandleFunc("/", diaplayPage)
    http.ListenAndServe(":8080", nil)
}
```

Creates a buffer to store the output of the executed template

Handles any errors from template execution

Copies the buffered output to the response writer

When the template is executed, a buffer is written to instead of http.Response-Writer. If any errors occur, those are handled before copying the contents of the buffer to the output http.ResponseWriter.

6.1.5   *Mixing templates*

The foundation of generating HTML output is the html/template package. It handles safely generating HTML output. But the documented use cases are simple. When building applications, you'll often want to mix templates together, have patterns for reusing and managing them, cache generated output, and more. In the following patterns, you'll see three ways to work with templates, built on top of the standard library, allowing you to use more-complex template handling. These patterns are template nesting, extending a base template through inheritance, and mapping a data object to a specific template (for example, a user object being mapped to a user template).

TECHNIQUE 35   Nested templates

Sharing and reusing sections of templates, like code reuse, is a common need. If you have an application with numerous web pages, you'll typically find that most elements are common across pages, and some elements are custom.

PROBLEM

You want to avoid duplicating the common sections of HTML markup in each template and the maintenance burden that goes along with that. Like the software you're developing, you want to take advantage of reuse.

SOLUTION

Use nested templates to share common sections of HTML, as shown in figure 6.1. The subtemplates enable reuse for sections of markup, cutting down on duplication.

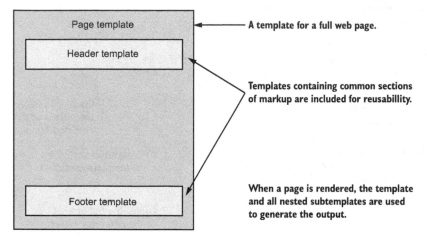

Figure 6.1   Using nested subtemplates to share common template code

DISCUSSION

The template system in Go is designed to handle multiple templates and allow them to work together. A parent template can import other templates. When the parent is executed to render the output, the subtemplates are included as well. The following listing shows how this works, touching on some important nuances.

Listing 6.6   Index template including head template: index.html

```html
<!DOCTYPE HTML>
<html>
  {{template "head.html" .}}
  <body>
      <h1>{{.Title}}</h1>
      <p>{{.Content}}</p>
  </body>
</html>
```

⬅ **Includes another template in this one, passing in entire dataset**

This nested template example starts out with index.html. This is similar to the simple template from listing 6.1. The difference is that instead of a <head> section, there's a directive to include another template.

The directive {{template "head.html" .}} has three parts. template tells the template engine to include another template, and head.html is the name of that template. The final part is the . after head.html. This is the dataset to pass to the template. In this case, the entire dataset from the parent template is passed to this template. If a property on the dataset contained a dataset for a subtemplate, that could be passed in (for example, if {{template "head.html" .Foo}} were used, the properties on .Foo would be the ones available inside head.html). See the following listing.

Listing 6.7   Head template included in the index: head.html

```
<head>
  <meta charset="utf-8">
  <title>{{.Title}}</title>          ◁─┐  Title is the same value
</head>                                    used in index.html.
```

When head.html, as seen in listing 6.7, is invoked by index.html, the entire dataset is passed in. When Title is used, it's the same Title used in index.html, as head.html has access to the entire dataset.

The next listing brings the example together.

Listing 6.8   Using the nested templates: nested_templates.go

```
package main

import (
    "html/template"
    "net/http"
)
                                            Loads the two templates
var t *template.Template                     into a template object

func init() {
    t = template.Must(template.ParseFiles("index.html", "head.html"))  ◁─┘
}

type Page struct {
    Title, Content string
}

func diaplayPage(w http.ResponseWriter, r *http.Request) {
    p := &Page{
            Title:   "An Example",
            Content: "Have fun stormin' da castle.",
    }
    t.ExecuteTemplate(w, "index.html", p)    ◁─┐  Invokes the template
}                                                 with the page data

func main() {
    http.HandleFunc("/", diaplayPage)
    http.ListenAndServe(":8080", nil)            Serves the page on the
}                                                 built-in web server
```

This listing starts by parsing the two templates to the same template object. This allows head.html to be accessible to index.html when it's executed. When the template is executed, ExecuteTemplate is used so that the template name to execute can be specified. If Execute had been used, as in the previous listings, the first template listed in ParseFiles would be used. ExecuteTemplate provides control over the template file when multiple ones are available.

TECHNIQUE 36   **Template inheritance**

Many template systems implement a model with a base template and other templates that fill in the missing sections of the base template. They extend the base template. This is different from the previous technique, in which subtemplates were shared among a group of different top-level templates. In this case, the top-level template is shared.

PROBLEM

You want to have a base template and have other templates extend the base template. The templates would have multiple sections that can be extended.

SOLUTION

Instead of thinking of a file as a template, think of sections of a file as templates. The base file contains the shared markup and refers to other templates that haven't yet been defined, as shown in figure 6.2. The templates extending the base file provide the missing subtemplates or override those in the base. After they're combined, you have a fully working template with a shared base.

DISCUSSION

The template system enables some inheritance patterns within templates. It doesn't represent the full range of inheritance available in other template systems, but patterns can be applied. The following listing shows a base template for others to inherit from.

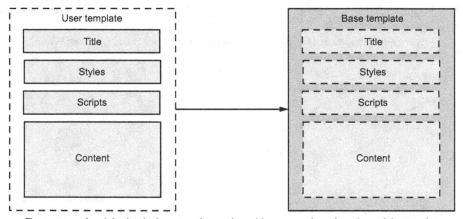

The user template inherits the base template and provides content for subsections of the template.

Figure 6.2   **A shared based template**

Listing 6.9 A base template to inherit from: base.html

```
{{define "base"}}<!DOCTYPE HTML>          ◁─┐ Starts a new base
<html>                                       │ template with define
  <head>
    <meta charset="utf-8">                          Invokes the title template,
    <title>{{template "title" .}}</title>    ◁───    which is defined elsewhere
    {{ block "styles" . }}<style>
      h1 {                                   Defines and
         color: #400080                      immediately invokes
      }                                      the styles template
    </style>{{ end }}
  </head>
  <body>                                     Defines and invokes the scripts
    <h1>{{template "title" .}}</h1>          template, which is currently
    {{template "content" .}}                 empty. An extending template can
    {{block "scripts" .}}{{end}}         ◁─  redefine the contents of scripts.
  </body>
</html>{{end}}                  ◁─────── End of the base template
```

Instead of the entire file being a template, the file contains multiple templates. Each template starts with a define or block directive and closes with an end directive. The block directive defines and immediately executes a template. This file opens by defining a base template. The base template, which can be referred to by name, invokes other templates but doesn't necessarily define them. Templates that extend this one, such as listing 6.10, will need to fill in the missing templates. In other cases, you may have a section with default content that you want to allow to be overridden by an extending template. Some sections may be optional. For those sections, you can create empty templates to be used by default.

NOTE The block directive and ability to redefine template sections that have content was introduced in Go 1.6. Prior to this, you couldn't redefine templates that had content.

Listing 6.10 Inheriting required sections: user.html

```
{{define "title"}}User: {{.Username}}{{end}}     ◁─────── Defines a title template
{{define "content"}}
<ul>
  <li>Userame: {{.Username}}</li>
  <li>Name: {{.Name}}</li>                        Defines a content
</ul>                                             template
{{end}}
```

Templates extending the base need to make sure all of the subtemplates without a default are filled out. Here the title and content sections need to be defined because they're required. You'll notice that the optional sections with empty or default content defined from listing 6.9 don't need to have sections defined.

The following listing showcases filling in an optional template in addition to the required sections.

Listing 6.11   Inheriting with optional section: page.html

```
{{define "title"}}{{.Title}}{{end}}
{{define "content"}}
<p>
  {{.Content}}
</p>
{{end}}
{{define "styles"}}
<style>
h1 {
    color: #800080
}
</style>
{{end}}
```

Defines a template to
fill in an optional
section of the parent

Here the styles template is defined. This overrides the default supplied in listing 6.9.
The following listing brings the templates together.

Listing 6.12   Using template inheritance: inherit.go

```
package main

import (
    "html/template"
    "net/http"
)

var t map[string]*template.Template

func init() {
    t = make(map[string]*template.Template)
    temp := template.Must(template.ParseFiles("base.html", "user.html"))
    t["user.html"] = temp
    temp = template.Must(template.ParseFiles("base.html", "page.html"))
    t["page.html"] = temp
}

type Page struct {
    Title, Content string
}

type User struct {
    Username, Name string
}

func displayPage(w http.ResponseWriter, r *http.Request) {
    p := &Page{
            Title:   "An Example",
            Content: "Have fun stormin' da castle.",
    }
    t["page.html"].ExecuteTemplate(w, "base", p)
}

func displayUser(w http.ResponseWriter, r *http.Request) {
    u := &User{
            Username: "swordsmith",
```

A map to store
templates in a
map of named
templates

Sets up the
template map

Loads templates along
with base into the map

Data objects to pass
into templates

Populates a dataset
for the page

Invokes the
template for
the page

```
         Name:        "Inigo Montoya",
    }
    t["user.html"].ExecuteTemplate(w, "base", u)
}
func main() {
    http.HandleFunc("/user", displayUser)          ┤ Serves pages via the
    http.HandleFunc("/", displayPage)              │  built-in web server
    http.ListenAndServe(":8080", nil)
}
```

This listing starts by creating a map to hold the templates. Each template is stored separately from the others. The map is populated with the template instances by using a key for the template name. When the templates user.html and page.html are loaded, the base.html file is loaded with each of them. This allows for the inheritance in each case.

Preparing to render a page happens in a similar manner to the normal template usage. A dataset is defined and populated. When it's time to render a response, the template to use is selected from the map of templates and the base template is invoked. The base is the root of the page and needs to be the one invoked. It will invoke the subtemplates defined in the inheritance.

TECHNIQUE 37 Mapping data types to templates

The previous two template techniques rendered all the output together. A dataset consisting of the entire page needs to be passed in, and the template setup needs to handle the variations to the full page.

An alternative approach is to render parts of the page, such as a user object instance, on its own and then pass the rendered content to a higher-level template. The higher-level template doesn't need to know the data type or how to render it. Figure 6.3 represents this concept.

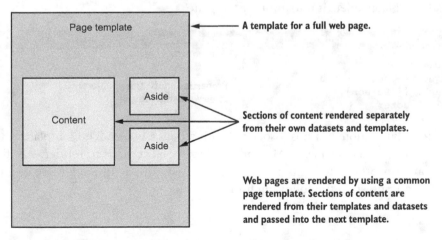

Figure 6.3 HTML rendered objects passed into the template

PROBLEM

You want to render an object to HTML and pass the rendered object to a higher-level template, where it can be part of the output.

SOLUTION

Use templates to render objects as HTML. Store the HTML in a variable and pass the HTML to higher-level templates wrapped in template.HTML, marking it as safe HTML that doesn't need to be escaped.

DISCUSSION

There are a couple reasons to have multiple rendering steps. First, if part of the page is expensive to generate a dataset for or render to HTML, it's worth not repeating when each page is generated.

For example, imagine you have a directory listing for a user. The listing contains information about a user and their activity that can be viewed by many other users. Obtaining the dataset to render would require multiple data source lookups. If that were cached, you could skip loading this information each time the page is viewed.

Caching this dataset would still require the dataset being rendered on each page load, and you'd need to store a complicated dataset somewhere. Rendering the data would mean the template package handles rendering in the right format and making sure everything is properly escaped. If the cache were instead populated with a rendered HTML snippet to reuse each time, more work on each page generation would be skipped due to better caching.

In a second case, say you have applications with complicated logic and have many pages to render. You could have many templates containing a lot of duplicate markup. If each template were instead scoped to render one thing—whether it be the main content, a piece of the sidebar, or the page wrapper—the templates could be easier to manage.

The following listing shows how to render an object from a template, store the HTML, and later inject it into another template.

Listing 6.13   A Quote **object template: quote.html**

```
<blockquote>
&ldquo;{{.Quote}}&rdquo;
&mdash; {{.Person}}
</blockquote>
```
**Properties on the Quote object
to be written to output**

This template, quote.html, is associated with a Quote object. The template is used to render the Quote object as HTML and has Quote object fields to render. You'll notice there are no other elements for a complete page here. Instead those are part of index.html, shown in the following listing.

Listing 6.14   A generic page wrapper: index.html

```html
<!DOCTYPE HTML>
<html>
  <head>
    <meta charset="utf-8">
    <title>{{.Title}}</title>
  </head>
  <body>
    <h1>{{.Title}}</h1>
    <p>{{.Content}}</p>
  </body>
</html>
```

Properties related to displaying a generic page

The index.html file is a template for the page wrapper. It contains variables that make sense in the scope of a page. The variables printed out aren't specific to a user or anything else. The following listing pulls this together.

Listing 6.15   Bringing the templates together: object_templates.go

```go
package main

import (
    "bytes"
    "html/template"
    "net/http"
)

var t *template.Template
var qc template.HTML

func init() {
    t = template.Must(template.ParseFiles("index.html", "quote.html"))
}

type Page struct {
    Title   string
    Content template.HTML
}

type Quote struct {
    Quote, Name string
}

func main() {
    q := &Quote{
        Quote: `You keep using that word. I do not think
            it means what you think it means.`,
        Person: "Inigo Montoya",
    }
    var b bytes.Buffer
    t.ExecuteTemplate(&b, "quote.html", q)
    qc = template.HTML(b.String())

    http.HandleFunc("/", diaplayPage)
    http.ListenAndServe(":8080", nil)
}
```

Variables to hold persistent data shared between requests

Loads the two template files for later use

Types to store data for templates with differing and specific properties

Populates a dataset to supply to template

Writes template and data

Stores quote as HTML in global variable

Serves handler using built-in web server

```
func diaplayPage(w http.ResponseWriter, r *http.Request) {
    p := &Page{
            Title:    "A User",
            Content: qc,
    }
    t.ExecuteTemplate(w, "index.html", p)
}
```

Creates page dataset with quote HTML

◁—┐ **Writes quote and page to web server output**

This code starts out in a fairly typical manner. It begins by parsing the two templates, quote.html and index.html, into a variable. In this case, you have two data structures for use. The first is for the output of a web page. The second is Quote, which can be converted to HTML.

To create a piece of content separate from generating the page, a quote is instantiated as part of the main function. Quote is passed into ExecuteTemplate along with the quote.html template to render the quote as HTML. Instead of writing the template to output, the template is written to Buffer. Then Buffer is converted to a string and passed into template.HTML. The html/template package escapes most of the data sent into it. An exception to that is template.HTML, which is safe HTML. Because the content was generated from a template that performed escaping, you can store the output of the quote.html template as safe HTML to use later.

In the Page type, you'll notice that the Content property is the type template.HTML. When the dataset used to generate the page is created, the HTML generated from the Quote object is set as the Content. When the index.html template is invoked with the dataset, the template system knows to skip escaping anything of the type template.HTML. The quote HTML is used as is. This provides a clean way to store and pass around safe HTML.

> **WARNING**   User input HTML should never be considered safe. Always escape user input information, such as information gathered from a form field, before presenting.

6.2 *Using templates for email*

Email is one of the staples of modern communication. It's often used for service notifications, registration verification, and more. Even services looking to take over where email has dominated will end up using it in some capacity.

The Go standard library doesn't provide a special template package for email as it does for HTML. Instead, the text and html template packages provide what you need to send text and HTML email.

TECHNIQUE 38   **Generating email from templates**

Email is one of the places templates can be used. Sometimes email is generated as text and other times as HTML. These happen to be the two template packages provided by the standard library.

PROBLEM

When creating and sending email, you want to incorporate templates.

SOLUTION

Use the template packages to generate the email text into a buffer. Pass the generated email in the buffer to the code used to send the email, such as the smtp package.

DISCUSSION

Templates can be used for a wide variety of things, and email messages are a great place to use them. To illustrate this, the following listing creates email messages from a template and sends them using the net/smtp package.

Listing 6.16   Send email from a template: email.go

```go
package main

import (
    "bytes"
    "net/smtp"              Uses text templates to
    "strconv"          ◁── send plain text email
    "text/template"
)

type EmailMessage struct {
    From, Subject, Body string          The data structure
    To                  []string        for an email
}

type EmailCredentials struct {
    Username, Password, Server string
    Port                       int
}

const emailTemplate = `From: {{.From}}
To: {{.To}}
Subject: {{.Subject}}          The email template
                               as a string
{{.Body}}
`

var t *template.Template

func init() {
    t = template.New("email")
    t.Parse(emailTemplate)
}

func main() {
    message := &EmailMessage{
        From:    "me@example.com",
        To:      []string{"you@example.com"},     Populates a dataset with
        Subject: "A test",                        the email for the template
        Body:    "Just saying hi",                and mail client
    }

    var body bytes.Buffer          Populates a buffer with the rendered
    t.Execute(&body, message)      message text from the template
```

```
        authCreds := &EmailCredentials{
                Username: "myUsername",
                Password: "myPass",
                Server:   "smtp.example.com",
                Port:     25,
        }
        auth := smtp.PlainAuth("",
                authCreds.Username,
                authCreds.Password,
                authCreds.Server,
        )
        smtp.SendMail(authCreds.Server+":"+strconv.Itoa(authCreds.Port),
                auth,
                message.From,
                message.To,
                body.Bytes())
}
```

Sets up the SMTP mail client

Sends the email

The bytes from the message buffer are passed in when the message is sent.

This code sends a simple email generated from a template. You'll notice the listing is using the `text/template` package instead of the `html/template` package used in the previous listings in the chapter. The `html/template` package is built on top of the `text/template` package. It provides HTML-specific features such as context-aware escaping on top of the `text/template` package.

Using the `text/template` package means the injected properties (for example, `.Body`) aren't escaped. If you need to escape anything injected into the template, you can use escape functions from the `text/template` package.

When you execute the template with a dataset, pass in a buffer to store the rendered template. The buffer provides the source of the content to send from the mail client.

This concept can be expanded to send a variety of email in a variety of ways. For example, you could use the `html/template` package to send HTML email. Or you could combine this with the other template techniques to create complex templates.

6.3   Summary

Using and extending template patterns for both HTML and email allows you to handle complexity in a more maintainable manner. This is useful as complexity grows within an application. These patterns include the following:

- Extending the functionality within templates through the use of piping commands.
- Caching and buffering templates.
- Having reusable sections within templates that can be shared across templates. For HTML templates, this includes having reusable sections such as a header or footer.
- Starting with a base or master template that's extended by other templates used.

- Mapping templates to objects, such as a user template for a user object, and rolling the templates up into a page-level output.
- Generating email output with templates.

In the next chapter, you'll explore serving static content and handling user input from HTML forms. This includes serving files such as JavaScript files, stylesheets, and images in several ways. You'll cover HTML form-handling patterns that can take the pain out of working with user input, especially when it comes to files.

Serving and receiving assets and forms

If you think about it, the original web service was serving files. This is what was first created back in 1991 when the web began. The interaction we enjoy today wasn't there at the beginning. When interaction came, it did so through web forms. These constructs, created decades ago, are still synonymous with the modern web and foundational to modern web applications.

This chapter starts by presenting methods to serve static files for your Go application. Because Go is a web server, rather than running behind a web server such as Apache or Nginx, you need to set up how you want files such as Cascading Style Sheets (CSS), JavaScript, images, or other files to be served. You'll learn several ways to store and serve files that provide solutions for varying applications.

From there, we move into form handling. Form handling with Go may seem fairly straightforward, and for simple cases it is. Yet, cases such as handling files as multipart form data can require tapping into parts of Go not often touched or understood. This is especially true if you want to work with large files.

File serving and form handling combined with template handling from the previous chapter lay a foundation for building web applications in Go. You can use these techniques with your front-end technologies of choice to build rich web applications.

7.1 Serving static content

A website or web application built with Go doesn't need to sit behind a web server. Instead, it handles serving all of the content with its web server, whether that content is application pages or static files, such as CSS, images, or JavaScript. Figure 7.1 illustrates the difference between a Go application and one using a separate web server.

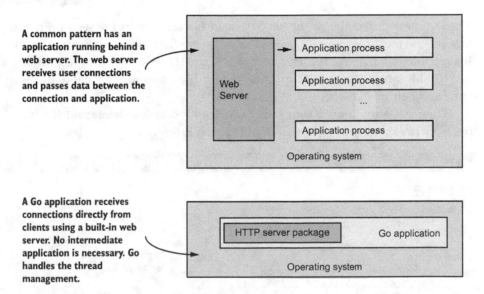

Figure 7.1 A Go application communicating over HTTP compared to a common web server model

Common Gateway Interface

Although Go is typically run as a server that serves all content, it can be used with a Common Gateway Interface (CGI) or FastCGI server. The `net/http/cgi` package works with the CGI interface, and the `net/http/fastcgi` package works with a Fast-CGI interface. In this environment, static content may be served by another web server. These packages are intended for compatibility with existing systems. CGI starts up a new process to respond to each request, which is less efficient than typical Go serving. This is a setup we don't recommend using.

To handle static files, the `http` package in the standard library has a series of functions that deal with file serving. Before you look into a few techniques to serve files within an application, it's important to know a little about the functionality built into the `http` package, shown in the next listing.

> **Listing 7.1   `http` package file serving: file_serving.go**

```go
package main

import (
    "net/http"
)

func main() {
    dir := http.Dir("./files")                              ◄  Uses a directory
    http.ListenAndServe(":8080", http.FileServer(dir))      ◄  on the filesystem
}                                                              Serves the
                                                              filesystem directory
```

The `FileServer` handler in the `http` package is a semi-smart file server. From a directory on the local filesystem, `FileServer` will serve files following proper permissions. It's capable of looking at the `If-Modified-Since` HTTP header and responding with a 304 Not Modified response if the version of the file a user already has matches the one currently being served.

When you want to write your own handler to serve files, the `ServeFile` function in the `http` package is useful, as shown in the next listing.

> **Listing 7.2   Serve file with custom handler: servefile.go**

```go
package main

import (
    "net/http"
)

func main() {
    http.HandleFunc("/", readme)              ◄  Registers a handler
    http.ListenAndServe(":8080", nil)            for all paths
}

func readme(res http.ResponseWriter, req *http.Request) {   ◄  Serves the contents
    http.ServeFile(res, req, "./files/readme.txt")             of a readme file
}
```

This example takes a different approach to serving a file. A basic web server has a single handler to serve all paths. This `readme` handler serves the content of a file located at ./files/readme.txt by using the `ServeFile` function. `ServeFile` takes a file or directory as its third argument to serve. And like `FileServer`, `ServeFile` looks at the `If-Modified-Since` HTTP header and responds with a 304 Not Modified response if possible.

This functionality, along with some of its underpinnings, enables you to serve content by using a variety of techniques.

TECHNIQUE 39   **Serving subdirectories**

A common practice, used in many frameworks and applications, is to serve files from the local filesystem where the application resides. This allows other applications to mount external filesystems as if they were local or have them local.

PROBLEM

You want to serve a directory and its subdirectories from the filesystem as part of your web application.

SOLUTION

Use the built-in file server or the file-serving handlers to serve the files from the local filesystem. For intimate control over error pages, including the case of a file not being found, you need to implement your own file server.

DISCUSSION

An easy way to understand file serving is to look at a simple example. Take the directory example_app/static/ and serve it from the path example.com/static/. This may seem fairly straightforward, and for some cases it is, but if you want intimate control over the experience, you'll see in a moment that you need to bypass some of the built-in file serving to have that control. First, let's look at a simple example.

> **Listing 7.3   Serving a subdirectory**

A directory and its subdirectories on the filesystem are chosen to serve.

The /static/ path serves the directory and needs to be removed before looking up file path.

```
func main() {
    dir := http.Dir("./files/")
    handler := http.StripPrefix("/static/", http.FileServer(dir))
    http.Handle("/static/", handler)

    http.HandleFunc("/", homePage)
    http.ListenAndServe(":8080", nil)
}
```

Serves a home page that may include files from the static directory

Here, the built-in web server is serving the ./files/ directory at the path /static/ by using the file server from the http package. The directory on the filesystem could be any directory and doesn't need to be within the source for the application. Strip-Prefix is used to remove any prefix in the URL before passing the path to the file server to find. When serving a subpath in your application, this is needed to find the right files.

This approach has two gotchas that you should be aware of. The first has to do with generating error pages, which includes the common 404 Not Found error. You may want to customize these pages in your website or application. It's common to have stylized or even specialized error pages to help end users. FileServer and ServeFile return a basic error message as text. It's not a web page, but rather English text that browsers display on a white background. There's no opportunity to change how these are displayed or what language they're displayed in while using `FileServer` or `Serve-File`. Technique 40 provides a method to make these changes.

The second gotcha when serving a directory of files is simpler to work around. When serving a directory and its subdirectories, you need a path-resolution method that will work for subdirectories. For example, if the `path` package is used in order to resolve wildcard paths, you'd be limited to the base directory. Paying attention to path resolution is important if your application serves files and generates other content. To illustrate the problem, let's look at the `pathResolver` from listing 2.17 along with the following `main` function in listing 7.4.

TIP   Wildcard path routing is covered in chapter 2. Listing 2.17 provides a simple example relating to the problem described here.

Listing 7.4   Using `path` package path resolution

```go
func main() {
    pr := newPathResolver()
    pr.Add("GET /hello", hello)

    dir := http.Dir("./files")
    handler := http.StripPrefix("/static/", http.FileServer(dir))
    pr.Add("GET /static/*", handler.ServeHTTP)

    http.ListenAndServe(":8080", pr)
}
```

This code is set up to serve both content and files. A file in the files directory will be served, but any subdirectories of files won't have their files served. This is because the `*` used as a wildcard in the `path` package stays at one directory level. The solution is to use a different method for path resolution, such as the regular expression method described in chapter 2.

TECHNIQUE 40   **File server with custom error pages**

The built-in file server in the Go standard library generates error pages, including the common 404 Not Found error for you. This is presented as English text, rather than a web page, and can't be changed.

What if you're building an application for those who don't know English? Or what if you want to build response pages to help people find the content they're looking for when they ended up with a Not Found error? These are common situations.

PROBLEM

How can you specify your own error pages, including a response to a file not being found, when your application is serving files?

SOLUTION

Use a custom file server that allows you to specify handlers for error pages. The `github.com/Masterminds/go-fileserver` package provides functionality to complement the built-in file server while enabling custom error handling.

DISCUSSION

FileServer and ServeFile both rely on the function ServeContent in the http package. That function calls private functions within the package that use the functions Error and NotFound to produce these responses. Error handling is baked in at the lowest levels. To alter these, you need to build your own file server. This can either be something entirely new or a fork of the file server from the standard library.

The package github.com/Masterminds/go-fileserver is a fork of the file server in the standard library. This fork adds the ability to use custom error handlers, including the common 404 Not Found response. It's designed to be used alongside the http package in the standard library, only providing file-serving elements not already in the standard library. To illustrate how this file server works, let's look at the following listing.

Listing 7.5   Custom file server error pages: file_not_found.go

```
package main

import (
    "fmt"
    fs "github.com/Masterminds/go-fileserver"          ◁——  Imports the file
    "net/http"                                               server package
)
                                                        Sets a function to call
func main() {                                              when no file found
    fs.NotFoundHandler = func(w http.ResponseWriter, req *http.Request)
        w.Header().Set("Content-Type", "text/plain; charset=utf-8")
        fmt.Fprintln(w, "The requested page could not be found.")
    }

    dir := http.Dir("./files")
    http.ListenAndServe(":8080", fs.FileServer(dir))   ◁——  Uses built-in web
}                                                            server and custom
                                                             file server
```

Sets up a directory to
serve files from

This example is similar to the file server in the standard library, with a couple of differences. First, a handler function is set for the case when no file is found. Anytime a file isn't found, this function will write the response. Although it's not used here, a custom function can be set for all error responses as well. The setup to serve a directory of files is the same as the file server in the standard library. An http.Dir instance is created for the directory of files to serve. The second difference has to do with serving the files. Rather than using http.FileServer, the function fs.FileServer is used. This function will make sure the proper error handlers are called.

NOTE   github.com/Masterminds/go-fileserver was created for this book. Because of the size of the codebase, which would have spanned many pages, and the useful nature of the file server, it was released as a package to be used in applications.

TECHNIQUE 41   **Caching file server**

In some cases, it's too time-consuming to read a file from the filesystem or other file source each time you want to serve it. Instead, it would be faster to cache and serve some files from memory, skipping calls to disk altogether.

Speedy file serving can eliminate slowdowns on high-traffic websites. Web caches such as Varnish have become popular and are used on many of the most popular websites and applications. You could put a web cache in front of a Go application to cache files such as images, CSS, and JavaScript to serve them from memory. In some cases, a useful alternative to an external application is to store files in memory in your Go application and serve the files yourself.

PROBLEM

Instead of serving static files from the filesystem each time they're requested, you want to cache files in memory in order to quickly serve responses to requests.

SOLUTION

Store files in memory when they're first requested and serve responses using `Serve-Content` rather than a file server.

DISCUSSION

Most of the time, it's appropriate to use a reverse proxy, such as the popular open source project Varnish, to handle caching and serving of files quickly. For those occasions, it's appropriate to cache commonly used files in memory. The following listing shows how to load a file from disk and serve it from memory.

Listing 7.6   Load and serve static files from memory: cache_serving.go

```go
package main

import (
    "bytes"
    "io"
    "net/http"
    "os"
    "sync"
    "time"
)

type cacheFile struct {
    content io.ReadSeeker          Data structure to store
    modTime time.Time              a file in memory
}
var cache map[string]*cacheFile    Mutex to handle race
var mutex = new(sync.RWMutex)      conditions while handling
                                   parallel cache changes
func main() {
    cache = make(map[string]*cacheFile)    Makes the map usable
    http.HandleFunc("/", serveFiles)
    http.ListenAndServe(":8080", nil)
}
```

Map to store files in memory →

```
func serveFiles(res http.ResponseWriter, req *http.Request) {
    mutex.RLock()
    v, found := cache[req.URL.Path]
    mutex.RUnlock()

    if !found {
        mutex.Lock()
        defer mutex.Unlock()
        fileName := "./files" + req.URL.Path
        f, err := os.Open(fileName)
        defer f.Close()

        if err != nil {
            http.NotFound(res, req)
            return
        }

        var b bytes.Buffer
        _, err = io.Copy(&b, f)
        if err != nil {
            http.NotFound(res, req)
            return
        }
        r := bytes.NewReader(b.Bytes())

        info, _ := f.Stat()
        v := &cacheFile{
            content: r,
            modTime: info.ModTime(),
        }
        cache[req.URL.Path] = v
    }

    http.ServeContent(res, req, req.URL.Path, v.modTime, v.content)
}
```

Annotations:
- **Loads from the cache if it's already populated**
- **When the file isn't in the cache, starts loading process**
- **Maps can't be written to concurrently or be read while being written to. Using a mutex prevents this from happening.**
- **Opens the file to cache, making sure to defer the close**
- **Handles an error when a file can't be opened**
- **Copies the file to an in-memory buffer**
- **Handles errors copying from file to memory**
- **Puts the bytes into a Reader for later use**
- **Populates the cache object and stores it for later**
- **Serves the file from cache**

This example opens with a data structure to hold the content in memory. When serving the data, the time and the content are important. The time can be sent to browsers and used as part of the If-Modified-Since HTTP header. Although it's not covered here, a time value can be used to look over the cache and clear old items from the cache. Monitoring the memory use of the cache and removing stale items can be useful.

Inside the server handler function serving the files, the first step is to try to get the file from the in-memory cache. Go's multiple return handling on a map allows you to find out whether an item was in the cache and get the value from the cache. Around the lookup, mutex.RLock and mutex.RUnlock calls are made as part of the setup to prevent race conditions by parallel requests modifying the cache. These calls are on a RWMutex object from the sync package. RWMutex enables an arbitrary number of readers or one writer to have access at a time. RLock and RUnlock are for readers. You'll see the writer in a moment.

If the file wasn't stored in the cache, the process begins to load the file and populate the cache. Because cache will be updated and you don't want parallel requests updating the same `cache` item, `mutex.Lock` is called. This waits for any current readers or writers to complete while blocking any future ones. Releasing the lock so that readers and other writers can access `cache` is done by deferring the `mutex.UnLock` call.

After the lock is in place, an attempt is made to load the file from the filesystem, with the closing of the file being deferred to the exit of the function. If the file isn't found or another error occurs, the 404 Not Found message is displayed. This is a place where you could optionally cache File Not Found responses and log the error messages.

The content of the file is copied into `Buffer`, and then the bytes are transferred into a `Reader` instance. This happens because `Buffer` can be written to. The content of the `File` can be copied into it. `Reader` implements both the `io.Reader` and `io.Seeker` interfaces needed by `ServeContent`. To take advantage of the `If-Modified-Since` HTTP header, the last modified time is retrieved from the file and stored in the cache alongside the content itself.

Finally, the cached file is served using `ServeContent`. This function does a lot of work for you. Looking at the requested filename, it attempts to figure out the MIME type and set the proper headers. It looks at the last modified time and sets the headers to provide 304 Not Modified HTTP responses where appropriate. When it serves the content, it figures out information such as the content length to set the appropriate headers.

> **TIP** Using a memory-caching service such as groupcache (https://github
> .com/golang/groupcache) can provide a shared memory cache between servers. This is useful when the file storage isn't local, a common situation in file serving at scale.

Serving files from memory is something that should be done with care. Loading many files into memory without monitoring runtime memory or cleaning up can cause problems. These should be monitored and managed, and what's kept in memory should be optimized for your use cases. You don't want a server running out of memory or an application's memory footprint to grow unwatched or unregulated.

TECHNIQUE 42   Embedding files in a binary

Sometimes you'll want to include assets right inside the application binary. Then, instead of looking for them on the filesystem, they're included in the application binary. This can be useful when distributing an application. The binary is the only thing needing to be distributed, rather than a collection of files to accompany it.

PROBLEM

You want to include static assets, such as images or stylesheets, in a Go binary.

SOLUTION

Store the assets as data assigned to variables in your application. Serve files from these variables instead of the filesystem. Because of the intricate nature of converting files' bytes and referencing them within your code, use the `github.com/GeertJohan/` `go.rice` package and command-line application to automate this process for you.

DISCUSSION

The idea is simple. Convert a file into bytes, store those bytes and the related information in a variable, and use the variable to serve the file via `ServeContent` from the `http` package. Implementing a conversion process yourself while taking into account the changing state of those files during development, testing, and builds isn't straight-forward. That's why we recommend using a package, such as `go.rice`, to handle this process for you.

go.rice enables you to work with files from the filesystem during development (for example, when using `go run`), to use files embedded in the built binary, and to build files into binaries. The following listing showcases simple file serving using `go.rice`.

Listing 7.7 Embedding files in binaries with `go.rice`: embedded_files.go

```
package main

import (
        "github.com/GeertJohan/go.rice"        <—┐  Imports go.rice to handle
        "net/http"                                │  file locations for you
)

func main() {                                        Creates a box to
        box := rice.MustFindBox("../files/")    <——  represent a location
        httpbox := box.HTTPBox()                      on the filesystem
        http.ListenAndServe(":8080", http.FileServer(httpbox))   <—┐
}
    └─> Serves files from the box           An HTTPBox provides files using
                                            the http.FileSystem interface
```

Using `go.rice` has a similar style to serving from the filesystem. Instead of using `http.Dir` to specify the directory, `rice.MustFindBox` is used with the filesystem location. Serving of the files happens using the built-in `FileServer` from the `http` package. Instead of passing in an `http.Dir` object, an `HTTPBox` object is passed in. `HTTPBox` provides the `http.FileSystem` interface that's needed for `FileServer`.

If this code is run using `go run`, it will get the files from the filesystem. Building a binary with the files included takes an extra step. For this extra step, you'll need the `rice` tool that can be installed from a command line as follows:

```
$ go get github.com/GeertJohan/go.rice/rice
```

After this tool is installed, you can build a Go binary with the following two commands:

```
$ rice embed-go
$ go build
```

The first command, `rice embed-go`, converts the real filesystem elements into a virtual filesystem inside Go files. This includes the content of the files. It's important to know that this command uses os.Walk, which doesn't walk symlinks. The go build command builds a binary normally. This binary will include the rice-built Go files containing the virtual filesystem.

> **TIP**   Using minification techniques on the files being embedded, such as removing unneeded whitespace from CSS and JavaScript files, can reduce the size of the Go binary that's generated.

The go.rice package can be used with templates. The following listing provides an example of loading a template from a box.

Listing 7.8   Templates as embedded files

```
box := rice.MustFindBox("templates")
templateString, err := box.String("example.html")
if err != nil {
    log.Fatal(err)
}
```

Gets a box pointing to a templates directory

Retrieves the template, which can be used with template Parse functions, as a string from the box

The go.rice package provides other helpers for the process of working with embedded files. The documentation at https://github.com/GeertJohan/go.rice gets into the specifics of what you can do with the helper functionality.

TECHNIQUE 43   **Serving from an alternative location**

At times you'll want to store and serve the files separately from the application. A common example is serving a web application's JavaScript, CSS, and other assets from a content delivery network (CDN).

PROBLEM

Instead of serving files through the same server as your application, you want to serve files through an alternative location. The alternative location needs to work with multiple environments such as your production, testing, and development environments.

SOLUTION

Serve the files from alternative locations, such as a CDN in production. For each environment, manage the deployment of files alongside the application and pass the location into the application as configuration. Use the location within your template files to tell browsers where to get the files from.

DISCUSSION

In each environment, you'll want to have a copy or a representative copy of the application's assets. Although these files may be served separately from the application pages, they shouldn't be used from a single source for all environments. This clean separation, illustrated in figure 7.2, allows any testing environments to be full testing environments, allows developers to be creative in development environments, and

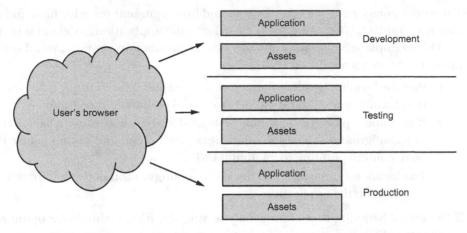

Figure 7.2   A browser fetches a different application and asset set in each environment.

enables safe development and testing whereby a slip-up in development or testing doesn't impact production users.

When the location of the files is different in each environment, the location needs to be passed into the application as configuration. This can happen via a shared configuration service such as etcd, in configuration files, as arguments passed into the application at startup time, or some other means of passing configuration. The following listing provides a basic example of passing a location in as a command-line argument.

Listing 7.9   Passing a URL location to a template

```go
var t *template.Template
var l = flag.String("location", "http://localhost:8080", "A location.")

var tpl = `<!DOCTYPE HTML>
<html>
  <head>
    <meta charset="utf-8">
    <title>A Demo</title>
    <link rel="stylesheet" href="{{.Location}}/styles.css">
  </head>
  <body>
    <p>A demo.</p>
  </body>
</html>`

func servePage(res http.ResponseWriter, req *http.Request) {
    data := struct{ Location *string }{
        Location: l,
    }
    t.Execute(res, data)
}
```

Gets the location of the static files from the application arguments

The path to the CSS is relative to the location.

An HTTP handler passing the location into the template

This rudimentary example takes a command-line argument for a location and uses it within a template. When no value is passed into the application, a default is used.

This example serves to illustrate the idea. In production software, you'd use something more complicated:

1 Pass the location in as configuration. See chapter 2 for multiple ways you can do this, including configuration files, etcd, and command-line arguments.
2 If no value is passed in, it should be logged and possibly cause a panic. The lack of a configuration value shouldn't allow production, and testing before that, to serve content pointing to an invalid URL.
3 The location can be attached to a global configuration object and reused across responses in the application.

If the server handling these files is only serving the files, it should be optimized for serving static files. For example, if you're using an Apache web server, you can turn off modules you don't need.

HTTP/2, the most recent version of the HTTP specification, provides features that may cause you to consider serving files along with application pages. For example, when a browser requests a page, an HTTP/2 server can respond with the page and any associated files for the page. The associated files can be sent to the browser even before it requests them, and all of the files can be sent over the original connection requesting the page. For this to happen, the server needs to serve the application and files.

> **NOTE** The HTTP/2 specification is documented in RFC 7540 by the Internet Engineering Task Force. You can read it at https://tools.ietf.org/html/rfc7540.

Serving content is only half of the process for modern interactive applications. To complete the cycle, the server needs to handle interaction from users.

7.2   Handling form posts

Working with HTML forms and POST or PUT requests in general is common in web applications and websites. Go provides much of what you need in the http package within the standard library. Although the functionality is available under the hood, it's not always obvious how you should use it. The following patterns highlight methods for working with data, whether it's a form submission or a multipart POST or PUT request.

7.2.1   Introduction to form requests

When a request is made to a server and it contains form data, that request isn't processed into a usable structure by default. Most of the request handling across most Go programs doesn't need to work with form data, so it's a feature you need to opt into. Opting in is fairly straightforward. The following example shows the simplest way to parse form data and get access to it:

```go
func exampleHandler(w http.ResponseWriter, r *http.Request) {
    name := r.FormValue("name")
}
```

Behind this call to `FormValue`, a lot is going on. `FormValue` starts by parsing the form data into a Go data structure. In this case, it's looking to parse text form data and multipart form data, such as files. After the data is parsed, it looks up the key (form field name) and returns the first value for the key, if one exists. If there's nothing with this key, an empty string is returned.

Although this case makes it look easy, a lot is going on that you may not want, and there are features that you can't access here. For example, what if you want to skip looking for multipart form data and trying to parse it because you know it won't be present? Or what if a form field has multiple values, and you want to get at all of them?

The first step to work with form data is to parse it (see listing 7.10). Inside a request handler are two methods on the `Request` object that can parse form data into a Go data structure. The `ParseForm` method parses fields that contain text. If you need to work with binary data or files from the form, you need to use `ParseMultipartForm`. As its name suggests, this method works on multipart form data (a form containing content with different MIME content types). `ParseMultipartForm` is called by `FormValue` in the preceding example if parsing hasn't happened yet.

The form data is parsed into two locations:

- The `Form` property on the `Request` object will contain the values from the URL query along with the values submitted as a `POST` or `PUT` body. Each key on `Form` is an array of values. The `FormValue` method on `Request` can be used to get the first value for a key. That's the value sitting in the `0` key of the array on `Form`.
- When you want the values from the `POST` or `PUT` body without those from the URL query, you can use the `PostForm` property on the `Request` object. Like `FormValue`, the `PostFormValue` method can retrieve the first value from `PostForm` for a key.

Listing 7.10 Parsing a simple form response

```go
func exampleHandler(w http.ResponseWriter, r *http.Request) {
    err := r.ParseForm()          ◄───────         Parses a simple form containing
    if err != nil {                                only text-based fields
        fmt.Println(err)
    }                                              Handles any errors that
    name := r.FormValue("name")   ◄───            occurred parsing the form
}
            Gets the first value for the
            name field from the form
```

This listing contains the handling for a simple form. This simple example works for forms with only text fields. If a file field were present, it wouldn't be parsed or accessible. And it works only for form values that have a single response. HTML forms allow for multiple responding values. Both of these are covered in the following techniques.

TECHNIQUE 44   Accessing multiple values for a form field

Form fields can have more than one value for a name. A common example is check boxes on a form. You can have a multiple select list using check boxes that, in the HTML, all have the same name.

PROBLEM

`FormValue` and `PostFormValue` each return the first value for a form field. When you have multiple values, how can you access all of them?

SOLUTION

Instead of using `FormValue` and `PostFormValue` to retrieve a field value, look up the field on the `Form` or `PostForm` properties on the `Request` object. Then iterate over all the values.

DISCUSSION

When a form field has more than one value, you'll need to do a little more work to access it. The following listing shows how to parse a form and retrieve multiple values for a field.

Listing 7.11   Parsing a form with multiple values for a field

```
func exampleHandler(w http.ResponseWriter, r *http.Request) {       ◁─────  The maximum memory to store file
    maxMemory := 16 << 20                                                   parts, where rest is stored to disk
    err := r.ParseMultipartForm(maxMemory)        ◁─────── Parses a multipart form
    if err != nil {
            fmt.Println(err)                      Handles any error
    }                                             parsing the form
    for k, v := range r.PostForm["names"] {       Iterates over all the POST
            fmt.Println(v)                        values of the names form field
    }
}
```

The HTTP handler function opens by defining a number for the maximum amount of memory to use when parsing a multipart form. In this case, the number is 16 megabytes. When `ParseMultipartForm` is called, the maximum amount of memory for storing file parts needs to be specified. Parts of files larger than this number will be stored to disk. The default number used when `FormValue` or `PostFormValue` needs to call `ParseMultipartForm` is 32 megabytes.

Instead of using `FormValue` or `PostFormValue` to obtain the first value for a form field, all the values of the `names` form field are iterated over. The `names` field on the `PostForm` property is used, limiting the values to just those submitted in the POST or PUT body.

> TIP   When presenting forms to users and processing forms, use security elements such as a cross-site request forgery (CSRF) token. For more information, see https://en.wikipedia.org/wiki/Cross-site_request_forgery.

7.2.2   *Working with files and multipart submissions*

After you move from text handling into file handling and multipart submissions that contain more than one type of content, the way you handle the processing changes. In its simplest form, you can see this when you upload a file via an online form. The file has a content type, such as an image, and the other text fields on the form. That's at least two types of content that need different handling.

In this section, you'll explore the handling of multipart submissions often thought of as file handling. These submissions can come in via simple and fast file uploads or large files that need special handling.

TECHNIQUE 45   Uploading a single file

Working with files is different from working with the input from text fields. Each file is a binary file with surrounding metadata.

PROBLEM

When a file is uploaded with a form, how to you process and save it?

SOLUTION

When a file is uploaded, process the form as a multipart form by using `Process-MultipartForm` on the `Request` object. This picks up the file parts. Then use the `FormFile` method on the `Request` object to access and file fields, uploading a single file. For each file, you can access the metadata and a file object that's similar to `File` objects from the `os` package.

DISCUSSION

Handling a file is nearly as straightforward as handling text form data. The difference lies in the binary file and the metadata surrounding it, such as the filename. The following listing presents a simple file-upload form.

Listing 7.12   A form with a single-value file-upload field

```
<!doctype html>
<html>
  <head>
    <title>File Upload</title>
  </head>
  <body>
    <form action="/" method="POST" enctype="multipart/form-data">
      <label for="file">File:</label>
      <input type="file" name="file" id="file">
      <br>
      <button type="submit" name="submit">Submit</button>
    </form>
  </body>
</html>
```

The form must be multipart for file uploads.

A single-value file field with the name "file"

A button is needed to submit the form.

This form has some important parts. The form method is POST, and its encoding is in multipart. Being multipart allows the text part of the form to be uploaded and processed as text, while the file is handled using its own file type. The input field is typed for a file, which tells browsers to use a file picker and upload the contents of the file. This form is served and processed by the handler function for the `http` package in the following listing.

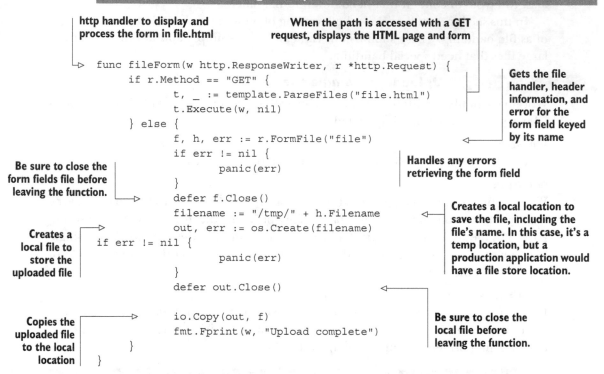

Listing 7.13 Handle a single file upload

```
                                When the path is accessed with a GET
http handler to display and     request, displays the HTML page and form
process the form in file.html

func fileForm(w http.ResponseWriter, r *http.Request) {
    if r.Method == "GET" {                              Gets the file
        t, _ := template.ParseFiles("file.html")        handler, header
        t.Execute(w, nil)                               information, and
    } else {                                            error for the
        f, h, err := r.FormFile("file")                 form field keyed
        if err != nil {                                 by its name
            panic(err)              Handles any errors
        }                          retrieving the form field
        defer f.Close()
        filename := "/tmp/" + h.Filename     Creates a local location to
        out, err := os.Create(filename)      save the file, including the
        if err != nil {                      file's name. In this case, it's a
            panic(err)                        temp location, but a
        }                                     production application would
        defer out.Close()                     have a file store location.

        io.Copy(out, f)
        fmt.Fprint(w, "Upload complete")
    }
}
```

Be sure to close the form fields file before leaving the function.

Creates a local file to store the uploaded file

Copies the uploaded file to the local location

Be sure to close the local file before leaving the function.

This handler, meant to be used with the web server in the `http` package, handles both displaying the form and processing the submitted form. It opens by detecting the method for the request. When a GET request is submitted, it returns the form from listing 7.12. When another HTTP method is used, such as a POST or PUT request, the form submission is processed.

The first step used to process the file field is to retrieve it by using the `FormFile` method on the `Request`. If the form hasn't been parsed, `FormFile` will call `ParseMultipartForm`. `FormFile` then returns a `multipart.File` object, a `*multipart.FileHeader` object, and an error if there is one. The `*multipart.FileHeader` object has a `Filename` property that it uses here as part of the location on the local filesystem to store the upload. To save the file locally, a new file is created on the filesystem and the contents of the upload are copied into this new file.

This solution works well for a field with a single file. HTML forms allow for multivalue fields, and this solution will pick up only the first of the files. For multivalue file uploads, see the next technique.

TECHNIQUE 46   **Uploading multiple files**

File fields on forms can optionally have the `multiple` attribute. When this attribute is on the input element, any number of files can be uploaded. In this case, using `Form-File` won't work to process the form. It assumes there's only one file per input field and will return only the first file.

PROBLEM

How do you process the files when multiple files are uploaded to a single file-input field on a form?

SOLUTION

Instead of using `FormFile`, which handles single files, parse the form and retrieve a slice with the files from the `MultipartForm` property on the `Request`. Then iterate over the slice, individually handling each file.

DISCUSSION

An input field handling multiple files needs to have only the `multiple` attribute on it. For example, the difference between the following listing and the single file-upload form in listing 7.12 is the `multiple` attribute.

> **Listing 7.14   A form with a multiple value file-upload field**

```
<!doctype html>
<html>
  <head>
    <title>File Upload</title>                       The form must be
  </head>                                        multipart for file uploads.
  <body>
    <form action="/" method="POST" enctype="multipart/form-data">  ◁─┐
      <label for="files">File:</label>
      <input type="file" name="files" id="files" multiple>
      <br>
      <button type="submit" name="submit">Submit</button>
    </form>
  </body>
</html>                                         A multivalue file field with
                                                 the name "files" and the
A button is needed to                              multiple attribute
submit the form.
```

This form, with the multipart encoding, has an input to handle multiple files. The `multiple` attribute turns a single file-input field into one accepting multiple files. The following listing processes this form to handle multiple files.

Listing 7.15   Process file form field with multiple files

http handler to display and process the form in file_multiple.html

When the path is accessed with a GET request, displays the HTML page and form

```go
func fileForm(w http.ResponseWriter, r *http.Request) {
    if r.Method == "GET" {
        t, _ := template.ParseFiles("file_multiple.html")
        t.Execute(w, nil)
    } else {
        err := r.ParseMultipartForm(16 << 20)
        if err != nil {
            fmt.Fprint(w, err)
            return
        }

        data := r.MultipartForm
        files := data.File["files"]
        for _, fh := range files {
            f, err := fh.Open()
            defer f.Close()
            if err != nil {
                fmt.Fprint(w, err)
                return
            }

            out, err := os.Create("/tmp/" + fh.Filename)
            defer out.Close()
            if err != nil {
                fmt.Fprint(w, err)
                return
            }

            _, err = io.Copy(out, f)

            if err != nil {
                fmt.Fprintln(w, err)
                return
            }
        }

        fmt.Fprint(w, "Upload complete")
    }
}
```

Parses the form in the request and handles any errors

Retrieves a slice, keyed by the input name, containing the files from the MultipartForm

Iterates over the files uploaded to the files field

Be sure to close and handle any errors opening a file handler.

Opens a file handler for one of the uploaded files

Creates a local file to store the contents of the uploaded file

Be sure to close and handle any errors when creating a local file.

Copies the uploaded file to the location on the filesystem

Handles any errors copying the uploaded file to the local file

This listing contains a handler function for the web server in the http package. It opens by presenting the form if the request is a GET request rather than one posting a form. When a request other than a GET request occurs, it handles the form submission.

Before you can work with the form fields, the form needs to be processed. Calling ParseMultipartForm on the Request object causes the form to be parsed. This is handled internally by methods such as FormFile used in previous techniques. The value passed in sets the amount of memory to use for holding form data in memory to 16 MB and the rest of the files will be written to disk as temporary files.

After the form has been parsed, the fields are available on `MultipartForm`. The uploads to the file-input field with the name `files` are available on the `File` property of `MultipartForm` as a slice of values. Each value is a `*multipart.FileHeader` object.

Iterate over the files to process each of them. Calling the `Open` method on a `*multipart.FileHeader` object returns `File`, a handler for the file. To save the file to disk, you need to create a new file somewhere to save the contents. The name of the uploaded file is available in the `Filename` property on the `*multipart.FileHeader`. After you have a local location to store the contents, copy the uploaded file to the local file by using `io.Copy`.

This solution requires moving a level lower in the package API. In doing so, you open up a little more power while needing to handle a little more on your own.

TECHNIQUE 47   Verify uploaded file is allowed type

When a file is uploaded, it could be any type of file. The upload field could be expecting an image, a document, or something else altogether. But is that what was uploaded? How would you handle an improper file being uploaded?

Client-side detection is sometimes seen as an option. For example, input fields with a type of file can have an `accept` property with a list of extensions or MIME types, also referred to as *content types*. Unfortunately, the `accept` property isn't implemented in all browsers. Even in the browsers where it works, the ability to easily alter the value makes it unreliable. Type checking needs to happen in your application.

PROBLEM

How can you detect the type of file uploaded to a file field inside your application?

SOLUTION

To get the MIME type for a file, you can use one of a few ways, with varying degrees of trust in the value:

- When a file is uploaded, the request headers will have a `Content-Type` field with either a specific content type, such as image/png, or a general value of application/octet-stream.
- A file extension is associated with a MIME type and can provide insight into the type of file being uploaded.
- You can parse the file and detect the content type based on the contents of the file.

DISCUSSION

The three solutions have varying degrees of trust. The `Content-Type` field is set by the application doing the uploading, and the file extension is set by the user uploading the file. These two methods rely on outside parties for accuracy and trust. The third solution requires parsing the file and knowing what to look for to map to a content type. This is the most difficult method and uses the most system resources, but is also the most trusted one. To understand how to use these methods, you'll look at each of them.

When a file is uploaded, as you saw in techniques 45 and 46, a *multipart.File-Header object is available to interact with. This is the second of the responses from FormFile on the Request object. The *multipart.FileHeader object has a property named Header with all of the uploaded header fields including the content type. For example:

```
file, header, err := r.FormFile("file")
contentType := header.Header["Content-Type"][0]
```

Here FormFile is called on a field with the name file. Header fields can be multivalue. In this case, you'll need to get the first one, even if there's only one value. The content type here will either be a specific MIME type, such as image/png, or a generic value of application/octet-stream when the type was unknown.

An alternative to the uploaded header value, the filename's file extension can provide insight into the type of file. The mime package includes the function TypeByExtension that attempts to return the MIME type based on the file extension. For example:

```
file, header, err := r.FormFile("file")
extension := filepath.Ext(header.Filename)
type := mime.TypeByExtension(extension)
```

Determining the type based on the file extension provides only some degree of accuracy. File extensions can be changed. The standard library contains a limited extension to MIME type mapping but is capable of reaching out to the operating system to retrieve a larger list.

Another option is to parse the file and determine the type from the file itself. You can perform this type of operation in two ways. The http package contains the function DetectContentType, capable of detecting the type for a limited number of file types. These include HTML, text, XML, PDF, PostScript, common image formats, compressed files such as RAR, Zip, and GZip, wave audio files, and WebM video files.

The following example showcases the DetectContentType function:

```
file, header, err := r.FormFile("file")
buffer := make([]byte, 512)
_, err = file.Read(buffer)
filetype := http.DetectContentType(buffer)
```

The buffer is only 512 bytes because DetectContentType looks at only up to the first 512 bytes when determining the type. When it isn't able to detect a specific type, application/octet-stream is returned.

The limited list of content types DetectContentType can detect means you'll need another method if you want to detect other common formats such as Microsoft Word documents, MP4 files, or many other common formats. To parse and detect these other formats, the easiest method is to integrate with an external MIME sniffing library such as the widely used libmagic. At the time of writing, several Go packages provide bindings to libmagic, making it easy to use from within Go.

> **NOTE**   A specification to sniff MIME types is available at http://mimesniff.spec .whatwg.org/.

7.2.3 Working with raw multipart data

The previous file-handling techniques work well when you're dealing with small files or files as a whole, but limit your ability to work with files while they're being uploaded. For example, if you're writing a proxy and want to immediately transfer the file to another location, the previous techniques will cache large files on the proxy.

The Go standard library provides both high-level helper functions for common file-handling situations, and lower-level access that can be used for the less common ones or when you want to define your own handling.

The handler function for a request is executed when a request begins, rather than when a request is completed. Many requests happen quickly, and the helper functions account for any delay. If you work with, for example, large files, you have an opportunity to act while uploads are happening.

Instead of using the `ParseMultipartForm` method on the `Request` object inside an `http` handler function, you can access the raw stream of the request by accessing the underlying `*multipart.Reader` object. This object is accessible by using the `MultipartReader` method on the `Request`.

The following technique uses the lower-level multipart handling. This illustrates how it works in addition to handling some common cases.

TECHNIQUE 48   Incrementally saving a file

Imagine that you're building a system meant to handle a lot of large file uploads. The files aren't stored on your API server but are instead stored in a back-end service designed for files. Using `ParseMultipartForm` is going to put those files into the temporary files directory on your API server while the uploads are in progress. To support large file uploads with `ParseMultipartForm` handling, your server would need a large disk cache for the files and careful handling to make sure it doesn't get full while parallel uploads are happening.

PROBLEM

You want to save the file, as it's being uploaded, to a location of your choice. That location could be on the server, on a shared drive, or on another location altogether.

SOLUTION

Instead of using `ParseMultipartForm`, read the multipart data from the request as it's being uploaded. This can be accessed with the `MultipartReader` method on the `Request`. As files and other information are coming in, chunk by chunk, save and process the parts rather than wait for uploads to complete.

DISCUSSION

Using an API server as a pass-through for data on its way to a final destination is a common model. You'll often see nonfile data being stored in a database. Large file handling or handling a lot of files concurrently presents a problem in local resources, in storing that much information as a cache on its way to the final location. An easy solution is to pass the problem on to the final destination, which should already be able to handle storing large files. Don't cache them locally if you don't need to.

The way to access the multipart stream directly, which is what `ParseMultipartForm` does, is to retrieve the reader from the `Request` with `MultipartReader`. After you have the reader, you can loop over the parts and read each one as it comes in.

When you process a multipart form, you'll often want to process file fields along with text fields. The following listing contains a simple form with a text field, file field, and Submit button.

> **Listing 7.16   HTML form containing a file and text field**

```
<!doctype html>
<html>
  <head>
    <title>File Upload</title>
  </head>
  <body>
    <form action="/" method="POST" enctype="multipart/form-data">
      <label for="name">Name:</label>
      <input type="text" name="name" id="name">          ⊲ A text input field
      <br>
      <label for="file">File:</label>
      <input type="file" name="file" id="file">          ⊲ A file field input field requiring
      <br>                                                    the form to be multipart
      <button type="submit" name="submit">Submit</button>  ⊲ A Submit button
    </form>                                                      also available as
  </body>                                                        a field
</html>
```

The next listing contains an `http` handler function to display and process the form in listing 7.16. This handler function displays the form, processes the form, and incrementally saves the file.

> **Listing 7.17   Incrementally save uploaded files**

http handler to display and
process the form in file_plus.html

When the path is accessed with a GET request,
displays the HTML page and form path is accessed
with a GET request, displays the HTML page and form

```
func fileForm(w http.ResponseWriter, r *http.Request) {
    if r.Method == "GET" {
        t, _ := template.ParseFiles("file_plus.html")
        t.Execute(w, nil)
    } else {
```

A map to store form field values not relating to files

10 megabyte counter for nonfile field size

Retrieves the name of the form field, continuing the loop if there's no name

If there's no filename, treats it as a text field

If there's an error reading the contents of the part, handles the error

Using a byte counter, makes sure the total size of text fields isn't too large

Puts the content for the form field into a map for later access

Closes the file when exiting the http handler

```go
mr, err := r.MultipartReader()
if err != nil {
        panic("Failed to read multipart message")
}

values := make(map[string][]string)
maxValueBytes := int64(10 << 20)
for {
        part, err := mr.NextPart()
        if err == io.EOF {
                break
        }

        name := part.FormName()
        if name == "" {
                continue
        }

        filename := part.FileName()
        var b bytes.Buffer
        if filename == "" {
                n, err := io.CopyN(&b, part, maxValueBytes)
                if err != nil && err != io.EOF {
                        fmt.Fprint(w, "Error processing form")
                        return
                }
                maxValueBytes -= n
                if maxValueBytes == 0 {
                        msg := "multipart message too large"
                        fmt.Fprint(w, msg)
                        return
                }
                values[name] = append(values[name],b.String())
                continue
        }

        dst, err := os.Create("/tmp/" + filename)
        defer dst.Close()
        if err != nil {
                return
        }
        for {
                buffer := make([]byte, 100000)
                cBytes, err := part.Read(buffer)
                if err == io.EOF {
                        break
                }
                dst.Write(buffer[0:cBytes])
        }
}

fmt.Fprint(w, "Upload complete")
}
}
```

Retrieves the multipart reader giving access to the uploaded files and handles any errors

Continues looping until all of the multipart message has been read

Attempts to read the next part, breaking the loop if the end of the request is reached

Retrieves the name of the file if one exists

A buffer to read the value of a text field into

Copies the contents of the part into a buffer

Creates a location on the filesystem to store the content of a file

As the file content of a part is uploaded, writes it to the file

This code opens with an `http` handler function. When it receives a GET HTTP request, it responds with an HTML form. When that form is posted, it processes the form.

Because the handler function parses the form, instead of relying on `Parse-MultipartForm`, you have a few elements to set up before working with the form itself. For access to the data on the form as it comes in, you'll need access to a reader. The `MultipartReader` method on the `Request` object returns `*mime.Reader`, which you can use to iterate over the multipart body of the request. This reader consumes input as needed. For the form fields not being handled as files, you need a place to store the values. Here a map is created to store the values.

After the setup is complete, the handler iterates over the parts of the multipart message. The loop starts by attempting to retrieve the next part of the multipart message. If there are no more parts, an `io.EOF` error is returned and the function breaks out of the parsing loop. *EOF* stands for the *end of the file.*

The parsing loop can now start handling the parts of the message. It first checks for the name of the form field by using the `FormName` method and continues the loop if there's no name. Files will have a filename in addition to the name of the field. This can be retrieved by using the `FileName` method. The existence of a filename is a way to distinguish between file and text-field handling.

When there's no filename, the handler copies the value of the content of the field into a buffer and decrements a size counter that starts at 10 megabytes. If the size counter runs down to 0, the parser returns and provides an error. This is put in place as a protection against text-field content being too large and consuming too much memory. 10 MB is quite large and is the default value inside `ParseMultipartForm` as well. If no errors occur, the content of the text form field is stored in the `values` map previously created and the parsing loop continues on the next part.

If the parsing loop has reached this point, the form field is a file. A file on the operating system is created to store the contents of the file. At this point, an alternative location such as cloud storage could be used to write the file to. Instead of creating a file on the operating system, a connection to another storage system could be opened. After the destination is opened, the handler loops over the content of the part, iteratively reading it as it comes in. Until a notification of the end of the part, designated with an `io.EOF` error, comes in, the bytes are written to the destination as they arrive. For example, if you use this to upload a large file, you can watch the data slowly being written to the output file while the upload is happening. After the loop completes, the files are all available on disk and the text fields are available on the `values` map.

7.3 Summary

Serving files and working with forms are common elements in any web application. They're staples of the web, and their use goes back decades. This chapter covered methods to use them while taking advantage of Go's helper functionality and power. These include the following:

- Uploading files to users from a Go server in a variety of ways, depending on your needs
- Using the Go helper functions for quick and easy access to form submissions
- Working with the underlying parts of the Go form parser and output it provides
- Getting access to the underlying multipart form handling and using it to parse and manipulate submissions

In the next chapter, you'll learn about working with REST APIs. You'll learn about building them, versioning them, and other characteristics needed to build stable, production-ready APIs that your applications can consume and that you can expose to others.

Working with web services

8

This chapter covers

- Making REST requests
- Detecting timeouts and resuming downloads
- Passing errors over HTTP
- Parsing JSON, including arbitrary JSON structures
- Versioning REST APIs

REST APIs are a cornerstone of the modern internet. They enable cloud computing, have been a pillar in the DevOps and automation movements, and set up client-side web development, among other things. They're one of the great enablers on the internet.

Although plenty of tutorials about creating and consuming simple APIs are available, what happens when things don't go as planned? The internet was designed to be fault-tolerant. API requests and servers need to enable that fault tolerance to work.

This chapter starts with the basics of REST APIs and quickly moves on to handling cases that don't go as planned. You'll look at detecting timeout failures, including those that Go doesn't formally flag as timeouts. You'll also look at resuming file transfers when timeouts happen, and you'll learn how to pass errors between an API endpoint and a requesting client.

Many APIs pass information as JSON. After a quick look at how JSON parsing works in Go, you'll learn about handling JSON structures when you don't know the structure of the data ahead of time. This is useful when you need to work with poorly defined or undefined JSON data.

Functionality within applications changes over time, and this often causes APIs to change. When APIs change, they need to be versioned. How can APIs be versioned? You'll learn a couple of methods for versioning REST APIs.

From this chapter, you'll learn how to move from the basics of API handling into more robust functionality.

8.1 Using REST APIs

The Go standard library includes an HTTP client that's pretty straightforward for most common use cases. After you move beyond the common use cases, you'll see rarer but still regularly needed cases without a clear solution. Before we touch on a couple of those, let's look at how the HTTP client works.

8.1.1 Using the HTTP client

The HTTP client is found in the net/http library within the standard library. It has helper functions to perform GET, HEAD, and POST requests, can perform virtually any HTTP request, and can be heavily customized.

The helper functions are http.Get, http.Head, http.Post, and http.PostForm. With the exception of http.PostForm, each function is for the HTTP verb its name suggests. For example, http.PostForm handles POST requests when the data being posted should be posted as a form. To illustrate how these functions work, the following listing shows a simple use of http.Get.

> **Listing 8.1 A simple HTTP get**

```
package main

import (
    "fmt"
    "io/ioutil"
    "net/http"
)

func main() {
    res, _ :=
    ➥http.Get("http://goinpracticebook.com")      ← Performs a GET request
    b, _ := ioutil.ReadAll(res.Body)              ← Reads the body of the response and closes
    res.Body.Close()                                  the Body reader when done reading it
    fmt.Printf("%s", b)                           ← Prints the body to Standard Output
}
```

The helper functions are all backed by the default HTTP client that's accessible and can perform any HTTP request. For example, the following listing shows how to use the default client to make a DELETE request.

Listing 8.2   DELETE request with default HTTP client

```
package main

import (
        "fmt"
        "net/http"
)

func main() {
        req, _ := http.NewRequest("DELETE",
        ➥"http://example.com/foo/bar", nil)
        res, _ := http.DefaultClient.Do(req)
        fmt.Printf("%s", res.Status)
}
```

- Creates a new request object set up for a delete HTTP method
- Performs the request with the default client
- Displays the status code from performing the request

Making a request is broken into two separate parts. The first part is the request, contained in `http.Request` instances. These contain the information about the request. The second part is the client that performs a request. In this example, the default client is used. By separating the request into its own object, you provide a separation of concerns. Both of these can be customized. The helper functions wrap creating a request instance and executing it with a client.

The default client has configuration and functionality to handle things like HTTP redirects, cookies, and timeouts. It also has a default transport layer that can be customized.

Clients can be customized to allow you to set up the client any way you need to. The following listing shows the creation of a simple client with a timeout set to one second.

Listing 8.3   A simple custom HTTP client

```
func main() {
        cc := &http.Client{Timeout: time.Second}
        res, err :=
        ➥cc.Get("http://goinpracticebook.com")
        if err != nil {
                fmt.Println(err)
                os.Exit(1)
        }
        b, _ := ioutil.ReadAll(res.Body)
        res.Body.Close()
        fmt.Printf("%s", b)
}
```

- Handles any errors such as a client timeout
- Performs a GET request using the custom client
- Creates a custom HTTP client with a timeout of one second

Custom clients allow numerous elements to be customized, including the transport layer, cookie handling, and the way that redirects are followed.

8.1.2   *When faults happen*

The internet was designed with fault tolerance in mind. Things break or don't work as expected, and you try to route around the problem while reporting it. In the age of cloud-native computing, this characteristic has been used to allow applications to move between locations and to be updated in place. When you're working with HTTP connections, it's useful to detect problems, report them, and try to fix them automatically when possible.

TECHNIQUE 49   Detecting timeouts

Connection timeouts are a common problem and useful to detect. For example, if a timeout error occurs, especially if it's in the middle of a connection, retrying the operation might be worthwhile. On retry, the server you were connected to may be back up, or you could be routed to another working server.

To detect timeouts in the `net` package, the errors returned by it have a `Timeout()` method that's set to `true` in the case of a timeout. Yet, in some cases, a timeout occurs and `Timeout()` doesn't return `true`, or the error you're working with comes from another package, such as `url`, and doesn't have the `Timeout()` method.

Timeouts are typically detected by the `net` package when a timeout is explicitly set, such as in listing 8.3. When a timeout is set, the request needs to complete in the timeout period. Reading the body is included in the timeout window. But a timeout can also happen when one isn't set. In this case, a timeout in the network occurs while the timeout checking isn't actively looking for it.

PROBLEM

How can network timeouts be reliably detected?

SOLUTION

When timeouts occur, a small variety of errors occurs. Check the error for each of these cases to see if it was a timeout.

DISCUSSION

When an error is returned from a `net` package operation or a package that takes advantage of `net`, such as `http`, check the `error` against known cases showing a timeout error. Some of these will be for the explicit cases where a timeout was set and cleanly detected. Others will be for the cases where a timeout wasn't set but a timeout occurred.

The following listing contains a function that looks at a variety of error situations to detect whether the error was caused by a timeout.

Listing 8.4   Detect a network timeout from error

A function whose response is true or false if a network timeout caused the error

```
func hasTimedOut(err error) bool {
    switch err := err.(type) {          Uses a type switch to detect
    case *url.Error:                    the type of underlying error
            if err, ok := err.Err.(net.Error); ok && err.Timeout() {
                    return true
            }
```

A url.Error may be caused by an underlying net error that can checked for a timeout.

```
    case net.Error:
        if err.Timeout() {
            return true
        }
    case *net.OpError:
        if err.Timeout() {
            return true
        }
    }

    errTxt := "use of closed network connection"
    if err != nil && strings.Contains(err.Error(), errTxt) {
        return true
    }

    return false
}
```

> **Looks for timeouts detected by the net package**

> **Some errors, without a custom type or variable to check against, can indicate a timeout.**

This function provides the capability to detect a variety of timeout situations. The following snippet is an example of using that function to check whether an error was caused by a timeout:

```
res, err := http.Get("http://example.com/test.zip")
if err != nil && hasTimedOut(err) {
    fmt.Println("A timeout error occured")
    return
}
```

Reliably detecting a timeout is useful, and the next technique highlights this in practice.

TECHNIQUE 50   Timing out and resuming with HTTP

If a large file is being downloaded and a timeout occurs, starting the download from the beginning isn't ideal. This is becoming truer with the growth of file sizes. In many cases, files are gigabytes or larger. It'd be nice to avoid the extra bandwidth use and time to redownload data.

PROBLEM

You want to resume downloading a file, starting from the end of the data already downloaded, after a timeout occurs.

SOLUTION

Retry the download again, attempting to use the Range HTTP header in which a range of bytes to download is specified. This allows you to request a file, starting partway through the file where it left off.

DISCUSSION

Servers, such as the one provided in the Go standard library, can support serving parts of a file. This is a fairly common feature in file servers, and the interface for specifying ranges has been a standard since 1999, when HTTP 1.1 came out:

```go
func main() {
    file, err := os.Create("file.zip")
    if err != nil {
        fmt.Println(err)
        return
    }
    defer file.Close()

    location := https://example.com/file.zip
    err = download(location, file, 100)
    if err != nil {
        fmt.Println(err)
        return
    }

    fi, err := file.Stat()
    if err != nil {
        fmt.Println(err)
        return
    }
    fmt.Printf("Got it with %v bytes downloaded", fi.Size())
}
```

Creates a local file to store the download

Downloads the remote file to the local file, retrying up to 100 times

Displays the size of the file after the download is complete

This snippet creates a local file location, downloads a remote file to it, displays the number of bytes downloaded, and will retry up to 100 times when a network timeout occurs. The real work is inside the download function spelled out in the following listing.

Listing 8.5 Download with retries

```go
func download(location string, file *os.File, retries int64) error {
    req, err := http.NewRequest("GET", location, nil)
    if err != nil {
        return err
    }
    fi, err := file.Stat()
    if err != nil {
        return err
    }
    current := fi.Size()
    if current > 0 {
        start := strconv.FormatInt(current, 10)
        req.Header.Set("Range", "bytes="+start+"-")
    }
    cc := &http.Client{Timeout: 5 * time.Minute}
    res, err := cc.Do(req)
    if err != nil && hasTimedOut(err) {
        if retries > 0 {
            return download(location, file, retries-1)
        }
        return err
    } else if err != nil {
        return err
    }
```

Creates a new GET request for the file being downloaded

Starts the local file to find the current file information

Retrieves the size of the local file

When the local file already has content, sets a header requesting where the local file left off. Ranges have an index of 0, making the current length the index for the next needed byte.

An HTTP client configured to explicitly check for timeout

Performs the request for the file or part if part of the file is already stored locally

When checking for an error, tries the request again if the error was caused by a timeout

```
                  if res.StatusCode < 200 || res.StatusCode >= 300 {          Handles
                          errFmt := "Unsuccess HTTP request. Status: %s"       nonsuccess HTTP
                          return fmt.Errorf(errFmt, res.Status)                status codes
                  }

                  if res.Header.Get("Accept-Ranges") != "bytes" {             If the server doesn't
                          retries = 0                                          support serving partial
                  }                                                            files, sets retries to 0

Copies            _, err = io.Copy(file, res.Body)
   the            if err != nil && hasTimedOut(err) {
remote                    if retries > 0 {
response                          return download(location, file, retries-1)
to the                    }
local file                return err
                  } else if err != nil {
                          return err                    If a timeout error occurs while
                  }                                     copying the file, tries retrieving
                                                        the remaining content
                  return nil
          }
```

Although the download function can handle timeouts in a fairly straightforward manner, it can be customized for your cases:

- The timeout is set to five minutes. This can be tuned for your application. A shorter or longer timeout may provide better performance in your environment. For example, if you're downloading files that typically take longer than five minutes, a timeout longer than most files take will limit the number of HTTP requests needed for a normal download.
- If a hash of a file is easily available, a check could be put in to make sure that the final download matches the hash. This integrity check can improve trust in the final download, even if it takes multiple attempts to download the file.

Checking for errors and attempting to route around the problem can lead to fault-tolerant features in applications.

8.2   *Passing and handling errors over HTTP*

Errors are a regular part of passing information over HTTP. Two of the most common examples are Not Found and Access Denied situations. These situations are common enough that the HTTP specification includes the capability to pass error information from the beginning. The Go standard library provides a rudimentary capability to pass errors. For example, the following listing provides simple HTTP generating an error.

Listing 8.6   Passing an error over HTTP

```
package main

import "net/http"                                                Returns an
                                                                 HTTP status
func displayError(w http.ResponseWriter, r *http.Request) {      403 with a
    http.Error(w, "An Error Occurred", http.StatusForbidden)     message
}
```

```
func main() {
    http.HandleFunc("/", displayError)          ←⌐ Sets up all paths to serve the
    http.ListenAndServe(":8080", nil)              HTTP handler displayError
}
```

This simple server always returns the error message An Error Occurred. Along with the custom message, served with a type of `text/plain`, the HTTP status message is set to 403, correlating to forbidden access.

The `http` package in the standard library has constants for the various status codes. You can read more about the codes at https://en.wikipedia.org/wiki/List_of_HTTP_status_codes.

A client can read the codes the server responds with to learn about what happened with the request. In listing 8.5, when the `res.StatusCode` is checked, the client is looking for a status in the 200 range, which signifies a successful request. The following snippet shows a simple example of printing the status:

```
res, _ := http.Get("http://example.com")
fmt.Println(res.Status)
fmt.Println(res.StatusCode)
```

The `res.Status` is a text message for the status. Example responses look like 200 OK and 404 Not Found. If you're looking for the error code as a number, `res.Status-Code` is the status code as an `int`.

Both the response code and the error message are useful for clients. With them, you can display error messages and automatically handle situations.

8.2.1   Generating custom errors

A plain text error string and an HTTP status code representing an error are often insufficient. For example, if you're displaying web pages, you'll likely want your error pages to be styled like your application or site. Or if you're building an API server that responds with JSON, you'll likely want error responses to be in JSON as well.

The first part of working with custom error responses is for the server to generate them.

TECHNIQUE 51   Custom HTTP error passing

You don't have much room for customization when using the `Error` function within the `http` package. The response type is hardcoded as plain text, and the `X-Content-Type-Options` header is set to `nosniff`. This header tells some tools, such as Microsoft Internet Explorer and Google Chrome, to not attempt to detect a content type other than what was set. This leaves little opportunity to provide a custom error, aside from the content of the plain text string.

PROBLEM

How can you provide a custom response body and content type when there's an error?

SOLUTION

Instead of using the built-in Error function, use custom functions that send both the correct HTTP status code and the error text as a more appropriate body for your situation.

DISCUSSION

Providing error responses that are more than a text message is useful to those consuming an application. For example, someone viewing a web page gets a 404 Not Found error. If this error page is styled like the rest of the site and provides information to help users find what they're looking for, it can guide users rather than only provide a surprise that what they're looking for wasn't found and that they can't easily find it.

A second example involves REST API error messages. APIs are typically used by software development kits (SDKs) and applications. For example, if a call to an API returns a 409 Conflict message, more detail could be provided to guide the user. Is there an application-specific error code an SDK can use? In addition to the error message, is there additional guidance that can be passed to the user?

To illustrate how this works, let's look at an error response in JSON. We'll keep the same response format as the other REST API responses that provide an application-specific error code in addition to the HTTP error. Although this example is targeted at API responses, the same style applies to web pages.

Listing 8.7   Custom JSON error response

JSONError function is similar to http.Error, but the response body is JSON

```go
type Error struct {
    HTTPCode int    `json:"-"`
    Code     int    `json:"code,omitempty"`
    Message  string `json:"message"`
}
```
A type to hold the information about an error, including metadata about its JSON structure

```go
func JSONError(w http.ResponseWriter, e Error) {
    data := struct {
        Err Error `json:"error"`
    }{e}
```
Wraps Error struct in anonymous struct with error property

```go
    b, err := json.Marshal(data)
    if err != nil {
```
Converts error data to JSON and handles an error if one exists

Makes sure the HTTP status code is properly set for the error

```go
        http.Error(w, "Internal Server Error", 500)
        return
    }
    w.Header().Set("Content-Type", "application/json")
    w.WriteHeader(e.HTTPCode)
```
Sets the response MIME type to application/json

Writes the JSON body as output

```go
    fmt.Fprint(w, string(b))
}

func displayError(w http.ResponseWriter, r *http.Request) {
    e := Error{
        HTTPCode: http.StatusForbidden,
        Code:     123,
        Message:  "An Error Occurred",
    }
```
Creates an instance of Error to use for the response error

```
        JSONError(w, e)
}
func main() {
    http.HandleFunc("/", displayError)
    http.ListenAndServe(":8080", nil)
}
```

> ← Returns the error message as JSON when the HTTP handler is called

This listing is conceptually similar to listing 8.6. The difference is that listing 8.6 returns a string with the error message, and listing 8.7 returns a JSON response like the following:

```
{
    "error": {
        "code": 123,
        "message": "An Error Occurred"
    }
}
```

After errors are passed as JSON, an application reading them can take advantage of the data being passed in this structured format. Using errors passed as JSON can be seen in the next technique.

8.2.2 Reading and using custom errors

Any client can work with HTTP status codes to detect an error. For example, the following snippet detects the various classes of errors:

```
res, err := http.Get("http://goinpracticebook.com/")

switch {
case 300 <= res.StatusCode && res.StatusCode < 400:
    fmt.Println("Redirect message")
case 400 <= res.StatusCode && res.StatusCode < 500:
    fmt.Println("Client error")
case 500 <= res.StatusCode && res.StatusCode < 600:
    fmt.Println("Server error")
}
```

The 300 range of messages has to do with redirects. You'll rarely see these because the default setting for the HTTP client is to follow up to 10 redirects. The 400 range represents client errors. Access Denied, Not Found, and other errors are in this range. The 500 range of errors is returned when a server error occurs; something went wrong on the server.

Using the status code can provide insight into what's going on. For example, if the status code is a 401, you need to log in to see the request. A user interface could then provide an opportunity to log in to try the request again, or an SDK could attempt to authenticate or re-authenticate and try the request again.

| TECHNIQUE 52 | **Reading custom errors** |

If an application responds with custom errors, such as those generated by technique 51, this presents an API response with a different structure from the expected response in addition to there being an error.

PROBLEM

When a custom error with a different structure is returned as an API response, how can you detect that and handle it differently?

SOLUTION

When a response is returned, check the HTTP status code and MIME type for a possible error. When one of these returns unexpected values or informs of an error, convert it to an error, return the error, and handle the error.

DISCUSSION

Go is known for explicit error handling, and HTTP status codes are no different. When an unexpected status is returned from an HTTP request, it can be handled like other errors. The first step is to return an error when the HTTP request didn't go as expected, as shown in the next listing.

| Listing 8.8   Convert HTTP response to an error |

```
type Error struct {
    HTTPCode int    `json:"-"`
    Code     int    `json:"code,omitempty"`
    Message  string `json:"message"`
}
```
> Structure to hold data from the error

```
func (e Error) Error() string {
    fs := "HTTP: %d, Code: %d, Message: %s"
    return fmt.Sprintf(fs, e.HTTPCode, e.Code, e.Message)
}
```
> The Error method implements the error interface on the Error struct.

```
func get(u string) (*http.Response, error) {
    res, err := http.Get(u)
    if err != nil {
        return res, err
    }
```
> The get function should be used instead of http.Get to make requests.

Uses http.Get to retrieve the resource and return any http.Get errors

```
    if res.StatusCode < 200 || res.StatusCode >= 300 {
        if res.Header.Get("Content-Type") != "application/json" {
            sm := "Unknown error. HTTP status: %s"
            return res, fmt.Errorf(sm, res.Status)
        }
```

Checks the response content type and returns an error if it's not correct

Checks if the response code was outside the 200 range of successful responses

Parses the JSON response and places the data into a struct and responds to any errors

```
b, _ := ioutil.ReadAll(res.Body)          Reads the body of the
res.Body.Close()                          response into a buffer
var data struct {
        Err Error `json:"error"`
}
err = json.Unmarshal(b, &data)
if err != nil {
        sm := "Unable to parse json: %s. HTTP status: %s"
        return res, fmt.Errorf(sm, err, res.Status)
}
data.Err.HTTPCode = res.StatusCode              Adds the HTTP
                                                status code to the
return res, data.Err                            Error instance
                        Returns the custom
}                       error and the response

    return res, nil
}                   When there's no error, returns
                    the response as expected
```

This code replaces the http.Get function for making a request to a server with the get function, which handles custom errors. The Error struct, which holds the data from the error, has the same structure as the error in technique 51. This custom error handling is designed to work with a server that emits errors in the same way as technique 51. These two techniques could share a common package defining the error.

Adding the Error() method to the Error type implements the error interface. This allows instances of Error to be passed between functions as an error, like any other error.

The main function in the following snippet illustrates using the get function instead of http.Get. Any custom errors will print the custom error details from the JSON and exit the application:

```
func main() {
    res, err := get("http://localhost:8080")
    if err != nil {
            fmt.Println(err)
            os.Exit(1)
    }

    b, _ := ioutil.ReadAll(res.Body)
    res.Body.Close()
    fmt.Printf("%s", b)
}
```

Using this technique for getting and passing HTTP errors around applications allows these errors to get the benefits of other error handling in Go. For example, using switch statements to test the type of error and reacting appropriately, as listing 8.4 showed, will work for the custom errors.

8.3   *Parsing and mapping JSON*

When communicating over REST APIs, the most common format to transfer informa-tion is JSON. Being able to easily and quickly convert JSON strings into native Go data structures is useful, and the Go standard library provides that functionality out of the box via the encoding/json package. For example, the following listing parses a simple JSON data structure into a struct.

Listing 8.9   A simple custom JSON-parsing example

```
package main
import (
    "encoding/json"
    "fmt"
)

type Person struct {              A struct that also represents information
    Name string `json:"name"`     in JSON. The json tag maps the Name
}                                 property to name in the JSON.

var JSON = `{                     JSON represented
  "name": "Miracle Max"           as a string
}`

func main() {                                      An instance of the
    var p Person                                   Person struct to hold
    err := json.Unmarshal([]byte(JSON), &p)        the parsed JSON data
    if err != nil {                                Parses the JSON data
        fmt.Println(err)                           into the instance of
        return                    Handles any      the Person struct
    }                             parsing
                                  errors
    fmt.Println(p)
}                   Acts on the now populated Person
                    object, in this case printing it
```

Although the standard library provides everything you need for the foundational JSON-parsing use cases, you may run into some known and common situations without an obvious solution.

TECHNIQUE 53   Parsing JSON without knowing the schema

The structure of JSON is often passed along via documentation, examples, and from reading the structure. Although schemas exist for JSON, such as JSON Schema, they're often not used. Not only is JSON schemaless, but API responses may vary the structure, and in some cases you may not know the structure.

When JSON data is parsed in Go, it goes into structs with a structure defined in the code. If you don't know the structure when the structs are being created, or the struc-ture changes, that presents a problem. It may seem as though it's difficult to intro-spect JSON or operate on documents with a varying structure. That's not the case.

PROBLEM

How can you parse a JSON data structure into a Go data structure when you don't know the structure ahead of time?

SOLUTION

Parse the JSON into an `interface{}` instead of a struct. After the JSON is in an interface, you can inspect the data and use it.

DISCUSSION

A little-known feature of the `encoding/json` package is the capability to parse arbitrary JSON into an `interface{}`. Working with JSON parsed into an `interface{}` is quite different from working with JSON parsed into a known structure, because of the Go type system. The following listing contains an example of parsing JSON this way.

Listing 8.10 Parse JSON into an `interface{}`

```go
package main

import (
      "encoding/json"
      "fmt"
      "os"
)

var ks = []byte(`{
"firstName": "Jean",                                    A JSON document to be
"lastName": "Bartik",                                   parsed and unmarshaled
"age": 86,
"education": [
      {
            "institution": "Northwest Missouri State Teachers College",
            "degree": "Bachelor of Science in Mathematics"
      },
      {
            "institution": "University of Pennsylvania",
            "degree": "Masters in English"
      }
],
"spouse": "William Bartik",
"children": [
      "Timothy John Bartik",
      "Jane Helen Bartik",
      "Mary Ruth Bartik"
]
}`)

func main() {
      var f interface{}                  ◁──  A variable instance of type
      err := json.Unmarshal(ks, &f)      ◁──  interface{} to hold the JSON data
      if err != nil {                         Parses the JSON data and puts it
            fmt.Println(err)                   into the interface{} type variable
            os.Exit(1)
      }                              Handles any errors,
                                     such as invalid JSON
      fmt.Println(f)          ◁──
}                          Accesses the JSON data
                           now on the interface{}
```

The JSON parsed here contains a variety of structure situations. This is important because working with the interface{} isn't the same as working with JSON parsed into a struct. You'll look at working with this data in a moment.

When JSON data is parsed into a struct, such as the example in listing 8.9, it's easily accessible. In that case, the name of the person from the parsed JSON is available at p.Name. If you tried to access firstName on the interface{} in the same way, you'd see an error. For example:

```
fmt.Println(f.firstName)
```

Accessing firstName like a property would generate an error:

```
f.firstName undefined (type interface {} is interface with no methods)
```

Before you can work with the data, you need to access it as a type other than interface{}. In this case, the JSON represents an object, so you can use the type map[string] interface{}. It provides access to the next level of data. The following is a way to access firstName:

```
m := f.(map[string]interface{})
fmt.Println(m["firstName"])
```

At this point, the top-level keys are all accessible, allowing firstName to be accessible by name.

To programmatically walk through the resulting data from the JSON, it's useful to know how Go treats the data in the conversion. When the JSON is unmarshaled, the values in JSON are converted into the following Go types:

- bool for JSON Boolean
- float64 for JSON numbers
- []interface{} for JSON arrays
- map[string]interface{} for JSON objects
- nil for JSON null
- string for JSON strings

Knowing this, you can build functionality to walk the data structure. For example, the following listing shows functions recursively walking the parsed JSON, printing the key names, types, and values.

Listing 8.11 Walk arbitrary JSON

```
func printJSON(v interface{}) {
    switch vv := v.(type) {
    case string:
        fmt.Println("is string", vv)
    case float64:
        fmt.Println("is float64", vv)
    case []interface{}:
        fmt.Println("is an array:")
```

Switch based on the data type for a value →

For each type of data from the JSON, displays information about the type and value. On objects and arrays from the JSON, recursively calls printJSON to display the properties inside them.

```
        for i, u := range vv {
            fmt.Print(i, " ")
            printJSON(u)
        }
    case map[string]interface{}:
        fmt.Println("is an object:")
        for i, u := range vv {
            fmt.Print(i, " ")
            printJSON(u)
        }
    default:
        fmt.Println("Unknown type")
    }
}
```

For each type of data from the JSON, displays information about the type and value. On objects and arrays from the JSON, recursively calls printJSON to display the properties inside them.

Although it's handy to be able to parse and work with JSON when you don't know the structure, it's useful to have known structures or to handle the version changes when those structures change. In the next section, you'll learn about versioning APIs that includes changes in JSON structures.

8.4   *Versioning REST APIs*

Web services evolve and change, which leads to changes in the APIs used to access or manage them. To provide a stable API contract for API consumers, changes to the API need to be versioned. Because programs are the users of an API, they need to be updated to account for changes, which takes time after an update is released.

APIs are typically versioned by major number changes such as v1, v2, and v3. This number scheme signifies breaking changes to the API. An application designed to work with v2 of an API won't be able to consume the v3 API version because it's too different.

But what about API changes that add functionality to an existing API? For example, say that functionality is added to the v1 API. In this case, the API can be incremented with a point version; feature additions can increment the API to v1.1. This tells developers and applications about the additions.

The following two techniques cover a couple of ways to expose versioned APIs.

TECHNIQUE 54   API version in the URL

A change in the API version needs to be easy to see and work with. The easier it is for developers to see, understand, and consume, the more likely they are to work with it and to fully use services.

Versioned APIs that easily work with existing tools are also important. For example, the ability to quickly test API calls with cURL or Postman, a popular API extension for Chrome, makes it easier for developers to develop and test APIs.

PROBLEM
What is an easily accessible method to provide versioned APIs?

SOLUTION

Provide the API version in the REST API URL. For example, instead of providing an API of https://example.com/api/todos, add a version to the path so it looks like https://example.com/api/v1/todos.

DISCUSSION

Figure 8.1 illustrates an incredibly popular method for versioning APIs: via the URL. Google, OpenStack, Salesforce, Twitter, and Facebook are a few examples that use APIs versioned this way.

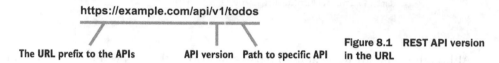

The URL prefix to the APIs   **API version Path to specific API**   Figure 8.1   REST API version in the URL

As the following listing shows, implementing this URL structure is done when the mapping between path and handlers occurs.

Listing 8.12   Register the API path including a version

```go
package main

import (
    "encoding/json"
    "fmt"
    "net/http"
)

type testMessage struct {
    Message string `json:"message"`
}

func displayTest(w http.ResponseWriter, r *http.Request) {    // An example handler function returning a JSON response
    data := testMessage{"A test message."}
    b, err := json.Marshal(data)
    if err != nil {
            http.Error(w, "Internal Server Error", 500)
            return
    }
    w.Header().Set("Content-Type", "application/json")
    fmt.Fprint(w, string(b))
}

func main() {
    http.HandleFunc("/api/v1/test", displayTest)    // When the handler function is mapped to the URL, the API version is included.
    http.ListenAndServe(":8080", nil)
}
```

In this example, the way the handler function is mapped to the path doesn't allow you to easily handle different request methods such as POST, PUT, or DELETE. If an endpoint represents a resource, the same URL typically handles all these requests. You can find techniques for handling multiple HTTP methods being mapped to the same URL in chapter 2.

Although this is an easy method for passing an API version, it's not technically semantic. A URL doesn't represent an object. Instead, it represents accessing an object within a version of an API. The trade-off is developer ease. Specifying an API version in the URL is easier for developers consuming the API.

TECHNIQUE 55   API version in content type

Although the previous technique focused on a method that was easy for developers, the method wasn't semantic. Part of the original theory of REST was that a URL represented something. That could be an object, list, or something else. Based on the details in the request, such as the requested content type or HTTP method, the response or action to that object would be different.

PROBLEM

How can API versions be handled in a semantic manner?

SOLUTION

Instead of referencing JSON in the request and response, use a custom content type that includes the version. For example, instead of working with `application/json`, use a custom content type such as `application/vnd.mytodo.v1.json` or `application/vnd.mytodo.json; version=1.0`. These custom types specify the intended schema for the data.

DISCUSSION

To handle multiple API versions at a single path, as seen in figure 8.2, the handling needs to take into account the content type in addition to any other characteristics. Listing 8.13 showcases one method for detecting the content type and using that to generate the response.

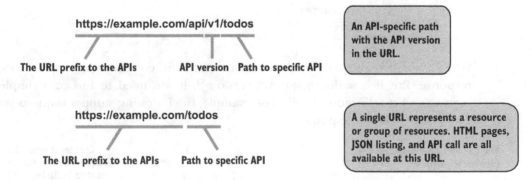

Figure 8.2   Differences between semantic URLs and API version in URL

Listing 8.13   Pass the API version in the content type

```go
func main() {
    http.HandleFunc("/test", displayTest)
    http.ListenAndServe(":8080", nil)
}

func displayTest(w http.ResponseWriter, r *http.Request) {
    t := r.Header.Get("Accept")
    var err error
    var b []byte
    var ct string
    switch t {
    case "application/vnd.mytodos.json; version=2.0":
        data := testMessageV2{"Version 2"}
        b, err = json.Marshal(data)
        ct = "application/vnd.mytodos.json; version=2.0"
    case "application/vnd.mytodos.json; version=1.0":
        fallthrough
    default:
        data := testMessageV1{"Version 1"}
        b, err = json.Marshal(data)
        ct = "application/vnd.mytodos.json; version=1.0"
    }

    if err != nil {
        http.Error(w, "Internal Server Error", 500)
        return
    }
    w.Header().Set("Content-Type", ct)
    fmt.Fprint(w, string(b))
}

type testMessageV1 struct {
    Message string `json:"message"`
}

type testMessageV2 struct {
    Info string `json:"info"`
}
```

- Registers a path that can have multiple content types
- Detects the content type that was requested
- Generates different content to return based on different content types
- If an error occurs in creating the JSON, returns it
- Sets the content type to the type that was generated
- Sends the content to the requestor

When a client requests the content, it can specify no content type to get the default response. But if it wants to use API version 2, it will need to forego a simple GET request and specify more details. For example, the following snippet requests version 2 and prints out the response:

- The content type with the API version to request
- Creates a new GET request to the server created in listing 8.13

```go
ct := "application/vnd.mytodos.json; version=2.0"
req, _ := http.NewRequest("GET", "http://localhost:8080/test", nil)
req.Header.Set("Accept", ct)
res, _ := http.DefaultClient.Do(req)
```

- Adds the requested content type to the request headers
- Performs the request

```
if res.Header.Get("Content-Type") != ct {
    fmt.Println("Unexpected content type returned")
    return
}
b, _ := ioutil.ReadAll(res.Body)
res.Body.Close()
fmt.Printf("%s", b)
```

Verifies that the response used the expected content type

Prints the response body

Although this method provides the capability to have multiple API versions from a single endpoint, you need to be aware of the following considerations:

- Content types in the vnd. namespace are supposed to be registered with the Internet Assigned Numbers Authority (IANA).
- When making a request for a nondefault version, you need to add extra steps to specify the content type for the version. This adds more work to applications consuming the API.

8.5 Summary

In this chapter, you started with the basics of working with web services such as making REST requests. You quickly moved from the basics to elements of building robust web service interactions that included the following:

- Detecting network timeouts, even when the network layer doesn't formally flag them, and resuming downloads when timeouts occur.
- Passing errors between API endpoints and client requestors by using and going beyond the HTTP status header.
- Parsing JSON, even when you don't know the structure ahead of time.
- Using two methods for versioning REST APIs and working with versioned APIs.

In the next chapter, you'll learn about working with cloud services. Running applications effectively in the cloud involves more than working with the APIs that let you configure them. In chapter 9, you'll learn techniques to help your Go applications be effective in the cloud.

Part 4

Taking your applications to the cloud

Cloud computing is changing the way applications are built and operated. Go is an ideal language for building computing systems and applications that run in the cloud. Part 4 dives headlong into cloud computing.

Chapter 9 opens part 4 by describing what cloud computing is and the considerations for building applications running in the cloud. The patterns in this chapter make it easier to run and monitor applications in the cloud. Chapter 10 continues the cloud theme by showing you services working together and providing high-performance API communication. This is especially powerful when a microservice architecture is used.

Chapter 11 closes out part 4 and the book by looking at reflection and metaprogramming. Reflection makes working with static types easier and is widely used in Go because it's inexpensive and accessible. Metaprogramming enables code generation, which opens a new door to the way some applications and libraries can be written.

Using the cloud

This chapter covers

- Introducing cloud computing
- Working with multiple cloud providers
- Gathering information on the cloud host
- Compiling to various operating systems and architectures
- Monitoring the Go runtime in an application

Cloud computing has become one of the buzzwords of modern computing. Is it just a buzzword or something more? This chapter opens with an introduction to cloud computing that explores this question and what cloud computing looks like in a practical sense. You'll see how it relates to the traditional models working with hardware servers and virtual machines.

Cloud computing is a space filled with various cloud providers. It's easy to build an application that ends up being locked into a single vendor. You'll learn how to avoid cloud vendor lock-in while architecting code in a manner that's easier to develop locally and test.

When you're ready to run your application in the cloud, you'll find situations you need to work with, such as learning about the host your application is running on, monitoring the Go runtime inside every application, and cross-compiling to various systems before deploying. You'll explore how to do this while avoiding pitfalls that can catch you off guard.

This chapter rounds out some key cloud concepts. After you've completed this chapter and the previous chapters, you'll have what you need to build and operate cloud-based applications written in Go.

9.1   *What is cloud computing?*

This is one of the fundamental questions that can make all the difference in both software development and operating applications. Is *cloud* a marketing term? Yes. Is there something else fundamentally different going on? Yes. Given the way the term is thrown around for use in everything from web applications and phone applications to physical servers and virtual machines, its meaning can be difficult to navigate for someone not familiar with the space. In this introductory section, you'll learn about cloud computing in a way that you can apply to software development and operations.

9.1.1   *The types of cloud computing*

In the simplest form of cloud computing, part of a system is managed by someone else. This can be someone else in your company, an outside service provider, an automation system, or any combination of these. If an outside service provider is providing part of the stack, what parts are they providing? Figure 9.1 shows the three forms of cloud computing and how they compare to an environment where you own the entire stack.

With a traditional server or rack of servers, you need to manage all of the components of the stack, right down to the physical space holding the hardware. When changes are needed, someone needs to order the hardware, wait for it to show up, connect it, and manage it. This can take a bit of time.

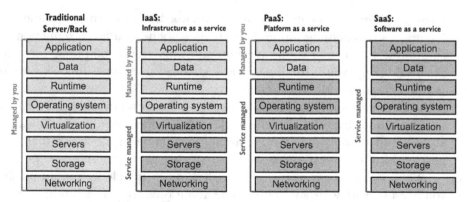

Figure 9.1   The types of cloud computing

INFRASTRUCTURE AS A SERVICE

Accessing *infrastructure as a service* (IaaS) is different from previous forms of working with virtual machines. Sure, services have been providing virtual machines and colocated servers for years. When IaaS came into being, the change was the way those servers were used and accessed.

Prior to IaaS, you'd typically get a server and then continue to use that server for months or years. IaaS turned that on its head. Under an IaaS setup, virtual servers are created and destroyed as needed. When you need a server, it's created. As soon as you no longer need it, you return it to the pool of available resources. For example, if you need to test an idea, you might create many servers, test the idea, and then immediately get rid of the servers.

Creating and working with IaaS resources happens via a programmable API. This is typically a REST API that can be used by command-line tools and applications to manage the resources.

IaaS is about more than servers. Storage, networking, and other forms of infrastructure are accessible and configurable in the same way. As the name suggests, the infrastructure is the configurable part. The operating system, runtime environment, application, and data are all managed by cloud consumers and their management software.

Examples of an IaaS include services provided by Amazon Web Services, Microsoft Azure, and Google Cloud.

PLATFORM AS A SERVICE

Platform as a service (PaaS) differs from IaaS in some important ways. One of the simplest is in how you work with it. To deploy an application to a platform, you use an API to deploy your application code and supporting metadata, such as the language the application was written in. The platform takes this information and then builds and runs the application.

In this model, the platform manages the operating system and runtime. You don't need to start virtual machines, choose their resource sizes, choose an operating system, or install system software. Handling those tasks is left up to the platform to manage. You gain back the time typically spent managing systems so you can focus on other tasks such as working on your application.

To scale applications, instances of the application are created and run in parallel. In this way, applications are scaled horizontally. A PaaS may be able to do some scaling automatically, or you can use an API to choose the number of instances yourself.

Heroku, Cloud Foundry, and Deis are three of the most widely known examples of a PaaS.

SOFTWARE AS A SERVICE

Say your application needs a database to store data in. You could create a cluster of virtual machines using IaaS, install the database software and configure it, monitor the database to make sure everything works properly, and continually update the system software for security. Or you could consume a database as a service and leave the

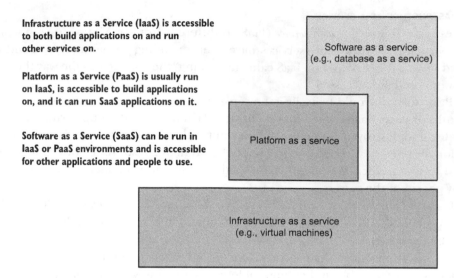

Infrastructure as a Service (IaaS) is accessible to both build applications on and run other services on.

Platform as a Service (PaaS) is usually run on IaaS, is accessible to build applications on, and it can run SaaS applications on it.

Software as a Service (SaaS) can be run in IaaS or PaaS environments and is accessible for other applications and people to use.

Software as a service
(e.g., database as a service)

Platform as a service

Infrastructure as a service
(e.g., virtual machines)

Figure 9.2   The layers of cloud services can sit on each other.

operations, scale, and updates to a service provider. Using APIs, you set up a database and access it. This ladder case is an example of *software as a service* (SaaS), shown in figure 9.2.

SaaS comprises a wide range of software, from the building blocks to other applications to consumer applications. Using SaaS for application building blocks, such as databases and storage, allows teams to focus on the activities that make their applications different.

SaaS examples are wide-ranging and include Salesforce, Microsoft Office 365, and the payment processor Stripe.

9.1.2 *Containers and cloud-native applications*

When Docker, the container management software, came into the public eye, using containers to run and distribute applications became popular. Containers are different from virtual machines or traditional servers.

Figure 9.3 compares virtual machines and containers. On the left is a system, going all the way down to the hardware server, that runs virtual machines. On the right is a separate system running containers. Each is running two applications as workloads, with App A being scaled horizontally to have two instances, for a total of three workload instances.

When virtual machines run, the hypervisor provides an environment for an operating system to run in that emulates hardware or uses special hardware for virtual machines. Each virtual machine has a guest operating system with its own kernel. Inside the operating system are all the applications, binaries, and libraries in the operating system or set up by the users. Applications run in this environment. When two instances

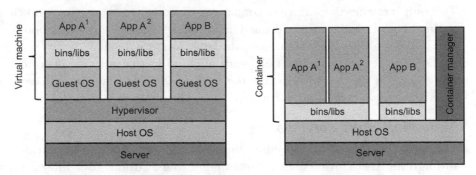

Figure 9.3 Comparing containers and virtual machines

of an application run in parallel (which is how horizontal scaling works), the entire guest operating system, applications, libraries, and your application are replicated.

Using virtual machines comes with certain architectural elements worth noting:

- When a virtual machine starts up, the kernel and guest operating system need time to boot up. This takes time because computers take time to boot up.
- Hypervisors and modern hardware can enforce a separation between each virtual machine.
- Virtual machines provide an encapsulated server with resources being assigned to it. Those resources may be used by that machine or held for that machine.

Containers operate on a different model. The host server, whether it's a physical server or virtual machine, runs a container manager. Each container runs in the host operating system. When using the host kernel, its startup time is almost instantaneous. Containers share the kernel, and hardware drivers and the operating system enforce a separation between the containers. The binaries and libraries used, commonly associated with the operating system, can be entirely separate. For example, in figure 9.3, App A could be using the Debian binaries and libraries, and App B could be running on those from CentOS. The applications running in those containers would see their environment as Debian or CentOS.

Cloud-native applications is a term that tends to be used alongside containers. Cloud-native applications take advantage of the programmatic nature of the cloud to scale with additional instances on demand, remediate failures so many problems in the systems are never experienced by end users, tie together microservices to build larger applications, and more. Containers, with their capability to start almost instantly while being more densely placed on the underlying servers than virtual machines, provide an ideal environment for scaling, remediation, and microservices.

> **DEFINITION** *Remediation* is the automatic correction of problems in running applications. *Microservices* are small, independent processes that communicate with other small processes over defined APIs. Microservices are used together to create larger applications. Microservices are covered in more detail in chapter 10.

This only scratches the surface of containers, cloud-native computing, and cloud computing in general. If you're interested in more information, numerous books, training courses, and other information cover the topic in more detail.

One of the most important elements of cloud services that we need to look at in more detail is the way you manage the services. The interface to manage cloud services provides a point of interaction for Go applications.

9.2   Managing cloud services

Managing cloud services, whether they're IaaS, PaaS, or SaaS, typically happens through an API. This enables command-line tools, custom user interfaces, autonomous applications (bots), and other tools to manage the services for you. Cloud services are programmable.

Web applications, such as the web console each cloud service vendor provides, appear to be simple and effective ways to view and manage cloud services. For some simple cases, this works. But the full power of the cloud is in the ability to program it. That includes automatically scaling horizontally, automatically repairing problems, and operating on large numbers of cloud assets at the same time.

Each of the cloud providers offers a REST API, and most of the time an SDK is built to interact with the API. The SDK or the API can be used within your applications to use the cloud services.

9.2.1   Avoiding cloud provider lock-in

Cloud services are like platforms, and each has its own API. Although they provide the same or similar feature sets, their programmable REST API is often quite different. An SDK designed for one service provider won't work against a competitor. There isn't a common API specification that they all implement.

TECHNIQUE 56   **Working with multiple cloud providers**

Many cloud service providers exist, and they're distributed all over the world. Some are region-specific, conforming to local data-sovereignty laws, whereas others are global companies. Some are public and have an underlying infrastructure that's shared with others; others are private, and everything down to the hardware is yours. These cloud providers can compete on price, features, and the changing needs of the global landscape.

Given the continuously changing landscape, it's useful to remain as flexible as possible when working with cloud providers. We've seen code written specifically for one cloud provider that has caused an application to become stuck on that provider, even when the user wanted to switch. Switching would be a lot of work, causing delays in new features. The trick is to avoid this kind of lock-in up front.

PROBLEM

Cloud service providers typically have their own APIs, even when they offer the same or similar features. Writing an application to work with one API can lead to lock-in with that API and that vendor.

SOLUTION

The solution has two parts. First, create an interface to describe your cloud interactions. If you need to save a file or create a server instance, have a definition on the interface for that. When you need to use these cloud features, be sure to use the interface.

Second, create an implementation of the interface for each cloud provider you're going to use. Switching cloud service providers becomes as simple as writing an implementation of an interface.

DISCUSSION

This is an old model that's proven to be effective. Imagine if computers could work with only a single printer manufacturer. Instead, operating systems have interfaces, and drivers are written to connect the two. This same idea can apply to cloud providers.

The first step is to define and use an interface for a piece of functionality rather than to write the software to use a specific provider's implementation. The following listing provides an example of one designed to work with files.

Listing 9.1   Interface for cloud functionality

```go
type File interface {                            ⟵── An interface for working with files
    Load(string) (io.ReadCloser, error)
    Save(string, io.ReadSeeker) error            Generic methods for working with files.
}                                                The names contain no details of the
                                                 underlying implementations.
```

File handling is a useful case to look at because cloud providers offer different types of file storage, operators have differing APIs, and file handling is a common operation.

After an interface is defined, you need a first implementation. The easiest one, which allows you to test and locally develop your application, is to use the local filesystem as a store. This allows you to make sure the application is working before introducing network operations or a cloud provider. The following listing showcases an implementation of the `File` interface that loads and saves from the local filesystem.

Listing 9.2   Simple implementation of cloud file storage

```go
type LocalFile struct {          A struct for the foundation of the
    Base string                  implementation. The Base property          Opens a file stored
}                                stores the base path for file storage.      locally or returns an
                                                                             error. os.File
                                                                             instances implement
func (l LocalFile) Load(path string) (io.ReadCloser, error) {                the io.ReadCloser
    p := filepath.Join(l.Base, path)                                         interface, allowing a
    return os.Open(p)                                                        return from os.Open
}                                                                            to work.
```

```go
func (l LocalFile) Save(path string, body io.ReadSeeker) error {

    p := filepath.Join(l.Base, path)
    d := filepath.Dir(p)
    err := os.MkdirAll(d, os.ModeDir|os.ModePerm)
    if err != nil {
        return err
    }

    f, err := os.Create(p)
    if err != nil {
        return err
    }
    defer f.Close()

    _, err = io.Copy(f, body)
    return err
}
```

> Saving files requires making sure the local directory exists for the requested path and copying the contents to the saved file location.

After you have this basic implementation, you can write application code that can use it. The following listing shows a simple example of saving and loading a file.

Listing 9.3   Example using a cloud provider interface

```go
func main() {
    content := `Lorem ipsum dolor sit amet, consectetur` +
        `adipiscing elit. Donec a diam lectus.Sed sit` +
        `amet ipsum mauris. Maecenascongue ligula ac` +
        `quam viverra nec consectetur ante hendrerit.`
    body := bytes.NewReader([]byte(content))

    store, err := fileStore()
    if err != nil {
        fmt.Println(err)
        os.Exit(1)
    }

    fmt.Println("Storing content...")
    err = store.Save("foo/bar", body)
    if err != nil {
        fmt.Println(err)
        os.Exit(1)
    }

    fmt.Println("Retrieving content...")
    c, err := store.Load("foo/bar")
    if err != nil {
        fmt.Println(err)
        os.Exit(1)
    }
    o, err := ioutil.ReadAll(c)
    if err != nil {
        fmt.Println(err)
        os.Exit(1)
    }
    fmt.Println(string(o))
}
```

> Example content placed in an instance implementing the io.ReadSeeker interface

> Retrieves a store implementing the File interface from listing 9.1 and handles any errors

> Saves the example content to the file store

> Retrieves and prints out content from the file store

The `fileStore` function retrieves an object implementing the `File` interface from listing 9.1. That could be an implementation connected to a cloud provider such as Amazon Web Services, Google Cloud, or Microsoft Azure. A variety of types of cloud file storage are available, including object storage, block storage, and file storage. The implementation could be connected to any of these. Although the implementation can vary, where it's used isn't tied to any one implementation.

The file store to use can be chosen by configuration, which was covered in chapter 2. In the configuration, the details of the type and any credentials can be stored. The credentials are important because development and testing should happen by using different account details from production.

In this example, the following function uses the local filesystem to store and retrieve files. In an application, the path will likely be a specific location:

```
func fileStore() (File, error) {
    return &LocalFile{Base: "."}, nil
}
```

This same concept applies to every interaction with a cloud provider, whether it's adding compute resourcing (for example, creating virtual machines), adding users to an SaaS customer relationship management (CRM) system, or anything else.

9.2.2 Dealing with divergent errors

Handling errors is just as important as handling successful operations when interacting with different cloud providers. Part of what has made the internet and those known for using the cloud successful is handling errors well.

TECHNIQUE 57 Cleanly handling cloud provider errors

In technique 56, errors from the `Load` and `Save` methods were bubbled up to the code that called them. In practice, details from the errors saving to the local filesystem or any cloud provider, which are different in each implementation, were bubbled up to the application code.

If the application code that calls methods such as `Load` and `Save` is going to display errors to end users or attempt to detect meaning from the errors in order to act on them, you can quickly run into problems when working with multiple cloud providers. Each cloud provider, SDK, or implementation can have different errors. Instead of having a clean interface, such as the `File` interface in listing 9.1, the application code needs to know details about the implementations errors.

PROBLEM

How can application code handle interchangeable implementations of an interface while displaying or acting on errors returned by methods in the interface?

SOLUTION

Along with the methods on an interface, define and export errors. Instead of returning implementation-specific errors, return package errors.

DISCUSSION

Continuing the examples from technique 56, the following listing defines several common errors to go along with the interface.

> **Listing 9.4   Errors to go with cloud functionality interface**

```
var (
    ErrFileNotFound    = errors.New("File not found")
    ErrCannotLoadFile = errors.New("Unable to load file")
    ErrCannotSaveFile = errors.New("Unable to save file")
)
```
Three package-exported errors to go along with the interface in listing 9.1

By defining the errors as variables that are exported by the package, they can be used in comparisons. For example:

```
if err == ErrFileNotFound {
fmt.Println("Cannot find the file")
}
```

To illustrate using these errors in implementations of an interface, the following listing rewrites the Load method from listing 9.2 to use these errors.

> **Listing 9.5   Adding errors to file load method**

A variable to store the returned error. It defaults to nil.   **When a file isn't found, handles the error to return the File Not Found error**

```
func (l LocalFile) Load(path string) (io.ReadCloser, error) {
    p := filepath.Join(l.Base, path)
    var oerr error
    o, err := os.Open(p)
    if err != nil && os.IsNotExist(err) {
        log.Printf("Unable to find %s", path)
        oerr = ErrFileNotFound
    } else if err != nil {
        log.Printf("Error loading file %s, err: %s", path, err)
        oerr = ErrCannotLoadFile
    }
    return o, oerr
}
```

Returns the package error, if there is one, along with the file   **Handles errors other than files not being found with a similar pattern**

Logs the original error so it's not lost

Logging the original error is important. If a problem occurs when connecting to the remote system, that problem needs to be logged. A monitoring system can catch errors communicating with external systems and raise alerts so you have an opportunity to remediate the problems.

By logging the original error and returning a common error, the implementation error can be caught and handled, if necessary. The code calling this method can know how to act on returned errors without knowing about the implementation.

Logging is important to observe an application operating in its environment and debug issues, but that's just the beginning of operating in the cloud. Detecting the environment, building in environment tolerance, monitoring the runtime, detecting information when it's needed, and numerous other characteristics affect how well it runs and your ability to tune the application. Next you'll look at applications running in the cloud.

9.3   Running on cloud servers

When an application is being built to run in the cloud, at times you may know all the details of the environment, but at other times information will be limited. Building applications that are tolerant to unknown environments will aid in the detection and handling of problems that could arise.

At the same time, you may develop applications on one operating system and architecture but need to operate them on another. For example, you could develop an application on Windows or Mac OS X and operate it on Linux in production.

In this section, you'll explore how to avoid pitfalls that can come from assuming too much about an environment.

9.3.1   Performing runtime detection

It's usually a good idea to detect the environment at runtime rather than to assume characteristics of it in your code. Because Go applications communicate with the kernel, one thing you need to know is that if you're on Linux, Windows, or another system, details beyond the kernel that Go was compiled for can be detected at runtime. This allows a Go application to run on Red Hat Linux or Ubuntu. Or a Go application can tell you if a dependency is missing, which makes troubleshooting much easier.

TECHNIQUE 58   Gathering information on the host

Cloud applications can run in multiple environments such as development, testing, and production environments. They can scale horizontally, with the potential to have many instances dynamically scheduled. And they can run in multiple data centers at the same time. Being run in this manner makes it difficult to assume information about the environment or pass in all the details with application configuration.

Instead of knowing through configuration, or assuming host environment details, it's possible to detect information about the environment.

PROBLEM

How can information about a host be detected within a Go application?

SOLUTION

The os package enables you to get information about the underlying system. Information from the os package can be combined with information detected through other packages, such as net, or from calls to external applications.

DISCUSSION

The os package has the capability to detect a wide range of details about the environment. The following list highlights several examples:

- os.Hostname() returns the kernel's value for the hostname.
- The process ID for the application can be retrieved with os.Getpid().
- Operating systems can and do have different path and path list separators. Using os.PathSeparator or os.PathListSeparator instead of characters allows applications to work with the system they're running on.
- To find the current working directory, use os.Getwd().

Information from the os package can be used in combination with other information to know more about a host. For example, if you try to look up the IP addresses for the machine an application is running on by looking at all the addresses associated with all the interfaces to the machine, you can end up with a long list. That list would include the localhost loop-back and IPv4 and IPv6 addresses, even when one case may not be routable to the machine. To find the IP address to use, an application can look up the hostname, known by the system, and find the associated IP address. The following listing shows this method.

Listing 9.6   Look up the host's IP addresses via the hostname

```
func main() {
    name, err := os.Hostname()
    if err != nil {
            fmt.Println(err)
            return
    }

    addrs, err := net.LookupHost(name)
    if err != nil {
            fmt.Println(err)
            return
    }

    for _, a := range addrs {
            fmt.Println(a)
    }
}
```

Retrieves the hostname as the kernel knows it

Looks up the IP addresses associated with the hostname

Prints each of the IP addresses, as there can be more than one

The system knows its own hostname, and looking up the address for that hostname will return the local one. This is useful for an application that can be run in a variety of environments or scaled horizontally. The hostname and address information could change or have a high rate of variability.

Go applications can be compiled for a variety of operating systems and run in various environments. Applications can detect information about their environment rather that assuming it. This removes the opportunity for bugs or other unexpected situations.

Detecting dependencies

In addition to communicating with the kernel or base operating system, Go applications can call other applications on the system. This is typically accomplished with the os/exec package from the standard library. But what happens if the application being called isn't installed? Assuming that a dependency is present can lead to unexpected behavior, and a failure to detect any issues in a reportable way makes detecting the problem in your application more difficult.

PROBLEM

How can you ensure that it's okay to execute an application before calling it?

SOLUTION

Prior to calling a dependent application for the first time, detect whether the application is installed and available for you to use. If the application isn't present, log an error to help with troubleshooting.

DISCUSSION

We've already talked about how Go applications can run on a variety of operating systems. For example, if an application is compiled for Linux, it could be running on a variety of distributions with different applications installed. If your application relies on another application, it may or may not be installed. This becomes more complicated with the number of distributions available and used in the cloud. Some specialized Linux distributions for the cloud are small, with limited or virtually no commands installed.

Anytime a cloud application relies on another application being installed, it should validate that dependency and log the absence of the missing component. This is relatively straightforward to do with the os/exec package. The following listing provides a function to perform detection.

> Listing 9.7 Function to check whether the application is available

Checks whether the passed-in dependency is in one of the PATHs. When not present, an error is generated.

```
func checkDep(name string) error {
    if _, err := exec.LookPath(name); err != nil {        ◁
        es := "Could not find '%s' in PATH: %s"
        return fmt.Errorf(es, name, err)
    }

    return nil
}
```

Returns an error when the dependency isn't found

Returning nil if there was no error

This function can be used within the flow of an application to check whether a dependency exists. The following snippet shows an example of checking and acting on an error:

```
err := checkDep("fortune")
if err != nil {
    log.Fatalln(err)
}

fmt.Println("Time to get your fortunte")
```

In this example, the error is logged when a dependency isn't installed. Logging isn't always the action to take. There may be a fallback method to retrieve the missing dependency or an alternative dependency to use. Sometimes a missing dependency may be fatal to an application, and other times it can skip an action when a dependency isn't installed. When you know something is missing, you can handle the situation appropriately.

9.3.2 Building for the cloud

There's no one hardware architecture or operating system for the cloud. You may write an application for the AMD64 architecture running on Windows and later find you need to run it on ARM8 and a Linux distribution. Building for the cloud requires designing to support multiple environments, which is easier handled up front in development and is something the standard library can help you with.

TECHNIQUE 60   **Cross-compiling**

In addition to the variety of environments in cloud computing, it's not unusual to develop a Go application on Microsoft Windows or Apple's OS X and want to operate it on a Linux distribution in production, or to distribute an application via the cloud with versions for Windows, OS X, and Linux. In a variety of situations, an application is developed in one operating system but needs to run in a different one.

PROBLEM

How can you compile for architectures and operating systems other than the one you're currently on?

SOLUTION

The go toolchain provides the ability to cross-compile to other architectures and operating systems. In addition to the go toolchain, gox allows you to cross-compile multiple binaries in parallel. You also can use packages, such as `filepath`, to handle differences between operating systems instead of hardcoding values, such as the POSIX path separator /.

DISCUSSION

As of Go 1.5, the compiler installed with the go toolchain can cross-compile out of the box. This is done by setting the GOARCH and GOOS environment variables to specify the architecture and operating system. GOARCH specifies the hardware architecture such as amd64, 386, or arm, whereas GOOS specifies the operating system such as windows, linux, darwin, or freebsd.

The following example provides a quick illustration:

```
$ GOOS=windows GOARCH=386 go build
```

This tells go to build a Windows binary for the 386 architecture. Specifically, the resulting executable will be of the type "PE32 executable for MS Windows (console) Intel 80386 32-bit."

> **WARNING** If your application is using cgo to interact with C libraries, complications can arise. Be sure to test the applications on all cross-compiled platforms.

If you want to compile to multiple operating systems and architectures, one option is gox, which enables building multiple binaries concurrently, as shown in figure 9.4.

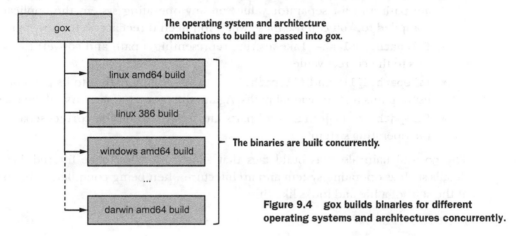

Figure 9.4 gox builds binaries for different operating systems and architectures concurrently.

You can install gox as follows:

```
$ go get -u github.com/mitchellh/gox
```

After gox is installed, you can create binaries in parallel by using the gox command. The following listing provides an example of building an application for OS X, Windows, and Linux on both the AMD64 and 386 architectures.

Listing 9.8 Cross-compile an application with gox

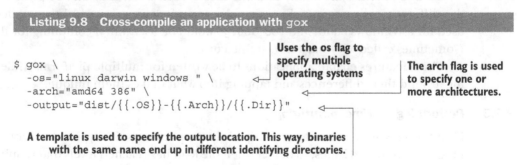

When building binaries in other operating systems—especially when operating them in the cloud—it's a best practice to test the result before deploying. This way, any environment bugs can be detected before deploying to that environment.

Besides compiling for different environments, differences between operating systems need to be handled within an application. Go has two useful parts to help with that.

First, packages provide a single interface that handles differences behind the scenes. For example, one of the most well-known is the difference between path and path list separators. On Linux and other POSIX-based systems, these are / and :, respectively. On Windows, they're \ and ;. Instead of assuming these, use the path/filepath package to make sure any paths are handled safely. This package provides features such as the following:

- filepath.Separator and filepath.ListSeparator—Represent the appropriate path and list separator values on any operating system the application is compiled to. You can use these when you need direct access to the separators.
- filepath.ToSlash—Take a string representing a path and convert the separators to the correct value.
- filepath.Split and filepath.SplitList—Split a path into its parts or split a list of paths into individual paths. Again, the correct separators will be used.
- filepath.Join—Join a list of parts into a path, using the correct separator for the operating system.

The go toolchain also has build tags that allow code files to be filtered, based on details such as operating system and architecture when being compiled. A build tag is at the start of a file and looks like this:

```
// +build !windows
```

This special comment tells the compiler to skip this file on Windows. Build tags can have multiple values. The following example skips building a file on Linux or OS X (darwin):

```
// +build !linux,!darwin
```

These values are linked to GOOS and GOARCH options.

Go also provides the ability to name files in such a way that they're picked up for the different environments. For example, foo_windows.go would be compiled and used for a Windows build, and foo_386.go would be used when compiling for the 386 (sometimes called x86) hardware architecture.

These features enable applications to be written for multiple platforms while working around their differences and tapping into what makes them unique.

9.3.3 *Performing runtime monitoring*

Monitoring is an important part of operating applications. It's typical to monitor running systems to find issues, to detect when the load has reached levels that require scaling up or down, or to understand what's going on within an application to speed it up.

The easiest way to monitor an application is to write issues and other details to a log. The log subsystem can write to disk and another application can read it or the log subsystem can push it out to a monitoring application.

TECHNIQUE 61 Monitoring the Go runtime

Go applications include more than application code or code from libraries. The Go runtime sits in the background, handling the concurrency, garbage collection, threads, and other aspects of the application.

The runtime has access to a wealth of information. That includes the number of processors seen by the application, current number of goroutines, details on memory allocation and usage, details on garbage collection, and more. This information can be useful for identifying problems within the application or for triggering events such as horizontal scaling.

PROBLEM

How can your application log or otherwise monitor the Go runtime?

SOLUTION

The `runtime` and `runtime/debug` packages provide access to the information within the runtime. Retrieve information from the runtime by using these packages and write it to the logs or other monitoring service at regular intervals.

DISCUSSION

Imagine that an imported library update includes a serious bug that causes the goroutines it created to stop going away. The goroutines slowly accumulate so that millions of them are being handled by the runtime when it should have been hundreds. (We, the authors, don't need to imagine this situation, because we've encountered it.) Monitoring the runtime enables you to see when something like this happens.

When an application starts up, it can start a goroutine to monitor the runtime and write details to a log. Running in a goroutine allows you to run the monitoring and write to the logs concurrently, alongside the rest of the application, as the following listing shows.

Listing 9.9 Monitor an application's runtime

A function to monitor the runtime ⟶

When monitoring starts, reports the number of processors available

```go
func monitorRuntime() {
    log.Println("Number of CPUs:", runtime.NumCPU())
    m := &runtime.MemStats{}
    for {
        r := runtime.NumGoroutine()
        log.Println("Number of goroutines", r)

        runtime.ReadMemStats(m)
        log.Println("Allocated memory", m.Alloc)
        time.Sleep(10 * time.Second)
    }
}

func main() {
    go monitorRuntime()
```

Logs the number of goroutines and amount of allocated memory

Loops continuously, pausing for 10 seconds between each iteration

When the application starts, begins monitoring the application

```
    i := 0
    for i < 40 {                                    Creates example
        go func() {                                 goroutines and memory
            time.Sleep(15 * time.Second)            usage while the
        }()                                         application runs for 40
        i = i + 1                                   seconds
        time.Sleep(1 * time.Second)
    }
}
```

It's important to know that calls to `runtime.ReadMemStats` momentarily halt the Go runtime, which can have a performance impact on your application. You don't want to do this often, and you may want to perform operations that halt the Go runtime only when in a debug mode.

Organizing your runtime monitoring this way allows you to replace writing to the log with interaction with an outside monitoring service. For example, if you were using one of the services from New Relic, a monitoring service, you would send the runtime data to their API or invoke a library to do this.

The `runtime` package has access to a wealth of information:

- Information on garbage collection, including when the last pass was, the heap size that will cause the next to trigger, how long the last garbage collection pass took, and more
- Heap statistics, such as the number of objects it includes, the heap size, how much of the heap is in use, and so forth
- The number of goroutines, processors, and `cgo` calls

We've found that monitoring the runtime can provide unexpected knowledge and highlight bugs. It can help you find goroutine issues, memory leaks, or other problems.

9.4   Summary

Cloud computing has become one of the biggest trends in computing and is something Go is quite adept at. In this chapter, you learned about using Go in the cloud. Whereas previous chapters touched on complementary topics to cloud computing, this chapter covered aspects for making successful Go applications in the cloud, including the following:

- Working with various cloud providers, while avoiding vendor lock-in
- Gathering information about the host rather than assuming details of it
- Compiling applications for varying operating systems and avoiding operating system lock-in
- Monitoring the Go runtime to detect issues and details about a running application

In the next chapter, you'll explore communicating between cloud services by using techniques other than REST APIs.

Communication between cloud services

This chapter covers

- Introducing microservice communication
- Reusing connections between services for faster performance
- Providing faster JSON marshaling and unmarshaling
- Using protocol buffers for faster payload transfer
- Communicating over RPC

Representational State Transfer (REST) is the most common form of communication between services, and the most common data format used to transfer information is JSON. REST is an incredibly powerful way to expose interacting with applications to developers and the applications they build.

When communicating between cloud services or microservices within a broader application, you have options besides REST. Some of these options provide for faster communication that uses less bandwidth. In a microservice architecture, in which network communications come into play and can make a real performance difference, some areas can be optimized.

In this chapter, you'll first learn about a microservice architecture and how the network can become a bottleneck or cause performance slowdowns when these services communicate. From there, you'll learn techniques that can speed up REST communications—in particular, JSON communications. Then you'll explore communication techniques other than REST and JSON that can provide an alternative approach.

After this chapter, you'll be able to move beyond the REST communication techniques covered in this book and into faster alternatives used by microservices operating quickly and at scale.

10.1   *Microservices and high availability*

Applications built with a microservice architecture are created as collections of independently deployable services. The rise of complex systems, the desire to independently scale parts of an application, and the need to have applications that are less brittle and more resilient have led to the rise of these microservices. Examples of microservices include configuration manager applications such as etcd, or applications that transcode media from one format to another. Microservices tend to have the following characteristics:

- Perform a single action. For example, store configuration or transcode media from one format to another.
- Elastic and can be horizontally scaled. As load on a microservice changes, it can be scaled up or down as needed.
- Resilient to failures and problems. The service can be deployed so that it doesn't go offline, even when instances of the application have problems.

This is similar to and inspired by the UNIX philosophy of *Do one thing and do it well.*

Imagine that you're building a service that transcodes media from one format to another. A user can upload media, the format is transcoded, and later the media in the new format is available for download. This could be built as a monolithic application in which all elements are part of the same application, or as microservices with different functional parts that are their own applications.

A simple transcoding application built using microservices is illustrated in figure 10.1.

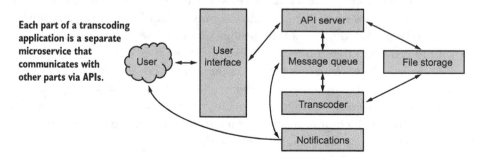

Figure 10.1   A simple transcoding application broken into microservices

In this application, media is uploaded through the user interface to the API server. The API server puts the media in the file store and places a job to transcode the media into a message queue. Transcoders pull the job from the message queue, transcode the media into a new format, place the new file into file storage, and place a job into the queue to notify the user that the transcoding is complete. From the user interface, the user can retrieve the transcoded file. The user interface communicates with the API server to retrieve the file from storage.

Each of these microservices can be written in a different programming language, reused on different applications, and may even be consumed as a service. For example, file storage could be an object storage consumed as software as a service.

Scaling each of these services depends on the needs of the service. For example, the transcoder service can scale depending on how much media needs to be transcoded. The API server and notifications service can scale differently from the transcoder, depending on the appropriate amount of resources they need.

Users have the expectation that services never go offline. The days of maintenance windows during which services aren't available are in the past. Accidental outages can lose user trust and reduce income. One of the advantages of microservices is that each service can be made highly available in a method most appropriate for that service. For example, keeping an API server highly available is different from keeping a message queue highly available.

10.2 Communicating between services

One of the key elements in a microservice architecture is communication between the microservices. If not well done, this can become a bottleneck in the performance of an application.

In the transcoding example in figure 10.1, four microservices are communicating with each other when uploading a new piece of media to be transcoded. If these used REST to communicate and the communications were over TLS, which is typical, a significant amount of time would be spent in network communications.

The performance of communications becomes more important when you use an increasing number of microservices. Companies such as Google, which are known for using microservice architectures, have gone so far as to create new, faster ways to communicate between microservices and build their own networking layer that outperforms what's being sold in the market.

Faster communication is something you can bring to your applications. As you'll see in this chapter, it isn't that complicated to implement.

10.2.1 Making REST faster

REST is the most common form of communication used in web and cloud services. Although transferring representational state data over HTTP is common, it's not efficient or as fast as other protocols. Most setups aren't optimized out of the box, either. This often makes communication a place to speed up application performance.

TECHNIQUE 62   **Reusing connections**

It's not unusual for each HTTP request to be made over its own connection. Negotiating each connection takes time, including the time to negotiate TLS for secure communications. Next, TCP slow-start ramps up as the message is communicated. *Slow-start* is a congestion-control strategy designed to prevent network congestion. As a slow-start ramps up, a single message may take multiple round-trips between the client and server to communicate.

PROBLEM

When each request is over its own connection, a significant amount of time is lost to network communication. How can an application avoid as much of this lost time as possible?

SOLUTION

Reuse connections. Multiple HTTP requests can be made over a single connection. That connection needs to be negotiated and ramped up for slow-start only once. After passing the first message, others happen more quickly.

DISCUSSION

Whether your application is using HTTP/2 (first available in Go 1.6) or HTTP/1 and HTTP/1.1 for your communications, you can reuse connections. Go tries to reuse connections out of the box, and it's the patterns in an application's code that can cause this to not happen.

When connections are reused, as shown in figure 10.2, the time spent opening and closing connections is reduced. Because TCP slow-start has already happened, the time to communicate future messages is faster as well. This is why the second, third, and fourth messages take less time when the connection is reused.

The server included in the net/http package provides HTTP keep-alive support. Most systems support TCP keep-alive needed to reuse connections out of the box. As of Go 1.6, the net/http package includes transparent support for HTTP/2, which has other communication advantages that can make communication even faster.

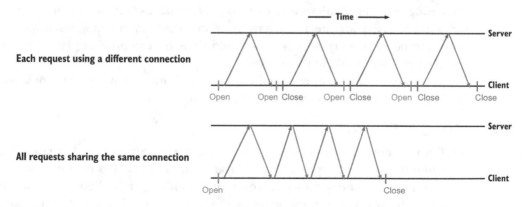

Figure 10.2   Messages being passed with and without connection reuse

NOTE HTTP keep-alive and TCP keep-alive are different. HTTP keep-alive is a feature of the HTTP protocol a web server needs to implement. The web server needs to periodically check the connection for incoming HTTP requests within the keep-alive time span. When no HTTP request is received within that time span, it closes the connection. Alternately, TCP keep-alive is handled by the operating system in TCP communications. Disabling keep-alive with DisableKeepAlives disables both forms of keep-alive.

Most of the problems preventing connection reuse are in the clients used to communicate with HTTP servers. The first and possibly most widespread problem happens when custom transport instances are used and keep-alive is turned off.

When the basic functions in the net/http package are used, such as http.Get() or http.Post(), they use http.DefaultClient, which is configured with keep-alive enabled and set up for 30 seconds. When an application creates a custom client but doesn't specify a transport, http.DefaultTransport is used. http.DefaultTransport is used by http.DefaultClient and is configured with keep-alive enabled.

Transporting without keep-alive can be seen in open source applications, examples online, and even in the Go documentation. For instance, the Go documentation has an example that reads as follows:

```
tr := &http.Transport{
    TLSClientConfig:    &tls.Config{RootCAs: pool},
    DisableCompression: true,
}
client := &http.Client{Transport: tr}
resp, err := client.Get("https://example.com")
```

In this example, a custom Transport instance is used with altered certificate authorities and compression disabled. In this case, keep-alive isn't enabled. The following listing provides a similar example, with the difference being that keep-alive is enabled.

```
tr := &http.Transport{
    TLSClientConfig:    &tls.Config{RootCAs: pool},
    DisableCompression: true,
    Dial: (&net.Dialer{
            Timeout:   30 * time.Second,
            KeepAlive: 30 * time.Second,
    }).Dial,
}
client := &http.Client{Transport: tr}
resp, err := client.Get("https://example.com")
```

The Dial function is configured with a keep-alive and timeout. This is the same configuration as the http.DefaultTransport.

One part of working with http.Transport can be confusing. Setting its DisableKeepAlives property to true disables connection reuse. Setting DisableKeepAlives to false doesn't mean that connections are explicitly reused. It means you can opt in to either HTTP or TCP keep-alive.

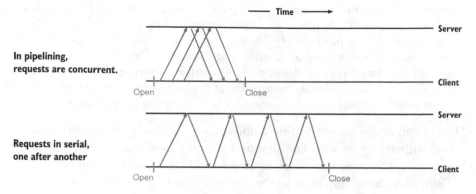

Figure 10.3   HTTP Pipelining compared to serial requests

Unless you have a reason to disable keep-alive, we suggest you use it. When making many HTTP requests to the same endpoint, it provides for faster performance.

The other behavior that can prevent connection reuse occurs when the body of a response isn't closed. Prior to HTTP/2, pipelining was almost never implemented or used. *Pipelining* allows multiple requests and their responses to be communicated in parallel rather than in serial, as you can see in figure 10.3. Prior to HTTP/2, one request and response needed to be completed before the next could be used. The body of the response would need to be closed before another HTTP request and response could use the connection.

The following listing illustrates a common case of one response body not being closed before another HTTP request is made.

Listing 10.2   Failing to close an HTTP response body

```
func main() {
r, err := http.Get("http://example.com")        ◁——  Makes an HTTP
if err != nil {                                        request and gets
        ...                                            a response
}
defer r.Body.Close()                             ◁——  Defers closing the
o, err := ioutil.ReadAll(r.Body)                       body until the main()
if err != nil {                                        function exits
        ...
}
// Use the body content

r2, err := http.Get("http://example.com/foo")    ◁——  Makes a second HTTP
if err != nil {                                        request. Because the body
        ...                                            isn't yet closed on the
}                                                      first, a new connection
defer r2.Body.Close()                                  needs to be made.
o, err = ioutil.ReadAll(r2.Body)
if err != nil {
        ...
}
...
}
```

In this case, using `defer` isn't optimal. Instead, the body should be closed when it's no longer needed. The following listing illustrates the same example, with the connection being shared because the body is closed.

Listing 10.3   Using and closing the HTTP response quickly

```go
func main() {
    r, err := http.Get("http://example.com")        ◄———  Makes an HTTP
    if err != nil {                                         request and gets
        ...                                                 a response
    }
    o, err := ioutil.ReadAll(r.Body)          ◄───┐
    if err != nil {                               Copies the response body to
        ...                                       another instance and closes
    }                                             the body when done with it
    r.Body.Close()                            ◄───┘
    // Use the body content

    r2, err := http.Get("http://example.com/foo")   ◄———  Makes another
    if err != nil {                                         HTTP request. This
        ...                                                 request reuses the
    }                                                       connection made
    o, err = ioutil.ReadAll(r2.Body)                        during the previous
    if err != nil {                                         request.
        ...
    }
    r2.Body.Close()
    ...
}
```

This subtle change to the application can impact how network connections behind the scenes are happening and can improve the overall performance of an application, especially as it scales.

TECHNIQUE 63   Faster JSON marshal and unmarshal

A majority of the communication that happens over REST involves passing data as JSON. The JSON marshaling and unmarshaling provided by the `encoding/json` package uses reflection to figure out values and types each time. Reflection, provided by the `reflect` package, takes time to figure out types and values each time a message is acted on. If you're repeatedly acting on the same structures, quite a bit of time will be spent reflecting. Reflection is covered in more detail in chapter 11.

PROBLEM

Instead of figuring out the types of data each time JSON is marshaled or unmarshaled, how can the type be figured out once and skipped on future passes?

SOLUTION

Use a package able to generate code that can marshal and unmarshal the JSON. The generated code skips reflection and provides a faster execution path with a smaller memory footprint.

DISCUSSION

Reflection in Go is fairly fast. It does allocate memory that needs to be garbage-collected, and there's a small computational cost. When using optimized generated code, those costs can be reduced, and you can see a performance improvement.

Several packages are designed to do this. In listing 10.4 you'll look at the package github.com/ugorji/go/codec, which is designed to work with Binc, MessagePack, and Concise Binary Object Representation (CBOR) in addition to JSON. Binc, MessagePack, and CBOR are alternative data exchange formats, though none is as popular as JSON.

> **Listing 10.4   A struct annotated for `codec`**

```
//go:generate codecgen -o user_generated.go user.go

package user

type User struct {
    Name  string `codec:"name"`
    Email string `codec:",omitempty"`
}
```

A code comment for the go generate command to know how to generate code from this file

The User struct is annotated for codec instead of JSON

codec can't generate code for main packages. Here the user functionality is in the user package.

The codec annotation will omit Email when it generates JSON output and the Email value is empty.

The Name property will be found as "name" in the JSON file. The difference is the case on the name.

A struct marked up for the `codec` package is almost the same as the `json` package. The difference is in the name `codec`.

To generate code, the `codecgen` command needs to be installed. This can be done as follows:

```
$ go get -u github.com/ugorji/go/codec/codecgen
```

After codecgen is installed, you can use it to generate code on this file, named user.go, by executing the following command:

```
$ codecgen -o user_generated.go user.go
```

The output file is named user_generated.go. In the generated file, you'll notice that two public methods have been added to the `User` type: `CodecEncodeSelf` and `Codec-DecodeSelf`. When these are present, the `codec` package uses them to encode or decode the type. When they're absent, the `codec` package falls back to doing these at runtime.

When the `codecgen` command is installed, it can be used with `go generate`. `go generate` will see the first comment line of the file, which is specially formatted for it, and execute `codecgen`. To use `go generate`, run the following command:

```
$ go generate ./...
```

NOTE The next chapter covers generators and reflection in depth.

After the `User` type is ready for use, the encoding and decoding can be incorporated into the rest of the application, as shown in the next listing.

Listing 10.5   Encode an instance to JSON with `codec`

```
jh := new(codec.JsonHandle)
u := &user.User{
    Name:  "Inigo Montoya",
    Email: "inigo@montoya.example.com",
}

var out []byte
err := codec.NewEncoderBytes(&out, jh).Encode(&u)
if err != nil {
    …
}

fmt.Println(string(out))
```

Creates an instance of User populated with data

Converts the byte slice to a string and prints it

Creates a byte slice to store the output in. This will be the generated JSON from the instance of User.

Creates a new JSON handler for the encoder. The codec package has handlers for each type it works with.

Encodes the instance of User into the output using the JSON handle. The codec package does this in two steps that can be done together.

Here's the output of this code:

```
{"name":"Inigo Montoya","Email":"inigo@montoya.example.com"}
```

Notice that the `name` key is lowercase, whereas the `Email` key has an uppercase first letter. The `User` type, defined in listing 10.4, has uppercase property names leading to key names that directly reflect that. But the `Name` property has a custom key of `name` used here.

The byte slice with the JSON that was created in listing 10.5 can be decoded into an instance of `User`, as shown in the following listing.

Listing 10.6   Decode JSON into an instance of a type

```
var u2 user.User
err = codec.NewDecoderBytes(out, jh).Decode(&u2)
if err != nil {
    …
}

fmt.Println(u2)
```

Creates a variable to hold the decoded JSON

Decodes the JSON by using the JSON handler, both created in listing 10.5, into the new instance of the User type. The decoder uses two steps that can be used together. The decoder can reuse the JSON handler.

Prints the populated instance of User

Although the API to `github.com/ugorji/go/codec` is different from the `encoding /json` package in the standard library, it's simple enough to be easily used.

10.2.2 *Moving beyond REST*

Although REST is common and usable for end-user-facing APIs, alternatives may be faster and more efficient for communication between your microservices. Given the rise of microservices, the amount of communication between them, and the manner in which network communication can be a bottleneck, exploring other options is worthwhile.

The network bottleneck has become enough of an issue that companies that operate on a large scale, such as Google and Facebook, have innovated new technologies to speed up communication between microservices.

TECHNIQUE 64   **Using protocol buffers**

JSON and XML are commonly used to serialize data. These formats are fairly easy to use and the transfer format is easy to read, but they're not optimized for transport over a network or for serialization.

PROBLEM

What formats that are optimized for network transfer and serialization are available for use in Go applications?

SOLUTION

Some more recent formats, including protocol buffers (a.k.a. protobuf) by Google and Apache Thrift and originally developed at Facebook, are faster in network transfer and serialization. These are available in Go, along with numerous other languages.

DISCUSSION

Protocol buffers, by Google, are a popular choice for a high-speed transfer format. The data in the messages being transferred over the network is smaller than XML or JSON and it can be marshaled and unmarshaled faster than XML and JSON as well. The transfer method isn't defined by protocol buffers. They can be transferred on a filesystem, using RPC, over HTTP, via a message queue, and numerous other ways.

Google provides support for working with protocol buffers in C++, C#, Go, Java, and Python. Other languages, such as PHP, have third-party libraries that provide support.

A protocol format is defined in a file. It contains the structure of the message and can be used to automatically generate the needed code. The following listing contains an example of the file user.proto.

Listing 10.7   Protocol buffer file

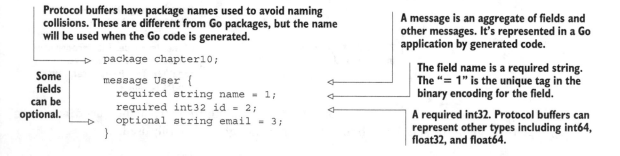

Protocol buffers have package names used to avoid naming collisions. These are different from Go packages, but the name will be used when the Go code is generated.

A message is an aggregate of fields and other messages. It's represented in a Go application by generated code.

```
package chapter10;

message User {
    required string name = 1;
    required int32 id = 2;
    optional string email = 3;
}
```

Some fields can be optional.

The field name is a required string. The "= 1" is the unique tag in the binary encoding for the field.

A required int32. Protocol buffers can represent other types including int64, float32, and float64.

TIP For more details regarding what can be passed in messages, including messages inside messages, see the protocol buffer documentation at https://developers .google.com/protocol-buffers/docs/overview.

Because the protocol buffer is used to generate Go code, it's recommended that it have its own package. In this Go package, the protocol buffer file and generated code can reside. As you'll see in listing 10.8, the directory in this case is userpb.

To compile the protocol buffer to code, you first need to install the compiler:

1 Download and install the compiler. You can get it at https://developers.google .com/protocol-buffers/docs/downloads.html.
2 Install the Go protocol buffer plugin. This can be done using `go get`:
    ```
    $ go get -u github.com/golang/protobuf/protoc-gen-go
    ```

To generate the code, run the following command from the same directory as the .proto file:

```
$ protoc -I=. --go_out=. ./user.proto
```

The command does a few things:

- `-I` specifies the input source directory.
- `--go_out` indicates where the generated Go source files will go.
- `./user.proto` is the name of the file to generate the source from.

After the generated code has been created, it can be used to pass messages between a client and server. The following listing provides the setup for a server to respond with protocol buffer messages.

Listing 10.8 Protocol buffer server setup

The messages are passed using a normal http server.

The import for the generated code and the custom messages

```
import (
    "net/http"

    pb "github.com/Masterminds/go-in-practice/chapter10/userpb"
    "github.com/golang/protobuf/proto"
)

func main() {
    http.HandleFunc("/", handler)
    http.ListenAndServe(":8080", nil)
}
```

The protobuf package needs to be imported to know how to work with the generated code.

A simple server with a single handler

WARNING Although this example communicates user information over HTTP for simplicity, in production applications, user information should be transported over encrypted communications for security.

Listing 10.8 opens in a similar manner to the web servers in earlier chapters. The same patterns there can be used here. The real work is done in the handler, shown in the following listing.

Listing 10.9   Protocol buffer server handler

Creates a pointer to a new instance of the generated User type in the protocol buffer package

Values are wrapped in calls to the proto package to return a reference to the value.

```go
func handler(res http.ResponseWriter, req *http.Request) {
    u := &pb.User{
        Name:  proto.String("Inigo Montoya"),
        Id:    proto.Int32(1234),
        Email: proto.String("inigo@montoya.example.com"),
    }
    body, err := proto.Marshal(u)
    if err != nil {
        http.Error(res, err.Error(), http.StatusInternalServerError)
        return
    }
    res.Header().Set("Content-Type", "application/x-protobuf")
    res.Write(body)
}
```

Marshals the instance into a message

Sets the content type and writes the message to output

Writing a response as a protocol buffer is fairly similar to writing a JSON or XML response. One difference is that values to properties on messages are pointers to a value rather than a value itself. Calls to proto.String, proto.Int32, and other functions return pointers to values rather than the values passed in.

A client can be used to retrieve and read the messages. The following listing showcases a simple client.

Listing 10.10   Protocol buffer client

```go
res, err := http.Get("http://localhost:8080")
if err != nil {
    ...
}
defer res.Body.Close()

b, err = ioutil.ReadAll(res.Body)
if err != nil {
    ...
}

var u pb.User
err = proto.Unmarshal(b, &u)
if err != nil {
    ...
}
```

Performs a GET request to the server from listings 10.8 and 10.9

Reads the response body to get one complete protocol buffer message

Creates a variable and unmarshals the message into it. The pb package is the same imported package from listing 10.8.

```
fmt.Println(u.GetName())
fmt.Println(u.GetId())
fmt.Println(u.GetEmail())
```

⊢ **Properties are pointers to values. The generated code has methods returning a value for each property that starts with Get. Use these to get the passed values.**

Protocol buffers are ideal when you need to pass messages between your microservices and are trying to limit the amount of time used to pass the message.

TECHNIQUE 65 Communicating over RPC with protocol buffers

Communicating requires more than just the payload passed between two endpoints. Communication includes the manner in which the payload is transferred. REST has certain semantics it enforces, which include a path and an HTTP verb, and are resource-based. At times, the semantics of REST aren't desired—for example, for an API call to restart a server. That's an operation, and at times operation-based semantics fit.

An alternative is to use a remote procedure call (RPC) instead. With an RPC, a procedure is executed in a subroutine that's often in a remote location. This is often another service altogether. The calls aren't tied to the semantics of the medium and are more closely related to executing a function on the remote system.

One of the potential issues of RPC is that both sides communicating with each other need to know about the procedure being executed. This is different from REST, in which the details of the communicated payload are enough. Knowing about the procedure can make working with RPC, especially when services are written in multiple languages, seem more difficult.

PROBLEM

How can you communicate over RPC in a manner that's portable across programming languages?

SOLUTION

Use gRPC and protocol buffers to handle defining the interfaces, generating the cross-language code, and implementing the RPC communications.

DISCUSSION

gRPC (www.grpc.io) is an open source, high-performance RPC framework that can use HTTP/2 as a transport layer. It was developed at Google and has support for Go, Java, Python, Objective-C, C#, and several other languages. Given the language support, you'll notice both server-side languages and languages used for building mobile applications. gRPC can be used for communication between mobile devices and supporting services.

gRPC uses code generation to create the messages and handle parts of the communication. This enables the communication to easily work between multiple languages, as the interfaces and messages are generated properly for each language. To define the messages and RPC calls, gRPC uses protocol buffers, as the following listing shows.

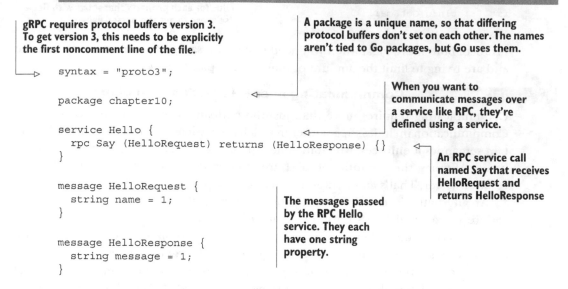

Listing 10.11   Define messages and RPC calls with a protocol buffer

gRPC requires protocol buffers version 3. To get version 3, this needs to be explicitly the first noncomment line of the file.

A package is a unique name, so that differing protocol buffers don't set on each other. The names aren't tied to Go packages, but Go uses them.

```
syntax = "proto3";

package chapter10;

service Hello {
  rpc Say (HelloRequest) returns (HelloResponse) {}
}

message HelloRequest {
  string name = 1;
}

message HelloResponse {
  string message = 1;
}
```

When you want to communicate messages over a service like RPC, they're defined using a service.

An RPC service call named Say that receives HelloRequest and returns HelloResponse

The messages passed by the RPC Hello service. They each have one string property.

TIP   For more details on version 3 of protocol buffers, see the version language guide at https://developers.google.com/protocol-buffers/docs/proto3.

Based on this protocol buffers file, messages and stub code can be generated to handle much of the work. The command to generate the code is a little different from the example in technique 64 to account for RPC generation.

The command (run here from the same directory as the hello.proto file) is shown here:

```
protoc -I=. --go_out=plugins=grpc:. ./hello.proto
```

The difference you'll see is in `--go_out=plugins=gprc:.`, where the gRPC plugin is specified as part of the Go output generation. Without specifying this, the output won't generate the service stub code. After this command is complete, code will be generated for the messages and to work with the Go gRPC package.

WARNING   To use protocol buffers version 3, you need at least version 3.0.0 of the protocol buffers application to be installed. That can be downloaded from https://github.com/google/protobuf/releases.

The following listing shows a simple Hello World server that accepts RPC messages and responds to them. This is an example of a microservice that responds over RPC.

Listing 10.12   gRPC server responding to requests

Imports the code generated from the
protocol buffer from listing 10.11

Imports the context and gRPC
packages that know how to work
with the generated code. You
need to fetch these packages.

```go
package main

import (
    "log"
    "net"

    pb "github.com/Masterminds/go-in-practice/chapter10/hellopb"
    "golang.org/x/net/context"
    "google.golang.org/grpc"
)

type server struct{}

func (s *server) Say(ctx context.Context, \
 in *pb.HelloRequest) (*pb.HelloResponse, error) {
    msg := "Hello " + in.Name + "!"
    return &pb.HelloResponse{Message: msg}, nil
}

func main() {
    l, err := net.Listen("tcp", ":55555")
    if err != nil {
        ...
    }
    s := grpc.NewServer()
    pb.RegisterHelloServer(s, &server{})
    s.Serve(l)
}
```

Creates an implementation of
the Say call defined as a service
in listing 10.11. It receives and
responds with the messages
from listing 10.11.

Starts a TCP server listening on
port 55555 and handles any
errors. The gRPC server will use it.

Creates a gRPC server and
handles requests over the
TCP connection

Registers the implementation of the hello
service on the RPC server. This ensures
that the interface matches properly.

The `golang.org/x/net/context` package is an important part of the communication, and gRPC depends on it. This package carries deadlines, cancelation signals, and other request-scoped values across API boundaries. For example, `context` could contain a timeout that the callee needs to know about. You'll explore more of this when you look at the client.

NOTE   The `context` package will be moving to the standard library for Go 1.7 and later.

To use the service in listing 10.12, you need a client. That client can be in any language, and client code can be generated by the protocol buffers. The following listing provides a Go client using the already generated Go code.

Listing 10.13   Request to a gRPC server with protocol buffers

Includes the generated code from the protocol
buffer for the messages and service

The gRPC package needed to
communicate with the server

```go
package main

import (
    "fmt"
    "os"

    pb "github.com/Masterminds/go-in-practice/chapter10/hellopb"
    "golang.org/x/net/context"
    "google.golang.org/grpc"
)

func main() {
    address := "localhost:55555"
    conn, err := grpc.Dial(address, grpc.WithInsecure())
    if err != nil {
        ...
    }
    defer conn.Close()
    c := pb.NewHelloClient(conn)

    name := "Inigo Montoya"
    hr := &pb.HelloRequest{Name: name}
    r, err := c.Say(context.Background(), hr)
    if err != nil {
        ...
    }
    fmt.Println(r.Message)
}
```

Connects to the other service and handles
any errors. Insecure communications
shouldn't be used in production. Be sure
to set up the connection to be closed.

Creates a new instance of a hello
client, defined in the protocol
buffer file from listing 10.11. It
communicates over the already
created connection.

Prepares a
HelloRequest
message to pass to
the other service

Passes a context and request to
Say and gets a response and
error. Notice the interface to Say
is the same as the server from
listing 10.12. Handles any errors
that may have occurred.

Prints the response that was
generated in the other service

The context being passed to Say is important. In this case, it's an empty context that's
never canceled and has no values. It's a simple background process. The context
package has other contexts, and you can read more about them in the package documentation at https://godoc.org/golang.org/x/net/context.

One example is using a context with a cancel function. This is useful if the caller
goes away (for example, the application is closed), and the callee needs to be
informed of this. The client could create a context like this:

```go
ctx, cancel := context.WithCancel(context.Background())
defer cancel()
```

When the function this code is in ends, the `cancel()` function is called. This tells the context to cancel the work. This is communicated to the other service, even when hosted on an entirely different system. On the server, this cancellation can be seen through a channel, which is how it's implemented in the client as well. For example, in an RPC function such as `Say`, there could be the following:

```
select {
case <-ctx.Done():
    return nil, ctx.Err()
}
```

When a message is sent over the channel available from `Done()`, which happens when the `cancel()` function is called, it will be received here. The `ctx.Err()` function is aware of the type of cancelation that was set up. In this case, the error sent back will note that the work was canceled.

Contexts are a powerful tool for passing information over the course of a remote call—especially when the remote call will take a good amount of time.

When the client and server are using HTTP/2, as they are by default when both ends are using gRPC, the communications use the connection reuse and multiplexing described earlier in the chapter. This enables a fast, modern transport layer for transferring the protocol buffer binary messages.

The advantages and disadvantages of RPC utilizing gRPC should be weighed before using them. The advantages include the following:

- Using protocol buffers, the payload size is smaller and faster to marshal or unmarshal than JSON or XML.
- The context allows for canceling, communicating timeouts or due dates, and other relevant information over the course of a remote call.
- The interaction is with a called procedure rather than a message that's passed elsewhere.
- Semantics of the transport methodology—for example, HTTP verbs—don't limit the communications over RPC.

The disadvantages include the following:

- The transport payload isn't human-readable as JSON or XML can be.
- Applications need to know the interface and details of the of the RPC calls. Knowing the semantics of the message isn't enough.
- Integration is deeper than a message, such as you'd have with REST, because a remote procedure is being called. Exposing remote procedure access to untrusted clients may not be ideal and should be handled with care for security.

In general, RPCs can be a good alternative for interactions between microservices you control that are part of a larger service. They can provide fast, efficient communication and will even work across multiple programming languages. RPCs shouldn't typically be exposed to clients outside your control, such as a public API. The information needed for those clients to be successful is more difficult to communicate, making REST and JSON better options.

10.3 Summary

In this chapter, you explored REST communications and faster alternatives. These alternatives, or similar options, are used by Google, Facebook, and others that operate using many discrete services that need to work together. The techniques you learned about include the following:

- Communications in a microservice architecture and how that can be a bottleneck
- Reusing connections to improve performance by avoiding repeated TCP slow-start, congestion-control ramp-ups and connection negotiations
- Faster JSON marshaling and unmarshaling that avoids extra time spent reflecting
- Using protocol buffering instead of JSON for messaging
- Communicating over RPC using gRPC

In the next chapter, you'll learn about reflection and metaprogramming in Go. That includes using tags on structs and code generation.

Reflection and code generation

11

This chapter covers

- Using values, kinds, and types from Go's reflection system
- Parsing custom struct annotations
- Writing code generators for use with the `go generate` tool

In this chapter, we turn our attention to some of Go's most interesting features. First, we present Go's reflection system. *Reflection*, in software development, refers to a program's ability to examine its own structure. Although Go's reflection subsystem isn't as versatile as Java's, it's still powerful. One feature that has enjoyed novel use is the annotation of structs. You'll see in this chapter how to write custom tags for struct fields. As useful as Go's reflection system is, though, sometimes it's cleaner to avoid complex and expensive runtime reflection, and instead write code that writes code. Code generation can accomplish some of the things that are typically done in other languages with generics. That practice, called *metaprogramming*, is the last thing you'll look at in this chapter.

11.1 *Three features of reflection*

Software developers use reflection to examine objects during runtime. In a strongly typed language like Go, you may want to find out whether a particular object satisfies an interface. Or discover what its underlying kind is. Or walk over its fields and modify the data.

Go's reflection tools are located inside the `reflect` package. To understand those tools, we need to define a few terms. You need to understand three critical features when working with Go's reflection mechanism: values, types, and kinds.

You might approach the first term, *value*, by thinking of a variable. A *variable* is a name that points to a piece of data, as illustrated in figure 11.1. (The figure labels this *Variable name*.) The piece of data that it points to is called a *value*. Depending on the type, the value may be nil. It may be a pointer, which in turn points to a value somewhere else. Or it may be a nonempty piece of data. For example, with x := 5, the value of x is 5. For var b bytes.Buffer, the value of b is an empty buffer. And with myFunc := strings.Split, the value of myFunc is a function. In the `reflect` package, the type `reflect.Value` represents a value.

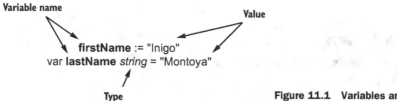

Figure 11.1   Variables and values

Go is a typed language. Each value in Go has a particular *type* associated with it. For example, with var b bytes.Buffer, the type is bytes.Buffer. For any reflect.Value in Go, you can discover its type. Type information is accessible through the `reflect` `.Type` interface.

Finally, Go defines numerous primitive *kinds*, such as struct, ptr (pointer), int, float64, string, slice, func (function), and so on. The reflect package enumerates all of the possible kinds with the type reflect.Kind. (Note that in figure 11.1, the value of type string also has the kind string.)

The typical tasks you perform when working with reflection use these three concepts. Usually, reflection begins by taking a value and then inspecting it to learn about its contents, its type, and its kind.

TECHNIQUE 66   Switching based on type and kind

One of the most frequent uses of Go's reflection system is identifying either the type or kind of a value. Go has various tools for learning about the type and kind of a particular value.

PROBLEM

You want to write a function that takes generic values (interface{}s), and then does something useful with them based on underlying types.

SOLUTION

Go provides various methods for learning this information, ranging from the type switch to the reflect.Type and reflect.Kind types. Each has subtle strong points. Here, you'll look at type switches and then employ the reflect package to build a kind switch.

DISCUSSION

Say you want to write a function with the signature sum(...interface{}) float64. You want this function to take any number of arguments of various types. And you want it to convert the values to float64 and then sum them.

The most convenient tool that Go provides for doing this is the type switch. With this special case of the switch control structure, you can perform operations based on the type of a value, instead of the data contained in a value. As you read through common Go libraries, you'll frequently encounter type switches (though using kinds and switches, which you'll see later in this section, is rare). Let's start with a simple (though incomplete) example in the next listing.

Listing 11.1 Sum with type switch

```go
package main

import (
    "fmt"
    "strconv"
)

func main() {
    var a uint8 = 2
    var b int = 37
    var c string = "3.2"
    res := sum(a, b, c)
    fmt.Printf("Result: %f\n", res)
}

func sum(v ...interface{}) float64 {
    var res float64 = 0
    for _, val := range v {
        switch val.(type) {
        case int:
            res += float64(val.(int))
        case int64:
            res += float64(val.(int64))
        case uint8:
            res += float64(val.(uint8))
        case string:
            a, err := strconv.ParseFloat(val.(string), 64)
            if err != nil {
                panic(err)
```

Sums a uint8, an int, and a string

Loops through all of the values given, and switches over them based on type

For each type that you support (int, int64, uint8, string), converts to float64 and sum

For a string, you use the strconv library to convert the string to a float64

```
        }
            res += a
    default:
            fmt.Printf("Unsupported type %T. Ignoring.\n", val)
        }
    }
    return res
}
```

> **If the type isn't one of the four you support, prints an error and ignores**

If you were to run this code, you'd get Result: 42.200000. This code illustrates the basic use of a type switch, as well as one of its limitations compared to regular switches.

In a standard switch statement, you might combine multiple values on a single case line: case 1, 2, 3: println("Less than four"). Combining types in a case statement introduces complications when assigning values, so typically a type switch has one type per line. If you were to support all of the integer types (int, int8, int16, int32, int64, uint, uint8, uint16, uint32, uint64), you'd need 10 separate case clauses. Although writing similar logic for 10 kinds may feel like an inconvenience, it isn't really a problem. But it's important to remember that type switches operate on *types* (not kinds).

Let's add a new type to the preceding example, as shown in the following listing.

Listing 11.2   Type switch with extra type

```
package main

import (
    "fmt"
    "strconv"
)

type MyInt int64                    ⟵────── MyInt is an int64.

func main() {

//...
    var d MyInt = 1
    res := sum(a, b, c, d)
    fmt.Printf("Result: %f\n", res)
}

func sum(v ...interface{}) float64 {
    var res float64 = 0
    for _, val := range v {
        switch val.(type) {
        case int:
            res += float64(val.(int))
        case int64:
            res += float64(val.(int64))
        case uint8:
            res += float64(val.(uint8))
        case string:
            a, err := strconv.ParseFloat(val.(string), 64)
```

> **Creates a new MyInt and gives it the value 1**

> **This will not match for a MyInt.**

```
                        if err != nil {
                                panic(err)
                        }
                        res += a                              This will catch the MyInt value.
                default:
                        fmt.Printf("Unsupported type %T. Ignoring.\n", val)
                }
        }
        return res
}
```

Running this program generates the following output:

```
$ go run typekind.go
Unsupported type main.MyInt. Ignoring.
Result: 42.200000
```

The type of var d MyInt isn't int64; it's MyInt. In the type switch, it matches the default clause instead of the int64 case. At times, this is precisely the behavior you'd desire. But for this case, it'd be better if sum() could tell what the underlying kind was, and work from that instead.

The solution to this problem is to use the reflect package, and work based on kind instead of type. The first part of our example will be the same, but the sum() function is different, as shown in the next listing.

Listing 11.3   A Kind switch

```
package main

import (
        "fmt"
        "reflect"
        "strconv"
)

type MyInt int64

func main() {
        //…var a uint8 = 2
        var b int = 37
        var c string = "3.2"
        var d MyInt = 1
        res := sum(a, b, c, d)
        fmt.Printf("Result: %f\n", res)
}

func sum(v ...interface{}) float64 {
        var res float64 = 0
        for _, val := range v {
                ref := reflect.ValueOf(val)          Gets the reflect.Value
                switch ref.Kind() {                   of the item

                                                      From the value, you can
                                                      switch on the Kind().
```

reflect.Kind is
a normal type,
so you can
switch on
multiple
values.

```
case reflect.Int, reflect.Int64:
        res += float64(ref.Int())
case reflect.Uint8:
        res += float64(ref.Uint())
case reflect.String:
        a, err := strconv.ParseFloat(ref.String(), 64)
        if err != nil {
                panic(err)
        }
        res += a
default:
        fmt.Printf("Unsupported type %T. Ignoring.\n", val)
}
```

The reflect.Value type provides convenience functions for converting related subkinds to their biggest version (e.g., int, int8, int16...to int64).

```
    }
    return res
}
```

In this revised version, you replace the type switch with a regular value-based switch, and you use the reflect package to take each val interface{} and get a reflect .Value describing it. One of the pieces of information you can learn from a reflect.Value is its underlying kind.

Another thing that the reflect.Value type gives you is a group of functions capable of converting related types to their largest representation. A reflect.Value with a uint8 or uint16 can be easily converted to the biggest unsigned integer type by using the reflect.Value's Uint() method.

With these features, you can collapse an otherwise verbose type switch to a more concise kind-based switch. Instead of needing 10 cases for the integer types, you could accomplish the same feature with only two cases (one for all the signed integers, and one for the unsigned integers).

But types and kinds are distinct things. Here, you've produced two cases that perform approximately the same task. Summing numeric values can be more easily done by determining kinds. But sometimes you're more concerned with specifics. As you've seen elsewhere in the book, type switches are excellent companions for error handling. You can use them to sort out different error types in much the same way that other languages use multiple catch statements in a try/catch block.

Later in this chapter, we return to examining types. In that case, you'll use the reflect.Type type to discover information about a struct. But before you get to that case, let's look at another common reflection task: determining whether a particular type implements an interface.

TECHNIQUE 67   Discovering whether a value implements an interface

Go's type system is different from the inheritance-based methods of traditional object-oriented languages. Go uses composition instead of inheritance. A Go interface defines a pattern of methods that another type must have before it can be considered to implement that interface. A concrete and simple example might help here. The fmt package defines an interface called `Stringer` that describes a thing capable of representing itself as a string:

```
type Stringer interface {
        String() string
}
```

Any type that provides a `String()` method that takes no arguments and returns a string is ipso facto a `fmt.Stringer`.

PROBLEM

Given a particular type, you want to find out whether that type implements a defined interface.

SOLUTION

There are two ways to accomplish this. One is with a type assertion, and the other uses the `reflect` package. Use the one that best meets your needs.

DISCUSSION

Go's view of interfaces differs from that of object-oriented languages like Java. In Go, a thing isn't declared to fulfill an interface. Instead, an interface is a description against which a type can be compared. And interfaces are themselves types. That is why when you write types in Go, you don't declare which interfaces they satisfy. In fact, as you saw in chapter 4, it's common to write interfaces to match existing code.

One easy way to conceptualize this is by considering how we, as humans, often generalize and categorize. If I were to ask you, "What do a swan, a snow drift, and a cloud have in common?" you would answer, "All are white." This doesn't mean that the three things have a common ancestor (the object-oriented approach). Instead, it means that all three share a commonality: whiteness. This is the way types work in Go. They express commonality, not inheritance.

Go makes it easy to determine whether a given interface matches another interface type. Determining the answer to this question can be done at the same time as converting that type, as shown in the next listing.

Listing 11.4 Checking and converting a type

```
package main

import (
    "bytes"
    "fmt"
)

func main() {
    b := bytes.NewBuffer([]byte("Hello"))
    if isStringer(b) {                              ⟵ Tests whether a
        fmt.Printf("%T is a stringer\n", b)            *bytes.Buffer is a
    }                                                  fmt.Stringer. It is.
    i := 123
    if isStringer(i) {                              ⟵ Tests whether an
                                                       integer is a
                                                       fmt.Stringer. It's not.
```

```
        fmt.Printf("%T is a stringer\n", i)
    }
}
func isStringer(v interface{}) bool {          Takes an interface{} value and runs a
    _, ok := v.(fmt.Stringer)                  type assertion to the desired interface
    return ok
}
```

Type assertions are one way of testing whether a given value implements an interface. But what if you want to test whether a type implements an interface, but determine which interface at runtime? To accomplish this, you need to use the reflect package and little bit of trickery.

Earlier in the chapter, you looked at the basic types in the reflect package. An astute reader might have noticed something missing. Go's reflection package has no reflect.Interface type. Instead, reflect.Type (which is itself an interface) provides tools for querying whether a given type implements a given interface type. To reflect on an interface type at runtime, you can use reflect.Type, as the following listing shows.

Listing 11.5   Determine whether a type implements an interface

```
package main

import (
    "fmt"
    "io"
    "reflect"
)

type Name struct {                          ←
    First, Last string
}                                                Creates a Name type and
                                                 gives it a String() method,
func (n *Name) String() string {          ←     then instantiates one
    return n.First + " " + n.Last
}

func main() {                             ←
    n := &Name{First: "Inigo", Last: "Montoya"}

    stringer :=                                     Creates a nil pointer
    (*fmt.Stringer)(nil)                            of type fmt.Stringer
    implements(n, stringer)
                                             ←    Tests whether n is a
                                                  fmt.Stringer (has a
    writer := (*io.Writer)(nil)                   String() method)
    implements(n, writer)           ←
}
```

Creates a nil pointer of type io.Writer

Tests whether n is an io.Writer (has a Write() method)

```
func implements(concrete interface{}, target interface{}) bool {
    iface := reflect.TypeOf(target).Elem()

    v := reflect.ValueOf(concrete)          Gets the reflect.Type of the
    t := v.Type()                           concrete type passed in

    if t.Implements(iface) {
            fmt.Printf("%T is a %s\n", concrete, iface.Name())
            return true
    }
    fmt.Printf("%T is not a %s\n", concrete, iface.Name())
    return false
}
```

Gets a reflect.Type that describes the target of the pointer

Tests whether the concrete instance fulfills the interface of the target

This example takes what may appear to be a roundabout method. The `implements()` function takes two values. It tests whether the first value (`concrete`) implements the interface of the second (`target`). If you were to run this code, you'd get the following output:

```
$ go run implements.go
*main.Name is a Stringer
*main.Name is not a Writer
```

Our `Name` type implements `fmt.Stringer` because it has a `String() string` method. But it doesn't implement `io.Writer` because it doesn't have a `Write([]bytes) (int, error)` method.

The `implements()` function does assume that the target is a pointer to a value whose dynamic type is an interface. With a few dozen lines, you could check that by reflecting on the value and checking that it's a pointer. As it stands now, it'd be possible to cause `implements()` to panic by passing a target that doesn't match that description.

To get to the point where you can test whether `concrete` implements the `target` interface, you need to get the `reflect.Type` of both the `concrete` and the `target`. There are two ways of doing this. The first uses `reflect.TypeOf()` to get a `reflect.Type`, and a call to `Type.Elem()` to get the type that the target pointer points to:

```
iface := reflect.TypeOf(target).Elem()
```

The second gets the value of `concrete`, and then gets the `reflect.Type` of that value. From there, you can test whether a thing of one type implements an interface type using the `Type.Interface()` method:

```
v := reflect.ValueOf(concrete)
t := v.Type()
```

The trickier part of this test, though, is getting a reference to an interface. There's no way to directly reflect on an interface type. Interfaces don't work that way; you can't just instantiate one or reference it directly.

Instead, you need to find a way to create a placeholder that implements an interface. The simplest way is to do something we usually recommend studiously avoiding: intentionally create a `nil` pointer. In the preceding code, you create two `nil` pointers, and you do so like this: `stringer := (*fmt.Stringer)(nil)`. In essence, you do this just to create a thing whose only useful information is its type. When you pass these into the `implements()` function, it'll be able to reflect on the `nil` pointers and determine the type. You need the `Elem()` call in order to get the type of the `nil`.

The code in listing 11.5 illustrates how working with Go's reflection system can require thinking creatively about how to set up various reflection operations. Tasks that might seem superficially simple may require some thoughtful manipulation of the type system.

Next, let's look at how to use Go's reflection system to take a struct and programmatically access its fields.

TECHNIQUE 68   Accessing fields on a struct

Go structs are the most commonly used tool for describing structured data in Go. Because Go can glean all of the important information about a struct's contents during compilation, structs are efficient. At runtime, you may want to find out information about a struct, including what its fields are and whether particular values of a struct have been set.

PROBLEM

You want to learn about a struct at runtime, discovering its fields.

SOLUTION

Reflect the struct and use a combination of `reflect.Value` and `reflect.Type` to find out information about the struct.

DISCUSSION

In the last few techniques, you've seen how to start with a value and reflect on it to get information about its value, its kind, and its type. Now you're going to combine these techniques to walk a struct and learn about it.

The tool you'll create is a simple information-printing program that can read a value and print information about it to the console. The principles will come in handy, though, in the next section, where you'll use some similar techniques to work with Go's annotation system.

First, let's start with a few types to examine in the following listing.

Listing 11.6   Types to examine

```
package main

import (
    "fmt"
    "reflect"
```

```
        "strings"
)
type MyInt int

type Person struct {
    Name    *Name
    Address *Address
}

type Name struct {
    Title, First, Last string
}

type Address struct {
    Street, Region string
}
```

Now you have an integer-based type and a few structs. The next thing to do is to write some code to inspect these types, as shown in the next listing.

Listing 11.7   Recursively examining a value

```
func main() {
    fmt.Println("Walking a simple integer")
    var one MyInt = 1
    walk(one, 0)                                          │ Shows details for a simple type

    fmt.Println("Walking a simple struct")
    two := struct{ Name string }{"foo"}
    walk(two, 0)                                          │ Shows details for a simple struct

fmt.Println("Walking a struct with struct fields")
    p := &Person{
            Name:    &Name{"Count", "Tyrone", "Rugen"},           Shows details
            Address: &Address{"Humperdink Castle", "Florian"},    for a struct with
    }                                                             struct fields
    walk(p, 0)
}

type MyInt int

type Person struct {
    Name    *Name
    Address *Address
}

type Name struct {                              The walk() function
    Title, First, Last string                   takes any value and
}                                               a depth (for
                                                formatting).
type Address struct {
    Street, Region string                                   For your unknown value u,
}                                                            you get the reflect.Value. If
                                                             it's a pointer, you
func walk(u interface{}, depth int) {      ◄──               dereference the pointer.
    val := reflect.Indirect(reflect.ValueOf(u))  ◄──
    t := val.Type()
    tabs := strings.Repeat("\t", depth+1)   ◄──   Depth helps you do some tab
                                                  indenting for prettier output.
```

Gets the type of this value

```
                fmt.Printf("%sValue is type %q (%s)\n", tabs, t, val.Kind())
                if val.Kind() == reflect.Struct {
                        for i := 0; i < t.NumField(); i++ {
                                field := t.Field(i)
                                fieldVal := reflect.Indirect(val.Field(i))

                                tabs := strings.Repeat("\t", depth+2)
                                fmt.Printf("%sField %q is type %q (%s)\n",
                                        tabs, field.Name, field.Type, fieldVal.Kind())

                                if fieldVal.Kind() == reflect.Struct {
                                        walk(fieldVal.Interface(), depth+1)
                                }
                        }
                }
        }
}
```

If the kind is struct, you examine its fields.

For each field, you need both the reflect.StructField and the reflect.Value.

If the field is also a struct, you can recursively call walk().

The preceding example combines just about everything you've learned about reflection. Types, values, and kinds all come into play as you walk through a value and examine its reflection data. If you run this little program, the output looks like this:

```
$ go run structwalker.go
Walking a simple integer
    Value is type "main.MyInt" (int)
Walking a simple struct
    Value is type "struct { Name string }" (struct)
            Field "Name" is type "string" (string)
Walking a struct with struct fields
    Value is type "main.Person" (struct)
            Field "Name" is type "*main.Name" (struct)
            Value is type "main.Name" (struct)
                    Field "Title" is type "string" (string)
                    Field "First" is type "string" (string)
                    Field "Last" is type "string" (string)
            Field "Address" is type "*main.Address" (struct)
            Value is type "main.Address" (struct)
                    Field "Street" is type "string" (string)
                    Field "Region" is type "string" (string)
```

In this output, you can see the program examine each of the values you've given it. First, it checks a `MyInt` value (of kind int). Then it walks the simple struct. Finally, it walks the more complex struct and recurses down through the struct until it hits only nonstruct kinds.

The `walk()` function does all of the interesting work in this program. It begins with an unknown value, u, and inspects it. While you're walking through an unknown value, you want to make sure that you follow pointers. If `reflect.ValueOf()` is called on a pointer, it will return a `reflect.Value` describing a pointer. That isn't interesting in this case. Instead, what you want is the value at the other end of that pointer, so you use `reflect.Indirect()` to get a `reflect.Value` describing the value pointed to. The `reflect.Indirect()` method is useful in that if it's called on a value that's not a pointer, it will return the given `reflect.Value`, so you can safely call it on all values:

```
val := reflect.Indirect(reflect.ValueOf(u))
```

Along with the value of u, you need some type and kind information. In this example, you get each of the three reflection types:

- The value (in this case, if you get a pointer for a value, you follow the pointer)
- The type
- The kind

Kinds are particularly interesting in this case. Some kinds, notably slices, arrays, maps, and structs, may have members. In this case, you're interested mainly in learning about the structure of your given value (u). Although you wouldn't need to enumerate the values in maps, slices, or arrays, you'd like to examine structs. If the kind is `reflect.Struct`, you take a look at that struct's fields.

The easiest way to enumerate the fields of a struct is to get the type of that struct and then loop through the fields of that type by using a combination of `Type.NumField()` (which gives you the number of fields) and `Type.Field()`. The `Type.Field()` method returns a `reflect.StructField` object describing the field. From there, you can learn about the field's data type and its name.

But when it comes to getting the value of a struct field, you can't get this from either the `reflect.Type` (which describes the data type) or the `reflect.StructField` (which describes the field on a struct type). Instead, you need to get the value from the `reflect.Value` that describes the struct value. Fortunately, you can combine your knowledge of the type and the value to know that the numeric index of the type field will match the numeric index of the value's struct field. You can use `Value.Field()` with the same field number as `Type.Field()`, and get the associated value for that field. Again, if the field is a pointer, you'd rather have a handle to the value at the other end of the pointer, so you call `reflect.Indirect()` on the field value. If you take a look at the output of the preceding program, you'll see this in action:

```
Field "Name" is type "*main.Name" (struct)
Value is type "main.Name" (struct)
```

The field Name is of type *main.Name. But when you follow the pointer, you get a value of type main.Name. This little program is dense, so to summarize what you've just seen:

- From interface{}, you can use `reflect.ValueOf()` to get `reflect.Value`.
- Sometimes a value might be a pointer. To follow the pointer and get the `reflect.Value` of the thing pointed to, you call `reflect.Indirect()`.
- From `reflect.Value`, you can conveniently get the type and kind.
- For structs (kind == `reflect.Struct`), you can get the number of fields on that struct by using `Type.NumField()`, and you can get a description of each field (`reflect.StructField`) by using `Type.Field()`.
- Likewise, with `reflect.Value` objects, you can access struct field values by using `Value.Field()`.

If you were interested in discovering other information, the `reflect` package contains tools for learning about the methods on a struct, the elements in maps, lists, and arrays, and even information about what a channel can send or receive. For all of Go's elegance, though, the reflection package can be difficult to learn and unforgiving to use: many of the functions and methods in that package will panic rather than return errors.

The example you've looked at here sets the stage for using one of our favorite Go features. Next, you'll look at Go's annotation system. You'll see how to build and access your own struct tags.

11.2 Structs, tags, and annotations

Go has no macros, and unlike languages such as Java and Python, Go has only Spartan support for annotations. But one thing you can easily annotate in Go is properties on a struct. You've already seen this practice for providing JSON processing information. Here's an example.

11.2.1 Annotating structs

In the previous chapter, you saw an example of using struct annotations with things like the JSON encoder. For example, you can begin with the struct from listing 11.5 and annotate it for the JSON encoder, as shown in the following listing.

Listing 11.8   Simple JSON struct

```
package main

import (
    "encoding/json"
    "fmt"
)

type Name struct {
    First string `json:"firstName"`      Annotates struct fields for JSON
    Last  string `json:"lastName "`      encoding and decoding
}

func main() {
    n := &Name{"Inigo", "Montoya"}
    data, _ := json.Marshal(n)
    fmt.Printf("%s\n", data)B            Marshals n to JSON and prints it
}
```

This code declares a single struct, Name, that's annotated for JSON encoding. Roughly speaking, it maps the struct member First to the JSON field firstName, and the struct field Last to lastName. If you were to run this code, the output would look like this:

```
$ go run json.go
{"firstName":"Inigo","lastName":"Montoya"}
```

The struct annotations make it possible to control how your JSON looks. Struct tags provide a convenient way to provide small bits of processing data to fields on a struct.

Practically speaking, annotations are a free-form string enclosed in back quotes that follows the type declaration of a struct field.

Annotations play no direct functional role during compilation, but annotations can be accessed at runtime by using reflection. It's up to the annotation parsers to figure out whether any given annotation has information that the parser can use. For example, you could modify the preceding code to include different annotations, as shown in the next listing.

Listing 11.9 A variety of annotations

```
type Name struct {
    First string `json:"firstName" xml:"FirstName"`
    Last  string `json:"lastName,omitempty"`
    Other string `not,even.a=tag`
}
```

These annotations are all legal, in the sense that the Go parser will correctly handle them. And the JSON encoder will be able to pick out which of those applies to it. It will ignore the xml tag as well as the oddly formatted annotation on the Other field.

As you can see from the tags in listing 11.9, an annotation has no fixed format. Just about any string can be used. But a certain annotation format has emerged in the Go community and is now a de facto standard. Go developers call these annotations *tags*.

11.2.2 Using tag annotations

The sample JSON struct you looked at earlier contained annotations of the form `json:"NAME,DATA"`, where NAME is the name of the field (in JSON documents), and DATA is a list of optional information about the field (omitempty or kind data). Figure 11.2 shows an example of a struct annotated for both JSON and XML.

Likewise, if you look at the encoding/xml package, you'd see a pattern similar to annotations for converting structs to and from XML. Tags for XML look like this: `xml:"body"` and `xml:"href,attr"`. Again, the pattern is similar to the JSON tag pattern: `xml:"NAME,DATA"`, where NAME is the field name, and DATA contains a list of

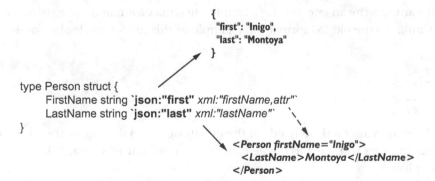

Figure 11.2 A struct marshaled to JSON and to XML

> ### Annotations for validation
>
> One of the most interesting uses for annotations that we've seen is for validating field data on a struct. By adding regular expressions in tags (`` `validate:"^[a-z]+$"` ``), and then writing code to run those regular expressions over struct data, you can write validation code easily and concisely. An example can be found in the Deis Router project at https://github.com/deis/router.

information about the field (though XML annotations are more sophisticated than JSON annotations).

This format isn't enshrined in the definition of a struct annotation, though. It's just a convention that has proven useful and thus enjoys widespread adoption. Go's reflection package even makes it easy to work with tags, as you'll see shortly.

TECHNIQUE 69   Processing tags on a struct

Annotations can be useful in a wide variety of situations. The preceding examples show how they can be used by encoders. Annotations can just as readily be used to describe how database field types map to structs, or how to format data for display. We've even seen cases in which annotations were used to tell Go to pass struct values through other filtering functions.

And because the annotation format is undefined, to build your annotations, you need only decide on a format and then write an implementation.

PROBLEM

You want to create your own annotations and then programmatically access the annotation data of a struct at runtime.

SOLUTION

Define your annotation format (preferably using the tag-like syntax described previously). Then use the `reflect` package to write a tool that extracts the annotation information from a struct.

DISCUSSION

Say you want to write an encoder for a simple file syntax for name-value pairs. This format is similar to the old INI format. An example of this file format looks like this:

```
total=247
running=2
sleeping=245
threads=1189
load=70.87
```

Here, the names are on the left side of the equals sign, and the values are on the right. Now imagine that you want to create a struct to represent this data. It looks like the following listing.

Listing 11.10   A bare Processes struct

```
type Processes struct {
    Total    int
    Running  int
    Sleeping int
    Threads  int
    Load     float32
}
```

To convert the plain file format into a struct like this, you can create a tag that fits your needs and then mark up your struct with them (see the following listing).

Listing 11.11   The Processes struct with annotations

```
type Processes struct {
    Total    int     `ini:"total"`
    Running  int     `ini:"running"`
    Sleeping int     `ini:"sleeping"`
    Threads  int     `ini:"threads"`
    Load     float32 `ini:"load"`
}
```

This tag structure follows the same convention as the JSON and XML tags you saw earlier. But there's no automatic facility in Go to handle parsing the file format and learning from the struct annotations how to populate a Processes struct. You'll do that work yourself.

As you design this, you can once again rely on existing conventions. Encoders and decoders in Go tend to provide marshal() and unmarshal() methods with a fairly predictable set of parameters and return values. So your INI file decoder will implement the same pattern, as shown in the following listing.

Listing 11.12   The marshal and unmarshal pattern

```
func Marshal(v interface{}) ([]byte, error) {}
func Unmarshal(data []byte, v interface{}) error {}
```

The bulk of both of these functions involves reflecting over the interface{} values and learning about how to extract data from or populate data into those values. To keep the code concise, the following example deals only with marshaling and unmarshaling structs.

Reflection tends to be a little verbose, so you'll split up the code for your program into smaller chunks, starting with a struct for your INI file and the main() function. In the first part, you'll create a new type (Processes), and then in the main() function you'll create a Processes struct, marshal it to your INI format, and then unmarshal it into a new Processes struct. See the next listing.

Listing 11.13   Processes and main()

```
package main

import (
        "bufio"                          ←  Most of these imports
        "bytes"                             are used later.
        "errors"
        "fmt"
        "reflect"
        "strconv"
        "strings"
)

type Processes struct {                   ←  You saw this struct in
        Total    int      `ini:"total"`       listing 11.11.
        Running  int      `ini:"running"`
        Sleeping int      `ini:"sleeping"`
        Threads  int      `ini:"threads"`
        Load     float64  `ini:"load"`
}

func main() {
        fmt.Println("Write a struct to output:")
        proc := &Processes{
                Total:    23,
                Running:  3,              Creates an instance
                Sleeping: 20,             of the Processes
                Threads:  34,             struct
                Load:     1.8,
        }                                        Marshals the struct
        data, err := Marshal(proc)       ←       into a []byte
        if err != nil {
                panic(err)
        }
        fmt.Println(string(data))        ←——— Prints the result

        fmt.Println("Read the data back into a struct")
        proc2 := &Processes{}                    Creates a new Processes struct
        if err := Unmarshal(data, proc2); err != nil {   and unmarshals the data into it
                panic(err)
        }
        fmt.Printf("Struct: %#v", proc2) ←——— Prints out the struct
}
```

The top-level code is straightforward. You begin with an instance of your `Processes`
struct and then marshal it into a byte array. When you print the results, they'll be in
your INI file format. Then you take that same data and run it back through the other
direction, expanding the INI data into a new `Processes` struct. Running the program
produces output like this:

```
$ go run load.go
Write a struct to a output:
total=23
running=3
```

```
sleeping=20
threads=34
load=1.8
```

```
Read the data back into a struct
Struct: &main.Processes{Total:23, Running:3, Sleeping:20, Threads:34,
    Load:1.8}
```

The first section of output shows your marshaled data, and the second shows your unmarshaled struct. Next you can look at the Marshal() function, which brings much of your reflection knowledge back to the forefront. See the following listing.

Listing 11.14 The `Marshal` function

A utility function to read tags off of struct fields

```
func fieldName(field reflect.StructField) string {        Gets the tag off the
    if t := field.Tag.Get("ini"); t != "" {              struct field
        return t
    }
    return field.Name        ←──────  If there is no tag, falls
}                                      back to the field name
func Marshal(v interface{}) ([]byte, error) {
    var b bytes.Buffer                             Gets a reflect.Value of the
    val :=                                         current interface.
    reflect.Indirect(reflect.ValueOf(v))    ←───   Dereferences pointers.
    if val.Kind() != reflect.Struct {
        return []byte{}, errors.New("unmarshal can only take structs")
    }
    t := val.Type()
    for i := 0; i < t.NumField(); i++ {      ←───  Loops through all of the
        f := t.Field(i)                            fields on the struct
        name := fieldName(f)                       Relies on the print
        raw := val.Field(i).Interface()            formatter to print the
        fmt.Fprintf(&b, "%s=%v\n", name, raw)  ←── raw data into the buffer
    }
    return b.Bytes(), nil        ←──────  Returns the contents of the buffer
}
```

For this program, you handle only structs.

Gets the name from tagName

This Marshal() function takes the given v interface{} and reads through its fields. By examining the type, it can iterate through all the fields on the struct, and for each field, it can access the annotation (via StructField.Tag()). As it loops through the struct fields, it can also fetch the relevant values for each struct field. Rather than manually convert these values from their native type to a string, you rely on fmt.Fprintf() to do that work for you.

Of note, the fieldName() function uses Go's automatic tag parsing. Although you can (if you desire) store any string data in an annotation, Go can parse tags for you. For any annotation tag that follows the format NAME:"VALUE", you can access the value by using StructField.Tag.Get(). It returns the value unprocessed. It's a common idiom for tag values to contain a comma-separated list of params (`json:"myField,omitempty"`). For our simple tags, though, you allow only a single field in the VALUE space. Finally, if you don't get any tag data for the field, you return the struct field's name.

> ## Ignoring struct fields with annotations
> Sometimes you want to tell encoders to ignore fields on a struct. The common idiom for doing this is to use a dash (-) in the name field of the annotation (`json:"-"`). Although we don't support this in the preceding code, you could extend the example to ignore fields whose name is -.

This `Marshal()` function isn't particularly flexible. For example, it'll read only structs. Maps, which could just as easily be converted to INI fields, aren't supported. Likewise, your `Marshal()` function is going to work well only on certain data types. It won't, for example, produce useful results for fields whose values are structs, channels, maps, slices, or arrays. Yet although those operations require lots of code, there's nothing particularly daunting about extending this `Marshal()` function to support a broader array of types.

In the next listing you can look at the process of taking an existing bit of INI data and turning it into a struct. Again, this uses annotations and the reflection subsystem.

Listing 11.15   The `Unmarshal` function

```go
func Unmarshal(data []byte, v interface{}) error {

    val := reflect.Indirect(reflect.ValueOf(v))      ⟵  Again, you begin with a
    t := val.Type()                                      (dereferenced)
                                                         reflect.Value.
    b := bytes.NewBuffer(data)
    scanner := bufio.NewScanner(b)                   From data, you use a scanner to
    for scanner.Scan() {                             read one line of INI data at a time.
        line := scanner.Text()
        pair := strings.SplitN(line, "=", 2)         ⟵  Splits a line at the
        if len(pair) < 2 {                               equals sign
            // Skip any malformed lines.
            continue
        }
        setField(pair[0], pair[1], t, val)           ⟵  Passes the task of setting
    }                                                    the value to setField()
    return nil
}
```

The `Unmarshal()` function reads `[]byte` and tries to convert the fields it finds there into matching fields on the supplied `v interface{}`. Your INI parser is trivially simple: it iterates through the lines of the file and splits name-value pairs. But when it comes time to populate the given struct with the newly loaded values, you have to do a fair amount of work.

The unmarshal() function relies heavily on the setField() helper, which uses most of the reflection strategies you've seen in this chapter. Again, you're going to switch on kinds, which make for verbose code. See the next listing.

Listing 11.16　The setField helper function

setField takes the raw name and value from the INI data, and also the type and value of the struct itself.

Iterates through each field on the struct, looking for one whose name matches the INI field's name

```
func setField(name, value string, t reflect.Type, v reflect.Value) {
    for i := 0; i < t.NumField(); i++ {
        field := t.Field(i)
        if name == fieldName(field) {
            var dest reflect.Value
            switch field.Type.Kind() {
            default:
                fmt.Printf("Kind %s not supported.\n",
                    field.Type.Kind())
                continue
            case reflect.Int:
                ival, err := strconv.Atoi(value)
                if err != nil {
                    fmt.Printf(
                        "Could not convert %q to int: %s\n",
                        value, err)
                    continue
                }
                dest = reflect.ValueOf(ival)
            case reflect.Float64:
                fval, err := strconv.ParseFloat(value, 64)
                if err != nil {
                    fmt.Printf(
                        "Could not convert %q to float64: %s\n",
                        value, err)
                    continue
                }
                dest = reflect.ValueOf(fval)
            case reflect.String:
                dest = reflect.ValueOf(value)
            case reflect.Bool:
                bval, err := strconv.ParseBool(value)
                if err != nil {
                    fmt.Printf(
                        "Could not convert %q to bool: %s\n",
                        value, err)
                    continue
```

Uses a kind switch to figure out how to take your value string and convert it to the right type

If you don't know about the kind, just skip the field. This isn't an error.

This version supports only a few kinds of values. Supporting other types is usually easy, but highly repetitive.

Once a raw value is converted to its type, wraps it in a value

```
            }
            dest = reflect.ValueOf(bval)
        }
        v.Field(i).Set(dest)                    ◁──┐ Sets the value for the
    }                                               │ relevant struct field
}
}
```

The `setField()` function takes the raw name-value pair, as well as the `reflect.Value` and `reflect.Type` of the struct, and attempts to match the pair to its appropriate field on the struct. (Again, you restrict the tool to working only with structs, though you could extend it to work with `map` types.) Finding the matching field name is relatively easy because you can reuse the `fieldName()` function defined in listing 11.14. But when it comes to the `value`, you need to convert the data from the string form you were given to whatever the data type of the struct field is. For the sake of space, the code in listing 11.14 handles only a few data types (`int`, `float64`, `string`, and `bool`). And you didn't explore types that extend from your base kinds. But the pattern illustrated here could be extended to handle other types. Finally, you store the newly converted value on the struct by first wrapping it in `reflect.Value()` and then setting the appropriate struct field.

One thing becomes clear when scanning the code you've written in this technique: because of Go's strong type system, converting between types often takes a lot of boilerplate code. Sometimes you can take advantage of built-in tools (for example, `fmt.Fprintf()`). Other times, you must write tedious code. On certain occasions, you might choose a different route. Instead of writing reflection code, you might find it useful to use Go's generator tool to generate source code for you. In the next section, you'll look at one example of writing a generator to do work that would otherwise require runtime type checking and detailed reflection code.

11.3 *Generating Go code with Go code*

Newcomers to Go often share a set of similar concerns. With no generics, how do you create type-specific collections? Is there an easier way to write typed collections instead of using reflection? The runtime cost of reflection is high. Is there a way to write better-performing code? Annotations have only limited capabilities; is there another way to transform code? As mentioned before, Go doesn't support macros, and annotations have only limited capabilities. Is there another way to transform code? How do you metaprogram in Go?

An often overlooked feature of Go is its capability to generate code. Go ships with a tool, `go generate`, designed exactly for this purpose. In fact, metaprogramming with generators is a powerful answer to the preceding questions. Generated code (which is then compiled) is much faster at runtime than reflection-based code. It's also usually much simpler. For generating a large number of repetitive but type-safe objects, generators can ease your development lifecycle. And although many programmers turn a jaundiced eye toward metaprogramming, the fact of the matter is that we use code generators frequently. As you saw in the previous chapter, Protobuf, gRPC, and Thrift use generators. Many SQL libraries are generators. Some languages even use generators behind the scenes for macros, generics, and collections. The nice thing about Go is that it provides powerful generator tools right out of the box.

At the root of Go's embracing of code generation is a simple tool called go generate. Like other Go tools, go generate is aware of the Go environment, and can be run on files and packages. Conceptually speaking, it's shockingly simple.

The tool walks through the files you've specified, and it looks at the first line of each file. If it finds a particular pattern, it executes a program. The pattern looks like this:

```
//go:generate COMMAND [ARGUMENT...]
```

The generator looks for this comment right at the top of each Go file that you tell it to search. If it doesn't find a header, it skips the file. If it does find the header, it executes the COMMAND. The COMMAND can be any command-line tool that the generator can find and run. You can pass any number of arguments to the command. Let's build a trivially simple example in the next listing.

Listing 11.17   A trivial generator

```
//go:generate echo hello
package main

func main() {
    println("Goodbyte")
}
```

This is legit Go code. If you compiled and ran it, it would print Goodbyte to the console. But it has a generator on the first line. The generator's command is echo, which is a UNIX command that echoes a string back to Standard Output. And it has one argument, the string hello. Let's run the generator and see what it does:

```
$ go generate simple.go
hello
```

All the generator does is execute the command, which prints hello to the console. Although this implementation is simple, the idea is that you can add commands that generate code for you. You'll see this in action in the next technique.

TECHNIQUE 70   Generating code with go generate

Writing custom type-safe collections, generating structs from database tables, transforming JSON schemata into code, generating many similar objects—these are some of the things we've seen developers use Go generators for. Sometimes Go developers use the Abstract Syntax Tree (AST) package or yacc tool to generate Go code. But we've found that one fun and easy way to build code is to write Go templates that generate Go code.

PROBLEM

You want to be able to create type-specific collections, such as a queue, for an arbitrary number of types. And you'd like to do it without the runtime safety issues and performance hit associated with type assertions.

SOLUTION

Build a generator that can create queues for you, and then use generation headers to generate the queues as you need them.

DISCUSSION

A *queue* is a simple data structure; you push data onto the front, and dequeue data off the back. The first value into the queue is the first value out (first in, first out, or FIFO). Usually, queues have two methods: `insert` (or enqueue) to push data onto the back of the queue, and `remove` (or dequeue) to get the value at the front of the queue.

What you want is to be able to automatically generate queues that are specific to the types you want to store in the queues. You want queues that follow a pattern like the next listing.

Listing 11.18   Simple queue

```
package main

type MyTypeQueue struct {
    q []MyType                              A simple queue backed
}                                           by a typed slice

func NewMyTypeQueue() *MyTypeQueue {
    return &MyTypeQueue{
        q: []MyType{},
    }
}
                                            Adds an item to the
func (o *MyTypeQueue) Insert(v MyType) {    ⬅  back of the queue
    o.q = append(o.q, v)
}
                                            Removes an item from
func (o *MyTypeQueue) Remove() MyType {     ⬅  the front of the queue
    if len(o.q) == 0 {
        panic("Oops.")                      ⬅  In production code, you'd
    }                                          replace the panic with an error.
    first := o.q[0]                            We simplify here to keep the
    o.q = o.q[1:]                              generator code smaller.
    return first
}
```

This code is a good representation of what you want to have generated for you. There are certain bits of information that you want to be filled in at generation time. The obvious example is the type. But you also want the package name to be filled out automatically. Your next step, then, is to translate the preceding code into a Go template. The next listing shows the beginning of your queue generator tool.

Listing 11.19   The queue template

```
package main

import (
    "fmt"
    "os"
    "strings"
    "text/template"
)

var tpl = `package {{.Package}}              ← .Package is your
                                              package placeholder
type {{.MyType}}Queue struct {           ← .MyType is your
    q []{{.MyType}}                          type placeholder
}

func New{{.MyType}}Queue() *{{.MyType}}Queue {
    return &{{.MyType}}Queue{
            q: []{{.MyType}}{},
    }
}

func (o *{{.MyType}}Queue) Insert(v {{.MyType}}) {
    o.q = append(o.q, v)
}

func (o *{{.MyType}}Queue) Remove() {{.MyType}} {
    if len(o.q) == 0 {
            panic("Oops.")
    }
    first := o.q[0]
    o.q = o.q[1:]
    return first
}
`
```

Your template is almost the same as the target code you wrote previously, but with the package name replaced with `{{.Package}}`, and the `MyType` prefix replaced with `{{.MyType}}`. From here, you need to write the code that performs the generation. This is a command-line tool designed to fit the `//go:generate COMMAND ARGUMENT...` pattern. Ideally, what you'd like is to be able to write something like this:

```
//go:generate queue MyInt
```

And as a result, the generator would generate a `MyIntQueue` implementation. It'd be even nicer if you could generate queues for multiple types at once:

```
//go:generate queue MyInt MyFloat64
```

You should be able to easily accommodate that, too, as shown in the next listing.

Listing 11.20   The main queue generator

```
func main() {
    tt := template.Must(template.New("queue").Parse(tpl))
    for i := 1; i < len(os.Args); i++ {
        dest := strings.ToLower(os.Args[i]) + "_queue.go"
        file, err := os.Create(dest)
        if err != nil {
            fmt.Printf("Could not create %s: %s (skip)\n", dest, err)
            continue
        }

        vals := map[string]string{
            "MyType":  os.Args[i],
            "Package": os.Getenv("GOPACKAGE"),
        }
        tt.Execute(file, vals)

        file.Close()
    }
}
```

Compiles the generator template → (points to `tt := template.Must(...)`)

Loops through the args, making a file named TYPE_queue.go for each

Sets .MyType to the type specified in the passed-in argument

Sets .Package to the value of the environment variable $GOPACKAGE

Executes the template, sending the results to the file (points to `tt.Execute(file, vals)`)

Because you want to accept multiple types at the command line, you start out by looping through os.Args. For each one, you automatically generate an output file with the name TYPE_queue.go. Though to be consistent with the Go file-naming conventions, you should lowercase the type name.

Your template had only two variables. One is the Go type that you want to handle. But the other is the package. One nice thing that the go generate command does for you is populate a few environment variables with useful information about the location of the generator file. The $GOPACKAGE environment variable is set to the name of the package where the go:generate header was found.

When the template is executed, the vals map is used to populate the template, and a complete Go file is generated.

To run this, you need to place the go:generate header in an appropriate file, as shown in the next listing.

Listing 11.21   Using the generator

```
//go:generate ./queue MyInt
package main

import "fmt"

type MyInt int

func main() {
    var one, two, three MyInt = 1, 2, 3
    q := NewMyIntQueue()
    q.Insert(one)
    q.Insert(two)
    q.Insert(three)

    fmt.Printf("First value: %d\n", q.Remove())
}
```

The generate header generates a queue for type MyInt

Defines the MyInt type

Uses the MyIntQueue

This is a good example of typical usage of a Go generator. In this one file, you declare a generator, you declare your type, and you even use the generator. Clearly, this code will not compile until you've run the generator. But because the generator doesn't depend on your code compiling, you can (and should) run it before building your package.

That raises an important point about generators: they're intended to be used as development tools. The Go authors intended that generation was part of the development lifecycle, not the build or runtime cycle. For example, you should always generate your code and then check the generated code into your VCS. You shouldn't require your users to run a generator (even if your users are other developers).

To run the preceding generator, you need to do a few things. First, compile the generator tool from listings 11.18 and 11.19. In order for the generator line to work, you need to have it in the local directory (because you called it as ./queue). Alternately, you could store the queue program anywhere on your path ($PATH), often including $GOPATH/bin, and call it as //go:generate queue.

With queue compiled and located where go generate can find it, you need to run your go generate tool, and then you can run the main program using the generated code:

```
$ ls
myint.go
$ go generate
$ ls
myint.go
myint_queue.go
$ go run myint.go myint_queue.go
First value: 1
```

After the generator has created your extra queue code, you can run the program in listing 11.21. Everything it needs has been generated.

The code you're using for this generator is basic. Instead of adding good error handling, you let the queue panic. And you don't handle the case where you'd want to queue pointers. But these problems are easily remedied by using the normal strategies. Adding pointers, for example, is just a matter of adding another template parameter that adds an asterisk (*) where appropriate.

Again, Go templates aren't the only way to generate code. Using the go/ast package, you can generate code by programming the abstract syntax tree. For that matter, you could just as easily write Python, C, or Erlang code that generated Go. You're not even limited to outputting Go. Imagine generating SQL CREATE statements by using a generator that reads structs. One of the things that make go generate so elegant is the versatility within its simplicity.

> ### Inspired by go generate
> We were inspired enough by the elegance of Go's generator that when we created the Helm package manager for Kubernetes (http://helm.sh), we implemented a similar pattern for transforming templates into Kubernetes manifest files.

Taking a higher-level view, generators can be a useful way of writing repetitive code that would otherwise use reflection. Go's reflection mechanism is useful, but it's tedious to write and limited in capabilities, and the performance of your application will suffer. That's not to say that reflection is bad. Rather, it's a tool designed to solve a specific set of problems.

On the other hand, generating code isn't always the best solution either. Metaprogramming can make debugging hard. It also adds steps to the development process. Just as with reflection, generation should be used when the situation calls for it. But it's not a panacea or a workaround for Go's strong typing.

11.4   Summary

This chapter has taken on two of the more difficult Go topics: reflection and metaprogramming. With reflection, you examined how types, values, kinds, fields, and tags can be used to solve a variety of programming problems. And with metaprogramming, you saw how the go generate tool can be used to write code that creates code.

During the course of this chapter, you saw how to do the following:

- Use kinds to identify critical details about types
- Determine at runtime whether a type implements an interface
- Access struct fields at runtime
- Work with annotations
- Parse tags within struct annotations
- Write marshal and unmarshal functions
- Use go generate
- Write Go templates that generate Go code

Over the course of this book, you've walked through a broad range of topics. We hope that the techniques we've demonstrated are as practical and applicable in your coding as they've been in ours. Go is a fantastic systems language. Part of the reason is the simplicity of Go's syntax and semantics. But more than that, Go developers built a programming language not as an academic exercise, but in an effort to solve real problems in elegant ways. We hope this book has illustrated both Go's elegance and its practicality.

index

MORE TITLES FROM MANNING

Go in Action

by William Kennedy
    with Brian Ketelsen and Erik St. Martin

  ISBN: 9781617291784
  264 pages
  $44.99
  November 2015

Go Web Programming

by Sau Sheong Chang

  ISBN: 9781617292569
  312 pages
  $44.99
  July 2016

For ordering information go to www.manning.com